Business
for Intermediate GNVQ

second edition

Chris J. Nuttall

Collins

Published by HarperCollins *Publishers* Limited
77–85 Fulham Palace Road
Hammersmith
London
W6 8JB

www.**Collins**Education.com
On-line support for schools and colleges

First published 2000
Reprinted 2000

ISBN 0 00 329105 7

British Cataloguing in Publication Data
A cataloguing record for this publication is available from the British Library

Series commissioned by Charis Evans
Edited and typeset by DSM Partnership
Cover design by Patricia Briggs
Cover picture by Tony Stone
Pictures by Helen Evans
Project managed by Kay Wright
Production by Emma Lloyd-Jones
Printed and bound by Scotprint

Contents

Acknowledgements and credits

Thanks to Trish for unfailing patience, support and love.

Chris

The author and publisher would like to thank the following for permission to reproduce photographs and other material.

Abbey National Group (pp. 18, 116)
Barking Dog Art (pp. 198, 199 and Trojan Horse logo)
Bluewater Management (p. 162)
British Telecommunications plc (pp. 18, 112)
Companies House (p. 113)
Esso (pp. 147, 148)
Greenpeace (p. 165)
Health and Safety Executive (p. 41)
Isleworth and Syon School (pp. 1, 8, 11)
J Sainsbury (p. 18)
John Birdsall (pp. 38, 58, 178)
John Walmsley (pp.32, 40, 44, 115)
Kay Wright (pp. 63, 190, 222)
Kelloggs (pp.180, 186)
London Docklands Development Corporation (p. 158)
Marks and Spencer (pp. 18, 20, 106, 107)
McDonald's (pp. 25, 66)
Nathan Betts (p. 40)
Nissan (UK) (p. 159)
Patricia Briggs (pp. 46, 71, 121, 137, 161, 191)
PC World (p. 222)
Pizza Hut (p. 125)
Red Cross, © Lars Scwhetje, International Federation (p. 24)
RJB Mining (p. 133)
Rover Group (p. 136)
Sally and Richard Greenhill (pp. 16–17, 28, 50, 56, 63, 88, 131, 211)
Stephen Barnes (pp. 55, 134)
Suma Co-operative (p. 122)
T&GW Union p. 43
Telegraph Colour Library (p. 39 Bluestone Prods, p. 68 Ron Chapple)
Telford Development Corporation (p. 152)
Tesco (p. 190)
Tony Stone (p.111, p. 172–3 Laurence Dutton, p. 201 Howard Kingsnorth)
Virgin Group (p. 118)
Woolworths (p. 116)

Every effort has been made to contact copyright holders, but if any have been overlooked, the publishers will be pleased to make the necessary arrangements at the first opportunity.

Introduction

Welcome to the second edition of the *Business for Intermediate GNVQ* students' textbook. Our aim is to provide you with interesting and easy-to-follow learning material so that you can develop and extend your knowledge and understanding of business. This introduction will help you to understand the GNVQ award and explains how to use the book most effectively.

Reading through this introduction will help you to understand more about where the GNVQ Intermediate Business award fits into the national framework of qualifications and how the award is organised. You will also learn about:

- the subjects that you'll cover in the course
- how to study on the course
- how your work will be assessed
- key skills
- what you might do when you have finished the course.

About GNVQ

The letters GNVQ stand for General National Vocational Qualification.

- **General:** GNVQ courses provide a broad general vocational education focused on a particular area of work, such as business.
- **National:** GNVQs are national qualifications, recognised by colleges and employers all over the country. When you complete the course you will receive your certificate from one of the three bodies (Edexcel, OCR, AQA) that award GNVQ certificates.
- **Vocational:** GNVQ courses are vocational or work-related. Your course relates to the world of work and employment in business. GNVQ courses are different to GCSE and A level courses in that they are concerned with developing practical knowledge and skills; in contrast GCSE and A level courses are more academic.
- **Qualification:** the GNVQ is a qualification or award which recognises your learning and achievement at pass, merit or distinction grade.

So GNVQs are directly relevant to the world of work and employment. They show that you have the knowledge and skills that employers are looking for. They can also lead on to higher level qualifications, if that is your aim.

What is GNVQ Intermediate Business?

The award is called **Intermediate** because it is the middle level of GNVQ qualifications, with GNVQ Foundation below it and GNVQ Advanced above. The Intermediate standard is about the same as GCSEs grade A* to C.

Your GNVQ Intermediate Business course will help you learn about:

- the different purposes for which businesses are set up
- how the different activities of a business are organised in order to help the business achieve its aims
- business ownership and how this affects what businesses do and how they develop
- how businesses are affected by the wider world in which they operate
- how businesses manage their money
- how decisions are made in business.

Course specifications

Ask your tutor for a copy of the specifications for the three compulsory units that you will be taking. Read through the first section of Unit 1, headed 'About this unit'.

1. Make a list of the main purposes for which you think businesses are set up. (These are the aims that they are trying to achieve.) For example, you might put down that you think one of the main purposes of businesses is 'to make a profit'.
2. For each of the entries on your list, try to say what a business will need to do in order to achieve that purpose.

Now, look through the next section of the specification (which is called 'What you need to learn') and see how many of your ideas you can find. What else is in the unit that you hadn't thought of? Can you find these points in the index of this book?

When you receive a copy of the three optional units that you will be studying, remember to read the 'About this unit' section carefully and spend a few minutes thinking about it before you look at the rest of the unit.

How is the qualification organised?

An Intermediate GNVQ is made up of six units. For the full award you must take and pass all six units. Three of the units are compulsory and three are optional. The **compulsory units** are the same for everyone taking the GNVQ. **Optional units** vary from one awarding body to another and you or your school or college can choose which three you will take. All the units are the same size. If you are studying for Part One Intermediate Business GNVQ, you will only need to cover the three compulsory units.

Each unit in this book gives you the background knowledge you need for one of the compulsory units of your GNVQ. The units also include many activities to help you with your learning and the written work that will be assessed. You should try to complete the activities when you come across them as they are an important way of learning.

How will I learn?

While you will learn a lot from this book, you will also learn a great deal by carrying out your own enquiries and investigations. These will often be a part of an assessment activity which counts towards your unit assignment and final result.

You may learn by:

- carrying out research in libraries and resource centres
- using the internet
- visiting and talking to the people working in business organisations
- hearing about the experiences of people who work in business organisations, and the people who buy things from them, either by conducting interviews or by watching films and videos
- using case studies to gain more understanding of what it is like to work in business
- arranging work experience with a local business organisation.

How long is the course?

Normally, you should complete your Intermediate GNVQ in one year of full-time study. However, this is not a fixed limit and some people may need longer to complete the qualification or might choose to spread their study over a longer period.

How will my work be assessed?

Four of the six units (two compulsory and two optional) will be assessed through your coursework, which you collect in a portfolio. Two units (Unit 3 and one of your optional units) will be assessed by external tests.

What is a portfolio?

Your **portfolio** is the folder where you keep the work you have done during the course and which counts towards your result. This work is called your **assessment evidence**. The portfolio is at the heart of your GNVQ course. Everything in it should be your own work.

Assessment evidence

Find your copy of the specifications for Unit 1. Look at the section on assessment evidence and at the box called 'What you need to produce'.

- What do you need to produce?
- How many businesses will you have to study?
- What will you have to show that you understand?
- What will you have to describe?
- What will you have to make a record of?
- What will your oral presentation have to compare?

Each time you begin work on a new unit that is assessed by portfolio, read the section on assessment evidence, and spend a few minutes thinking about the evidence you have to produce.

What is an external test

External tests are set by your Awarding Body and will assess your skills, knowledge and understanding of unit 3 (Business finance). There will be two opportunities each year to take the external assessment, in January and in June. The grade you achieve in the external assessment will be your grade for unit 3.

The external tests will be short-answer questions to case study material. Your teacher or tutor will be able to give you more information and help in preparing for the tests by giving you opportunities to practise short-answer questions.

What grades can I get?

There are three grades: **pass**, **merit** and **distinction**. Look again at the assessment evidence section in the Unit 1. It has three columns. The first one says all the things you have to do to get a pass. To get a merit, you have to do all the things required for a pass plus the things listed in the second column. For a distinction, you do everything you have to do for a merit plus the things listed in the third column.

To find out the difference between each grade you need to identify the key words in these columns. They are the ones which, for each bullet point, say what you actually have to do. For example, to achieve a pass in Unit 1, you have to:

- describe clearly...
- describe... explain... give examples of...
- describe...
- explain...
- compare... and explain...
- list...
- explain orally... and suggest...
- speak clearly...

Now look at the key words and phrases in the merit column, and then in the distinction column. You will see that, for these grades, you have to do things which are more difficult than for a pass.

You will be awarded a pass, merit or distinction for each unit, including the ones in which you take an external test. These results are then combined to give you the grade for the whole qualification. You have to pass every unit to achieve the qualification, but you don't have to get all merits or all distinctions to achieve these grades for the whole qualification.

Who will assess my work?

Normally, your tutor will be your **assessor**. He or she will discuss your coursework with you and assess it at the end of each unit. As you work through the course, you will know what standard you are reaching.

Your tutor is supported by an internal verifier. This is another tutor who works at your college or school. His or her job is to check that your assessor is making a fair assessment of the evidence in your portfolio. Finally, the awarding body checks that the work being done at your school or college is at the right standard.

The awarding body also marks your external tests.

What will it say on my certificate?

Your final certificate will list all the units you have completed and the grades you achieved for each unit. It will also say what grade you achieved for the whole qualification.

What happens if I don't finish the course?

If you are unable to complete all of the units in the course, you will be given a certificate showing which units you have passed, and at what grade.

What can I do when I have finished the course?

When you have gained your Intermediate GNVQ qualification, you can choose between:

- taking the next step up the GNVQ ladder (to Advanced GNVQ)
- changing to the academic route (for example, by taking an A level course)
- getting a job, probably with the opportunity to gain NVQ qualifications at a higher level.

What about key skills?

There are six **key skills** units. They are the same for everybody, regardless of the qualification they are taking. They are:

- communication
- application of number
- information technology (IT)
- working with others
- improving own learning and performance
- problem solving.

Key skills are the skills you need to succeed in your studies and when you get a job. They are the skills you need to get things done and to make things happen at work. You use and apply them in real situations (see Figure I.1)

Figure I.1: The applications of key skills in real situations

Key skill	Application
Communication	When you are working with customers or colleagues, writing a report or a letter you need to be able to communicate clearly and accurately.
Application of number	You will need number skills when you are carrying out research or making financial calculations.
Information technology	You can use your information technology skills to present written work, or to search for information in a database.
Working with others	You have to be able to work with others if you are to make a successful career in any business.
Improving own learning and performance	We can all improve how we learn and what we achieve, and you need this skill to ensure that you continue to develop professionally.
Problem solving	We are all faced with problems when studying or at work. You can get better at tackling problems if you work on this skill.

Although you don't have to achieve any key skills units to pass your GNVQ course, all schools and colleges are likely to expect you to aim for at least communication, application of number and information technology. If you achieve these, at any level, you will be awarded a key skills qualification.

How are key skills assessed?

Like the GNVQ, key skills are assessed through a combination of portfolio evidence and external tests. Your tutor will explain this to you. If you find that you need some extra help with your key skills, talk to your GNVQ tutor.

Build your learning

Summary points

- GNVQ stands for General National Vocational Qualification.
- Business is about different types of business organisations and how they work.
- GNVQ Intermediate Business is made up of three compulsory units and three optional units.
- During the course, you will make enquiries, talk to people in business, and learn from different sources.
- You will complete assignments for four units, and do an external test for each of the other two units.
- You can achieve a pass, merit or distinction grade.
- You may also achieve up to six key skills units.

Key words and phrases

You should know the meaning of these words and phrases as they relate to your GNVQ course. If you're not sure about any of them, go back through the last seven pages of this introduction to check or refresh your understanding.

- **Assessment evidence**
- **Assessor**
- **Compulsory units**
- **External test**
- **GNVQ**
- **Intermediate level**
- **Key skills**
- **Optional units**
- **Pass, merit, distinction**
- **Portfolio**

Student questions

1 What does GNVQ stand for?

2 Where can you find out about the course contents?

3 What happens if you don't finish the course in a year?

4 How many units are assessed through portfolio evidence?

5 Which is better, a merit grade or a distinction grade?

6 What does an internal verifier do?

7 What are key skills?

About this book

How is this book organised?

Each main section of this book has the same title as one of the three compulsory units in the Intermediate GNVQ specification. Look at the **preview** to Unit 1 (see pages 16–17) and compare it with the 'About this unit' and 'What you need to learn' sections in the specifications. How do they compare?

You will find that if you make similar comparisons for Units 2 and 3 (on pages 98–9 and pages 172–3 respectively), you will see that the book covers the material that you need to learn as set out in the specification for the qualification.

Before you start looking through these main sections, however, you should look at the 'Getting started' section which begins on page 1. This will help you to organise your learning, to find the information you need to undertake the activities and assignments, and to present your work well.

How does the book help me to learn?

The book includes three important features to help you learn and revise.

Activities

As you know, it is always easier to learn something by doing it than by just reading about it or being told about it. You have already done some **activities** in this introduction, but there are many more throughout the book. For example, have a look at the activity on page 18. Making lists like those asked for in this activity really makes you think about what you are learning. Other activities suggest some research you might do, or points to discuss, or notes to make, or things to think about.

Case studies

Turn to page 44 of the book and read through the **case study**. The names of the people in this study have been made up but the situations described are typical. After most case studies in the book, you are asked questions or given something to discuss with other people. So, though you probably don't yet have experience of working with real people in business situations, this is the next best thing. You can use the case studies so that when you go out on work placement or get your first job, you have some experience to draw on.

Build your learning

At the end of the main sections of each unit, you will find a section called 'Build your learning'. In fact, there is one earlier in this introduction. Have a look at the example on pages 72–3 now. These sections include summary points, key words and phrases, and student questions.

- **Summary points**. Use these to check that you have understood all the key points in the section.
- **Key words and phrases**. As you finish each section of the book, you can test your learning by checking that you understand the meaning of key words and phrases. Write down what you think each word or phrase means. Then find where it is explained in the book (maybe by using the index) and check whether you have got it right.
- **Student questions**. This is another way to test and improve your own learning. You should try to answer these questions. Your answers don't count towards your grade for the unit: the questions are to help you learn – not to test you. That's why the section is called build your learning.

It would be a good idea to keep a file of key words and phrases and your answers to student questions, with corrections where necessary, for revision.

How will the book help me to prepare my portfolio?

You have already looked at the assessment evidence you have to produce for Unit 1. This time let's look at the assessment evidence you need to produce for Unit 2. This is set out in the specifications for Unit 2 (ask your tutor for a copy if you do not have one).

Look at the box called 'What you need to produce' – this looks like a lot of work, and it is. However, you have about half a term in which to do it and this book is arranged to help make the job easier. It breaks down the work you have to do into smaller, more reasonably sized, sections. Let's see how this works.

Turn to page 97 of this textbook and look at the assessment grid. This analyses what you have to do, section by section. The first column shows the sections of the unit, the second column shows what you have to do to obtain a pass, the third column shows what you have to do in addition to obtain a merit, and the fourth column shows what you have to do in addition to that in order to achieve a distinction.

Throughout each unit in this book there are special activities called 'Collect the evidence'. Look at the 'Collect the evidence' activity on page 129 in the section on ownership. What does it ask you to do?

Now look at the assessment check list at the end of Unit 2 (on page 170), and you will see that it lists all the evidence from the unit specifications. Each bullet point gives a page reference to a 'Collect the evidence' activity. Find the bullet point that refers to the 'Collect the evidence' activity you looked at on page 129.

As Unit 3 is assessed externally rather than through your portfolio, the section at the end of this unit is called 'Assessment preparation'. This shows what you will have to answers questions about during the external assessment.

In this way, by working through each unit section by section and by completing all the 'Collect the evidence' activities, making sure that you have met the criteria for each section given in the assessment grid for each unit, you will know that you have produced all you need to achieve a pass, merit or distinction for the unit.

Build your learning

Summary points

- The contents of this book cover all you need to learn for the compulsory units of the GNVQ Intermediate Business.
- The 'Getting started' section helps you organise your learning.
- Activities help you to learn by giving you things to do.
- Case studies help you to think about real situations where care may be needed.
- 'Build your learning' summarises each section, lists key words and phrases and summary points and asks some questions.
- If you complete all the 'Complete the evidence' sections, you will have all you need for your portfolio.

Key words and phrases

You should know the meaning of the words and phrases listed below as they relate to the organisation of this book. If you're not sure about any of them, go back to check and refresh your understanding.

- **Activities**
- **Assessment check list**
- **Assessment preparation**
- **Case studies**
- **Key words and phrases**
- **Preview**
- **Student questions**
- **Summary points**
- **Work experience**
- **Work placement**

Student questions

1. How do activities help you learn?
2. How do case studies help you learn?
3. How does the 'Build your learning' section help you learn?
4. What do you have to do to complete your portfolio?

Answers to external tests (see page ix)

The answer to question 1 is 'receive more money from selling its products than it costs to make them'. This is because the profit of a business is the amount by which its income (the money it receives for the product it provides) exceeds its expenditure (the amount it spends on providing its product).

Answers to question 2 include discrimination on the grounds of sex, race, religion, sexual orientation and disability.

Finally...

Studying for GNVQ will probably be quite different from the kinds of studying you have been used to. Most importantly you will be responsible for a large part of your own learning and will have to do a lot of research for yourself. You will need discipline, commitment and sometimes just dogged persistence. We hope that you will find this book a useful and enjoyable guide to business and your GNVQ.

Work hard, enjoy yourself and good luck!

Getting started

You will probably find that studying for Intermediate GNVQ Business is different to the kinds of studying you have done before. For one thing, you are going to be responsible for a much larger part of your own learning. Besides attending lessons, you are going to have to carry out your own research. This calls for discipline, commitment and sometimes just dogged persistence! You must produce your own evidence and make sure it is well presented and properly referenced in your portfolio.

This section will help you:

- organise yourself and your learning
- find the information you need quickly and effectively
- present your work well.

Organising your learning

One of the first things you will need is somewhere to study when you are not at school or college. Try to find somewhere that you can call your own, where you can study quietly and without interruptions. It should be somewhere you can use whenever you want. Let the other people you live with know that it is your place of study so that they will not disturb you unnecessarily.

Make this place personal, whether it is in your bedroom, or a corner of another room. You should feel comfortable and it should be a place where you are able to work easily. You will need a desk or a table, and also somewhere handy to keep your textbooks, notes and other resources, and your portfolio.

Managing your time

A comfortable place to study will not help you much unless you learn to use time efficiently. This means planning your week so that you have time to study – and time to enjoy yourself.

At school or college, you have a timetable which shows what you should be doing at various times of the day. You should try to construct a similar plan of your week so that you can make full use of all the time you have. You may like to include your school or college timetable into a larger timetable of your week. By doing this, you will be able to make best use of any untimetabled periods as well as your own time.

You will find that your studies take up a lot of your time. It will help if you have a regular routine and you stick to it. But don't forget to set aside time to have fun, to go out with friends to a club or the cinema, or take time just to sit and read. Time to relax and recharge your batteries is important, and will help you to study better. Don't worry if you can't always stick to your timetable. If something crops up that you must – or want to – do, just make sure you rearrange your timetable so that you can catch up on your work later.

As well as planning your time on a daily and weekly basis, you will also have to do some long-term planning. For example, you will have to plan each assignment so that you complete it by its due date. If you don't, you will be putting yourself under a great deal of pressure and stress as you struggle to complete outstanding assignments before the end of the course. You must plan, too, for the external tests. Allowing yourself sufficient time to revise will help you pass them without last minute cramming.

Organise your notes and handouts

During your course you will accumulate a lot of paperwork. This may include:

- notes taken during lessons
- handouts given to you by your tutors
- articles from newspapers and magazines
- printouts of information downloaded from the internet
- pamphlets and booklets collected from business organisations.

The information will provide you with valuable background on business issues and examples of real business situations. It will be important in helping you to learn and understand the principles of business, complete your assignments, and prepare for your external tests. The information will only be useful to you, however, if you organise the paperwork so that you can find things easily and quickly.

In order to do this, you must establish a filing system for all these documents. An expanding file or a loose-leaf folder with plastic pockets is ideal. Use subject dividers labelled with the topic or unit that the documents refer to. By doing this, you will be able to find the information that you want when you want it.

Tackling assignments

A major part of your course will involve assignment work. Assignments are important: they are the basis for successfully completing the course and for determining your final grade. There are some things you must ask yourself in order to decide how you should go about tackling the assignment.

- What exactly are you expected to do for the assignment? Read the assignment brief carefully. What is it asking for? Break the assignment down into discrete tasks if you can. It is easier to attempt a series of small activities and integrate them at the end, than to try to work on a complex assignment all at once.
- How should you present your work? Do you need to write a report, produce an essay, make an oral presentation, or undertake a variety of tasks?
- When do you have to submit the assignment? Plan carefully so that you do not overrun and cause yourself problems completing the next assignment. If you cannot submit the assignment on its due date, perhaps because of illness, do you have to complete a form authorising an extension?

Think carefully about the information you will need in order to complete the assignment, where will you find it and what research you will need to undertake.

Read the specifications. These will give you vital guidance on the areas of knowledge and subject content that are covered by the assignment.

Undertaking research

To do well in this course you will have to find – and use – more information than your tutor can give you in the classroom. At first, this may seem rather daunting. Where do you find all the information you need? Fortunately we live in an age of information. The information you need will be easy to find if you know where – and how – to look for it. The main sources of information that you will use are:

- published materials, such as books, newspapers and magazines
- the internet
- business organisations.

Books, newspapers and magazines

Books are an important source of information. A good textbook, such as the one you are reading now, will give you the background theory and introduce ideas you will meet during your course. It will also provide case studies and real examples to show how the theories and ideas work in the business world.

There will be times, however, when you need more information than you can find in this textbook. On these occasions, you will need to refer to other books that deal in more detail with particular topics. You will find books on business topics in school, college and public libraries. As early in your course as possible, you should find out where these books are kept – they may be in both the lending and the reference sections. The library will become one of the main resource centres for your studies. Get to know it well.

As well as books, many newspapers and magazines carry articles on business. Get into the habit of looking at as many newspapers and magazines as you can. Information in articles and features is up to date, and will help you understand current trends and events in the business world. Again, school, college and public libraries usually have a good selection of newspapers and magazines.

These publications are particularly useful:

- **daily newspapers** – *The Times, Financial Times, The Guardian, Daily Telegraph, The Independent*
- **sunday newspapers** – *Sunday Times, Sunday Telegraph, Independent on Sunday, The Observer*
- **magazines** – *The Economist* (weekly), *Business Review* (four times a year)
- **professional journals** – *Accountancy* (monthly), *The Director* (monthly), *Management Today* (monthly), *People Management* (fortnightly).

The internet

The internet is a valuable source of information. We live in a fast changing world. Case studies, statistics and other data printed in books, while still valuable, rapidly become out of date. You will get the most out of your course, and be more successful, if the statistics and data you use are up to date.

The internet is a huge resource consisting of sites (or web pages) that individuals, businesses and other organisations have set up to make information about an almost infinite variety of topics easily available. Sites of interest to business students include those set up by individual businesses. These often provide useful background information about the company and its operations, including the latest company accounts and trends in the industry. Government departments and financial institutions have sites, many of which provide statistical information and data about business trends and forecasts.

Information that you find on the internet should help both in your coursework and assignments. You may be able to access the internet at school or college – check with your tutor whether this is possible. When you start to use the internet, you will quickly find out that there is an enormous amount of information about business and business organisations.

We have provided a directory of some websites that might help you in your research (see page 13). However, these are only a start!

Business and other organisations

Businesses and other organisations can provide much help and information to assist you in your studies. Some information is readily accessible in published reports, brochures and guides. For example, high street banks and firms of accountants publish booklets on starting a small business (which might

▼ You can pick up free booklets like this from many banks

come in useful for Unit 1); these publications are usually free. The annual reports and accounts of large public limited companies (plcs) can easily be obtained by contacting company head offices, and many will be available for reference at your local library.

Some assignments that you have to do as part of the course require you to find out how a real business operates. You will need to arrange meetings with people working in business organisations to complete these assignments. The human resources manager of a local business organisation or the local branch of a national or international company, such as Tesco or Marks and Spencer, may be happy to talk to you about job roles (useful for part of the assessment for Unit 2).

Getting in touch with real business organisations is not difficult. To get the most from using business organisations as a resource, you should follow these steps.

- Be clear about the type of information you want and what you want it for.
- Identify a suitable organisation to contact – your tutor or teacher will be able to help you. If you want to arrange to meet someone, you will need to contact a local business or the local branch of a national or international organisation. If, on the other hand, you want information in writing, it may be best to approach a company's head office.
- Try to find out the name of the person to contact for information or to arrange a meeting, and write a short letter addressed to that individual. Your letter should be polite and neat (word-processed if possible), and have correct grammar and spelling.
- Before a meeting, plan the questions that you want to ask in advance. You may find it useful to prepare a questionnaire, but don't be too rigid, and be prepared to ask additional questions to follow up on any points that interest you.

It will be useful to maintain contact with someone working in a business organisation who you can approach for further advice or information when you need it. When you contact someone in an organisation, ask if you can telephone or meet again if you want further information.

Don't forget that your school or college is an organisation. You may find out valuable information about business procedures by talking to people working in your school or college, especially those responsible for administration.

Getting the most from work experience

Work experience allows you to see business at first hand

Part of your course may consist of a period of work experience. This is an excellent opportunity for you to experience working in a business organisation at first hand, and to find out from the inside how businesses operate. You will also be able to see how some of the ideas and theories you have come across are put into practice. To get the most from your work experience, you should:

- try to make a good impression by being polite, smart, punctual and reliable
- use your initiative – look around, see what other people are doing and what needs to be done
- ask for help or advice if you are unsure about anything
- keep a log or diary and note down everything you do
- make notes about what you see and about how the business operates – try to see how it fits in with what you have learned about business
- at the end of each day, evaluate your contribution to the work of the organisation and what you are learning by being there
- set targets for the next day and write down any questions you want to ask
- enjoy yourself!

▶ Computers help you present your work neatly

Presenting your work

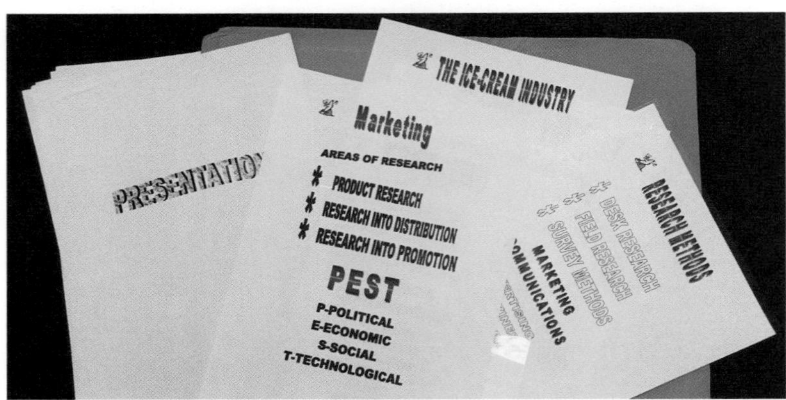

Writing analytically and evaluatively

Most assignments call for analysis and evaluation. When you analyse a problem or question, you examine all aspects of that question or problem, weighing up how each aspect affects the outcome. This usually involves considering causes, consequences and implications.

Evaluation means forming your own judgement and opinion of the evidence you have discovered. All evaluation must be based on analysis. Being able to analyse and form your own opinion about a problem or question is an important skill that takes practice.

Writing reports

Sometimes you will be asked to write a report as part of an assignment or coursework. You may be asked to write a report to communicate the results of your research and explain its implications. When writing a report, you must remember that it is very important to use an appropriate format for the report.

There are two basic types of report format – formal and informal. You will normally be told which format to use.

Informal reports

Informal reports are sometimes called memo reports. Each section of the report should be given a heading. An informal report normally contains:

- a title or subject
- a brief introduction, explaining what the report is about and your purpose in writing it
- a main section setting out the relevant facts and findings of your research
- a conclusion containing your own evaluation of the facts, or any recommendations you have been asked to make.

Formal reports

Formal reports are generally longer and more structured than informal reports. They are often bound documents. Like informal reports, formal reports should be structured in sections and each section should be given a heading.

A formal report should contain:

- a title page, stating the title of the report, who it has been written by, and who it has been written for
- terms of reference – the purpose of the report and what it covers
- the research methods you used to obtain the information needed
- your findings, including appropriate data or statistics
- an analysis of your findings
- your conclusions based on an evaluation of your analysis
- any recommendations you have been asked to make – again these must be firmly based on your analysis
- sometimes a formal report will have a summary of the main points of the report
- an appendix containing statistical or other data not contained in the main body of the report.

Note that tables, graphs and charts may, if you wish, be included in an appendix, but you should refer to them in the main body of your report and explain what they mean and their significance.

Tables, graphs and charts

Your assignments will often contain numerical data and statistics. Wherever possible, these should be presented as tables, graphs and charts, rather than as figures in the text, which are much harder to take in. You should be able to produce these by hand, although these days it is very easy to produce attractive tables, graphs and charts using an appropriate computer software package. Your tutor will help you with this.

When producing a table, graph or chart, always remember to give it a title and, where appropriate, a key. You should also give the source of the data shown.

You can present information in four ways (see Figure G.1, page 10):

- line graph
- bar chart
- pie chart
- table of figures.

Figure G.1: Four ways of presenting numerical information

Table of figures

	1 Qtr	2 Qtr	3 Qtr	4 Qtr	Total
N	65	50	65	85	265
S	45	40	45	70	200
E	70	30	40	20	160
W	90	20	30	45	185
Total	270	140	180	220	810

Pie chart

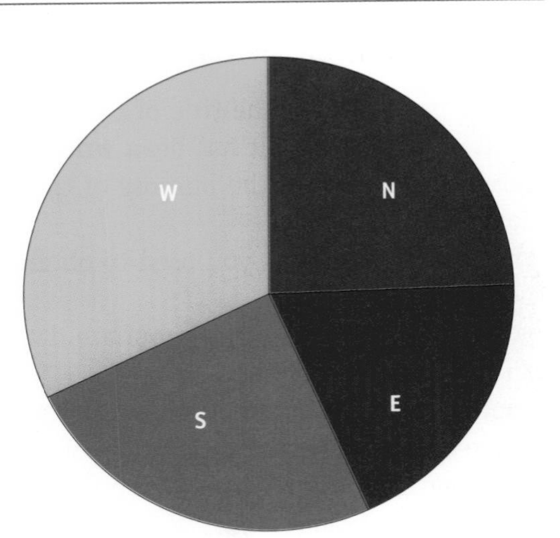

Line graph

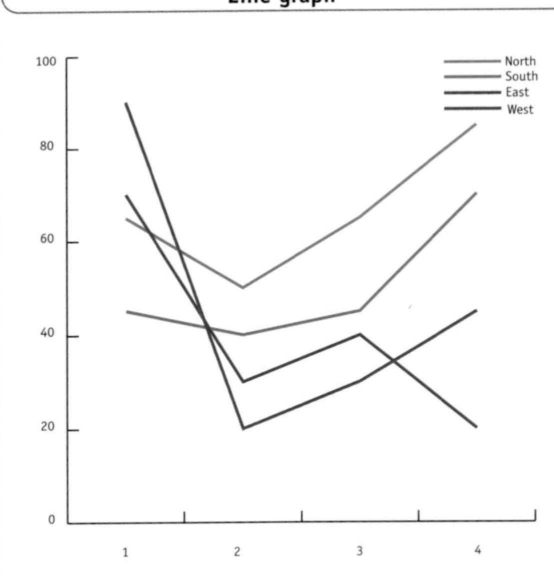

Bar chart

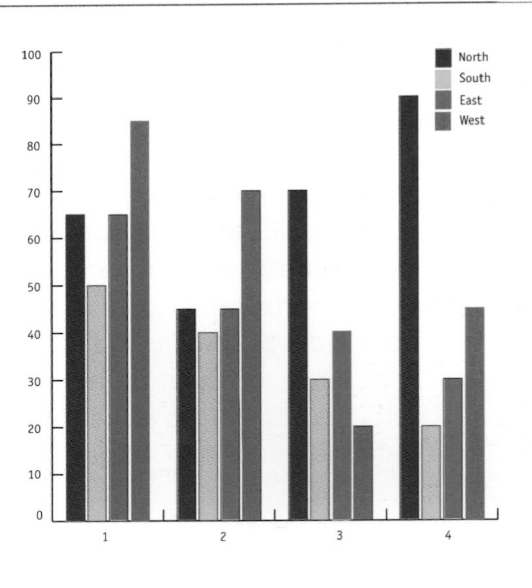

Making presentations

Sometimes as part of an assignment or coursework you will be asked to give a presentation using visual aids such as an overhead projector. Some software packages such as Microsoft Powerpoint or Corel Presentations allow you to prepare slides on a computer. If you have access to a computer-linked projector, you may be able to show these as part of your presentation, in stunning colour and complete with sound effects, graphics and animations. Check with your tutor if you do have access to this facility.

◀ Making a presentation in class

Everybody – even seasoned professionals – is nervous before having to make a presentation in front of an audience. So don't worry, you are not alone. But while nervousness is natural, there are some things you can do to make your presentation easier and a success.

- Decide what you are trying to do in your presentation. Are you trying to inform, persuade, or teach?
- Define your objectives. What is your presentation about? What do you want your audience to know at the end of the presentation?
- Prepare your presentation. This involves carrying out the necessary research, deciding exactly what you are going to say and preparing your visual aids. If you are going to use an overhead or computer-linked projector, make sure that you know how to use it.
- Give your presentation an attention-grabbing opening, perhaps an unexpected fact or statistic. Beware of using humour, as unless it is well done, it will fall flat. Introduce your subject and outline what you are going to say.

- Your opening should lead smoothly into the middle section of your presentation. Here you will give your core material – information, statistics, facts and so on. Make this section as interesting as possible, especially when presenting statistics. Visual aids will help focus and keep the attention of your audience, but they must be relevant and well produced.
- The conclusion of your presentation must follow logically from the material you have already given. You should present it so that your audience can see how you have arrived at your conclusion. Do not introduce any new facts at this stage. Finally, summarise the main findings and your conclusions to remind your audience of the things you have said.
- Once you have prepared your presentation you must practise it. Is it the right length? Does it say what you want it to? Does it work?
- When you actually make your presentation, be ready. Have your notes and visual aids ready and in the right order. Make sure that any equipment you are going to use is set up and works. Welcome your audience and introduce yourself. Be enthusiastic and confident – after all you have prepared and practised your presentation well. Vary the tone and pitch of your voice, but use gestures sparingly. Look at your audience. Ask them if they have any questions. Finish your presentation on time and thank your audience for listening.
- A final and essential element of making presentations is to review and evaluate your performance. This helps you improve your skills for next time. Ask yourself whether you achieved what you set out to? How did your audience react? What went well? What could you improve?

Few people find presentations easy to make. If you are systematic in your approach to making a presentation and review your performance you will develop both your skills and performance.

Internet directory

Biz/ed

Biz/ed is a website that has been set up by the Economics and Business Education Association (EBEA). It is an easy-to-use site with a wealth of valuable information for business studies students. There are well-written revision notes covering most topic areas, as well as links to other web sites of companies, financial institutions and government organisations. Biz/ed is well worth visiting and browsing – again and again.

- Biz/ed
  http://www.bized.ac.uk

Company websites

Most large companies have established their own websites. While they are principally aimed at marketing the company, many are well designed and contain a wealth of useful information about the company and the industry in which it operates. Company sites often contain both the company's annual report and the chairperson's report, and these are can be useful sources of information. Some interesting company websites are:

- Granada Group
  http://www.granada.co.uk
- Nike
  http://www.nike.com (go to nikebiz)
- Marks and Spencer
  http://www.marks-and-spencer.co.uk
- Sainsbury
  http://www.sainsbury.co.uk

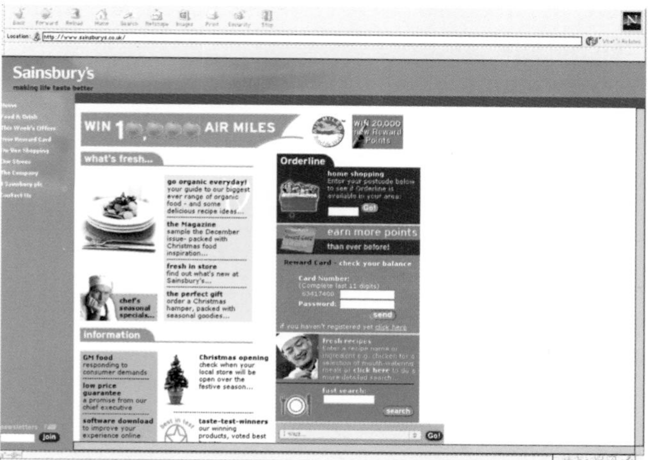

Financial institutions

Most financial institutions now have a website. Here are four useful sites:

- Bank of England
  http://www.bankofengland.co.uk
- European Central Bank
  http://www.ecb.int
- National Westminster Bank
  http://www.natwestgroup.com
- Lloyds TSB
  http://www.lloydstsb.co.uk

Government organisations

The government hosts several websites dedicated to individual government departments. Most of these contain information about the work of the department, as well as statistics and other information about British business, society and the economy.

- HM Treasury
  http://www.hm-treasury.gov.uk
- Department of Trade and Industry
  http://www.dti.gov.uk
- Office of Fair Trading
  http://oft.gov.uk

Worldwide organisations

Here are three international organisations that publish a range of financial information, statistics and business analysis.

- Organisation for Economic Co-operation and Development
  http://www.oecd.org
- United Nations Statistics Division
  http://www.un.org
- International Monetary Fund
  http://www.imf.org

Newspapers, magazines and television news

Newspapers and magazines are a valuable source of up-to-date information about what is happening in the business world. Most have websites that are searchable and contain many useful archive articles. In addition, both BBC News and ITN have websites that carry stories of interest to business students. Look up 'business' on their sites. Some useful sites are:

- *Daily Telegraph*
  http://www.telegraph.co.uk
- *Financial Times*
  http://www.ft.com
- *The Guardian*
  http://www.guardian.co.uk
- *The Times*
  http://www.the-times.co.uk
- *The Economist*
  http://www.economist.com
- BBC News
  http://www.bbc.co.uk/news
- ITN
  http://www.itn.co.uk

The internet sites given in this directory are only a small selection of all the interesting and valuable sites there are. Whatever you are looking for there is almost certain to be a site that will give you the information you want. Try searching using one of the search engines, such as Yahoo. Happy surfing!

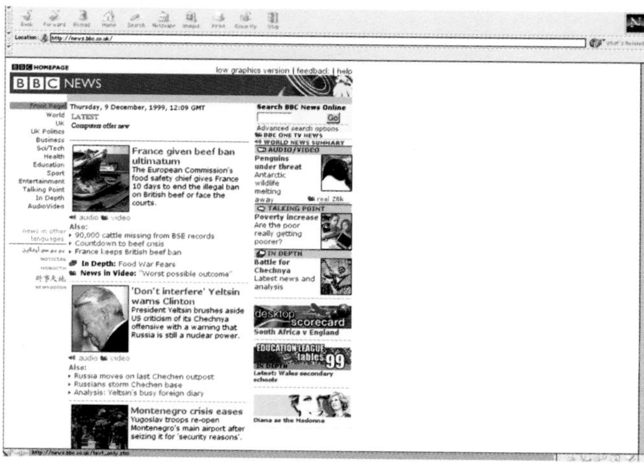

Investigating how businesses work 1

In this unit you will find out about the aims and objectives of businesses. You will study the functional areas that help businesses to achieve their aims and objectives. These functional areas are the different types of activities that must be carried out in order for the business to operate. You will see how businesses develop organisational structures that enable them to coordinate their activities. Measuring their actual performance against planned objectives enables businesses to evaluate their success in achieving their aims. Finally, you will examine the types and purposes of communications used in business.

You will be assessed through your portfolio work. In order to gather evidence you need to investigate a large or medium-sized business and show that you understand how it works. For example, you need to describe what the business does, its aims and objectives, describe the purposes and activities of four functional areas of the business, and show how different areas of the business communicate.

As part of your assessment evidence, you will make an oral presentation comparing the customer service of your selected business with best practice customer service. Completing the 'Collect the evidence' activities in this unit will help you gather the evidence you require.

The aims and objectives of businesses

A business is an organisation that has been set up to produce goods and services and supply them to individuals and other business organisations that want those goods and services and are willing to pay for them.

- **Goods** are things you can touch and use, such as clothes, computers and textbooks.
- **Services** are things that other people do for you, such as cutting your hair, looking after your money in a bank, or prescribing medicines for you when you are sick.

There is a vast number and variety of different business organisations around today. You are probably familiar with the names of many of them.

What is a business?

Make a list of all the business organisations you can think of. What are the goods or services that they supply?

▼ Some well-known businesses

The Abbey National Group

MARKS & SPENCER

Your list of business organisations probably contains well-known businesses such as Microsoft, Virgin, Nike, Coca-Cola and McDonald's. You may have included some smaller local businesses, for example shops, hairdressers, bus companies, and traders such as decorators and plumbers. But did you know that your school or college is also a business organisation, as are hospitals, libraries, leisure centres and similar organisations that provide services for the general public?

The main activity of a business is producing the goods or services it supplies. For example, the main activity of Ford is making cars (producing goods). The main activity of Tesco is selling food and household goods (providing a service). The main activity of your school or college is providing education (providing a service). Although the products that Tesco sells are goods, Tesco does not produce those goods itself but provides a service by selling them.

All businesses have aims that they want to achieve, and objectives that help them plan what they have to do to achieve those aims. **Aims** are the overall goals and purposes that the business was set up to fulfil. **Objectives** are specific targets that must be achieved if the business is to fulfil its aims.

Aims

Typical aims of a business might include:

- making a profit
- providing goods or services to the local or wider community
- surviving as a business, or expanding
- maximising sales or improving the quality of a product or service
- providing a highly competitive service
- providing charitable or voluntary services
- being environmentally friendly.

We shall look at these in turn, before we consider the type of objectives businesses must set in order to achieve their aims.

Making a profit

All business activity costs money. A business needs money to pay for:

- raw materials and components
- wages and salaries
- electricity and power
- factory and office costs
- other costs such as advertising and telephone charges.

Figure 1.1: The flow of money into and out of a business

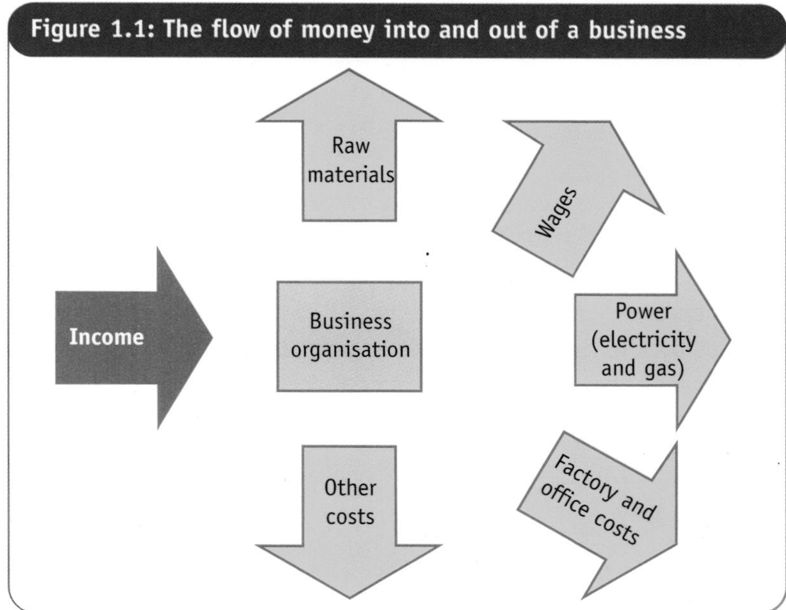

To cover these costs, a business sells the goods or services it produces. The money it receives in return for the goods or services it sells is called its **income**, or **revenue**. If the revenue of a business is more than its costs, it has made a **profit**. If the revenue of a business is less than its costs, it has made a **loss**.

A business that continues to make a loss over a period of time will go out of business since it will not have enough money coming in to pay its bills. One of the main aims of most businesses is therefore to make a profit, or at least to cover its costs. For example, an aim of Marks and Spencer is to make a profit. It achieves this very successfully. (In 1999, Marks and Spencer made a profit of £655.7 million – although this was a reduction of 41 per cent on the previous year!)

▶ One of the aims of Marks and Spencer is making a profit

The profit that a business makes may be:

- kept by the owners of the business (see Unit Two to find out who owns different types of business)
- distributed among the employees of the business, perhaps as bonuses
- kept by the business to meet any future emergencies, pay for new and up-to-date equipment, or perhaps fund expansion.

In practice, most businesses allocate their profits in more than one way, distributing some among the owners, paying bonuses to employees and retaining some within the business.

It is important to remember that the profits made by businesses also contribute to the wealth and economic strength of the nation. The higher the profits made by businesses in the United Kingdom, the more money they and their employees will have to buy goods and invest in British industry. This helps British industry become more competitive in Europe and the rest of the world.

Figure 1.2: The distribution of profits

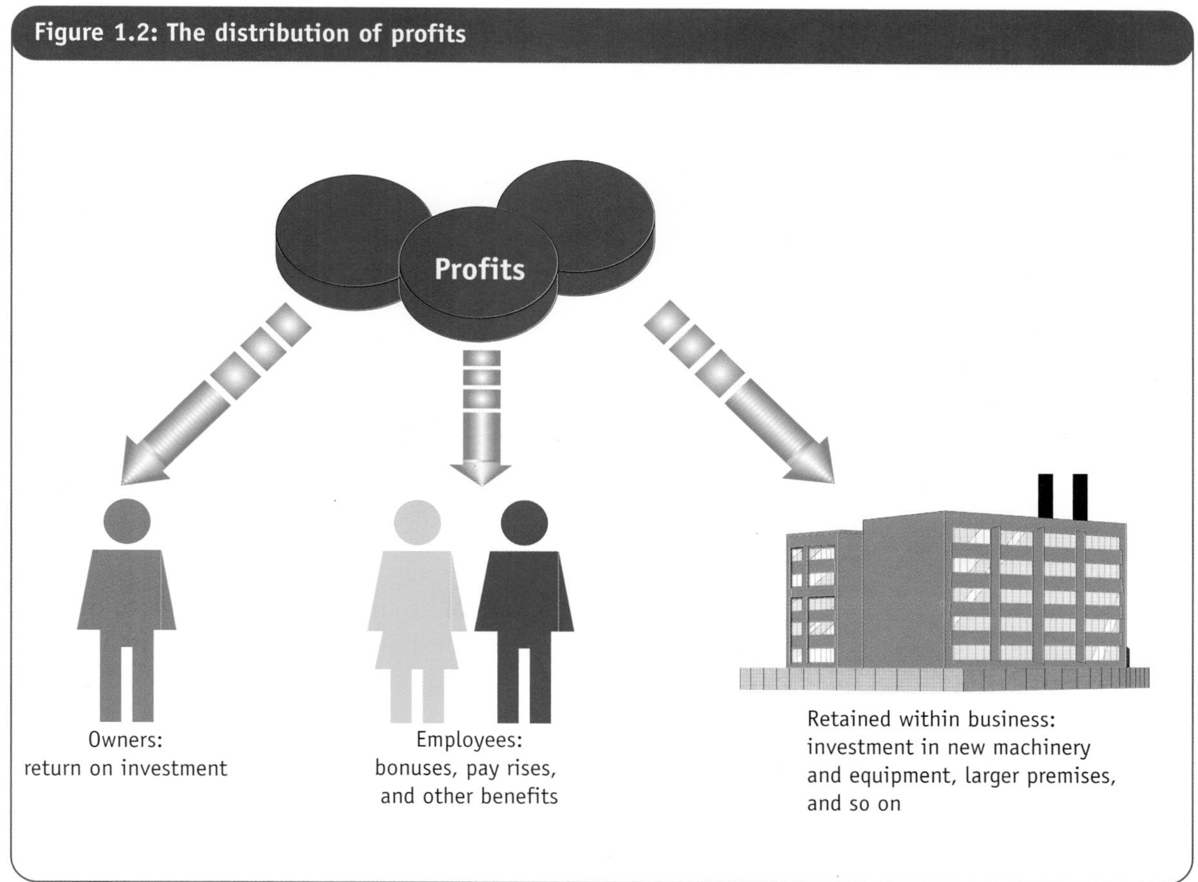

Providing goods or services to the community

All business organisations provide goods and services, and most, like Marks and Spencer, do this with the aim of making a profit. However, the principal aim of some business organisations is simply to provide a **service to the public**. This applies especially to organisations in the public sector – that is, businesses that are owned and run by local or national government.

For example, the aim of a state-run school or college is to provide education facilities for the local (and sometimes wider) community. In order to do this, it is allocated funds by the government. These government allocated funds are its income – the school or college does not have to sell its services to the public. However, a school or college may sell some services to boost its income so that it can provide more and better services. Many schools and colleges, for example, provide services such as market research and training in information technology to local businesses.

▲ Providing a service to the community

Although the main aim of an organisation may be to provide a service to the public, it still has to operate within its income. In other words, it must ensure that its costs do not exceed its income from all sources.

Survival or expansion

We have mentioned that although one of Marks and Spencer's aims is to make a profit, its profits fell by 41 per cent in 1999. The profit of a business can fall for many reasons and, when it does, it can give the business cause for concern. Sometimes a business's profits can fall so low, or it can make a loss, that the immediate aim of the business must be to survive.

When a business is in difficulty, **survival** can call for drastic measures, including reducing costs (perhaps by closing factories and laying employees off or making them redundant) or taking action to increase sales revenue. It is only when the survival of the business is assured that it is able to concentrate on other aims, such as increasing its profits.

A successful business will often try to increase its profits by **expanding**. There are two basic ways in which it can expand:

- by increasing its sales of goods and services to customers (and the profit it generates on these sales), so that it can grow as a company by increasing production, taking on more employees and, perhaps, opening new factories or sales outlets
- by taking over or merging with another business, so that the new combined business produces more goods and sells them at a more competitive price to more customers than either of the original businesses.

Maximising sales

The more sales a business makes, the greater will be its revenue. An aim of most businesses is therefore to make as many sales as possible – in other words to maximise sales. A business can **maximise sales** by:

- attracting new customers
- retaining, and selling more to, existing customers.

Customers want high-quality products and services. In order to attract new customers or retain existing customers, therefore, a business must continually try to **improve the quality** of its goods or services. If it doesn't, customers will simply go to a supplier that produces similar goods or services but of a higher quality.

Providing a competitive service

We live in an increasingly competitive world, in which many businesses compete to sell goods and services to the same customers. For example, Barclays, Lloyds TSB, HSBC and NatWest are all high street banks, providing a range of financial services both to private customers and to other businesses. A customer of one bank could just as well be a customer of one of the others. Where two or more businesses try to sell their goods or services to the same customers, those businesses are said to be competitors.

▼ Banks seek to attract customers by offering better services

In order to attract customers, therefore, a bank must strive to offer financial services that are at least as good as those provided by the other banks – its competitors. If it doesn't, customers looking for better financial services will switch to other banks that offer better products. The first bank will then lose customers and sales, resulting in a loss of sales revenue and falling profits.

Providing a highly **competitive service** means more than just offering a good quality product at the right price. It means giving good customer service by also providing the extra services that customers increasingly demand, such as help and advice, finance and after-sales services.

Providing charitable or voluntary services

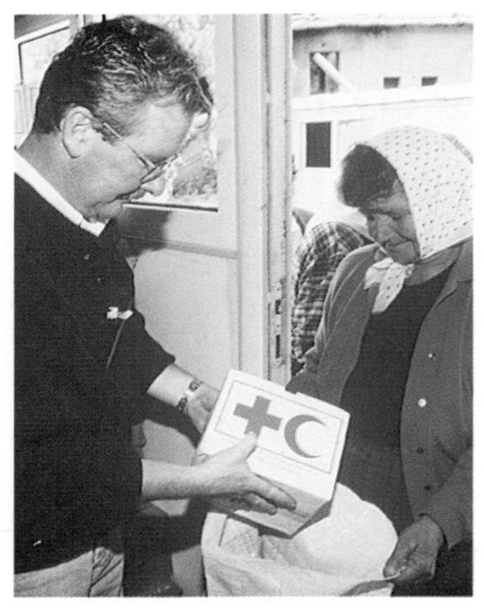

▲ Red Cross worker distributing relief parcels in Bosnia

Charities are set up to collect donations from the public and other business organisations. The donations are then spent on providing goods and services to the 'needy' – people who, without the help of the charity, would be unable to obtain or afford these goods and services.

Charities are normally established to fulfil a perceived social need, or to provide help to a specific section of the community. Many charities collect money in the UK to be spent abroad. The donations received by a charity are its revenue. The money left after the charity has paid its operating costs is used for **charitable services** (or purposes). It is essential, therefore, that the costs of any charity are kept as low as possible.

Other organisations are set up to provide **voluntary services**. These may be established by local or national government or by charities. Examples include Citizens Advice Bureaux (CAB), with around 1,000 branches staffed by more than 15,000 volunteers providing help and advice to members of the local community, and the Red Cross, the world's largest humanitarian organisation which is largely staffed by volunteers who provide first aid, community care, welfare and other services.

Being environmentally friendly

In recent years, people have become concerned about what is happening to the natural environment. People generally want more consideration to be given to preserving the environment in which we live. This trend in public opinion has meant that many businesses have had to take action to ensure that their operations do not harm the environment. New terms, such as **environmentally friendly** and 'green', are used to show that products have been developed and manufactured in ways that help to maintain – or do not harm –the environment.

▲ Businesses like McDonald's and The Body Shop publicise their green credentials

Pressure from the general public, environmentalists and environmental groups such as Greenpeace and Friends of the Earth, combined with new legal restrictions including European Union regulations, have brought about significant changes in production and consumption. For example, the introduction of lead-free petrol for cars is reducing pollution of the atmosphere, while the increasing use of cleaner forms of power is cutting the use of fossil fuels such as coal, which produce gases that contribute to global warming.

Many businesses now publicise the fact that their products and processes are green and environmentally friendly. The Body Shop is one of a growing number of businesses that have established their reputations and developed good customer relations with an increasingly environmentally aware public. Other businesses, such as Tesco and McDonald's, make information available to customers and potential customers about the effect their products have on the environment, and what they are trying to do to preserve the environment. Any business that fails to respond to public opinion by acting in an environmentally friendly manner is likely to lose customers to competitors that have a more green image and reputation. In this way, social aims such as being environmentally friendly also support other aims such as maximising sales.

Objectives

In order to achieve its aims, a business must identify and set specific practical objectives. Objectives are **targets** that must be met if the business is to achieve its aims. For example, in 1999, the internet service provider Freeserve announced that one of its aims was to expand its user base (number of customers). As of June 1999, Freeserve had approximately 1.32 million active accounts. In order to achieve its aim of increasing this number, Freeserve must attract more users. Its target, or objective, therefore, is to have more than 1.32 million active accounts within a specified time. By achieving this target, Freeserve will know that it is achieving its aim of expansion.

The objectives of a business are closely related to its aims and should fulfil two essential criteria. They should be:

- **quantifiable** – defined in way that can be measured
- **achievable** – they must be targets that the business can realistically meet.

Figure 1.3: Business aims can be broken down into objectives and targets

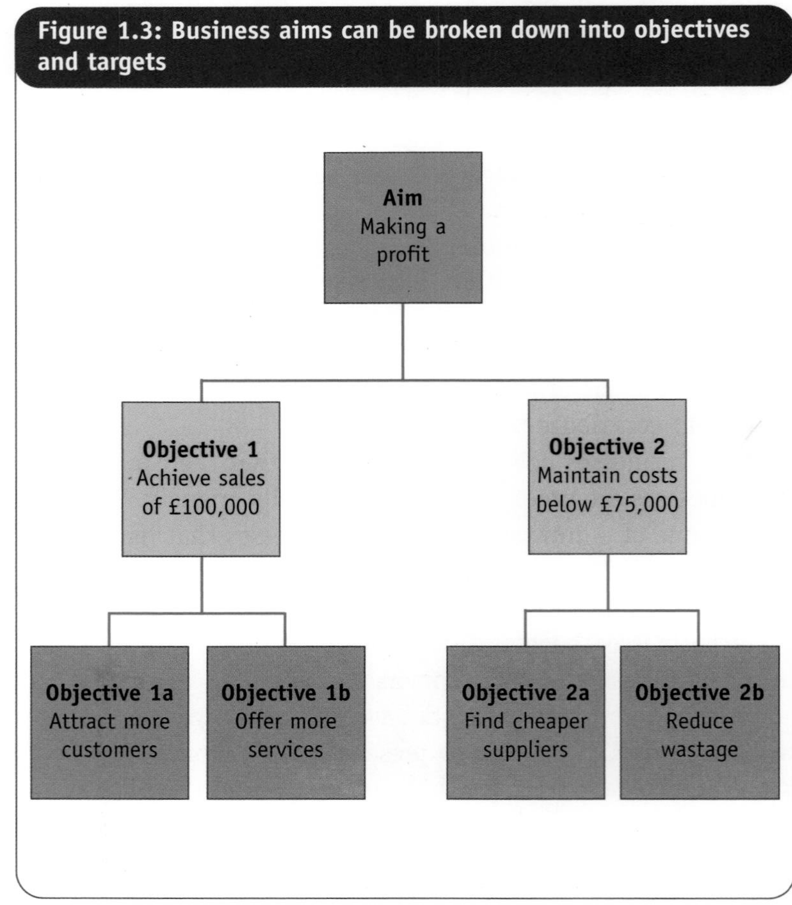

Some typical objectives of a business might include:

- to sell more of its products than a competitor
- to provide more goods or services this year than it did last year
- to produce a new product, or provide a new service that meets the needs of customers better than existing products or services
- to improve a product or service so that it meets the needs of customers more closely.

The importance of monitoring performance

Monitoring and evaluating its performance by comparing actual performance with its set targets enables a business to know if it has achieved its objectives. If the business has failed to achieve its objectives, it is able to make plans to take appropriate corrective action. Most businesses therefore **monitor** and **evaluate** their performance on a regular basis, so that any corrective action can be taken as quickly as possible. Monitoring and evaluation should be seen as a continuing process of updating and developing objectives according to the needs of the business.

Figure 1.4: By monitoring performance, businesses can revise targets to achieve their aims

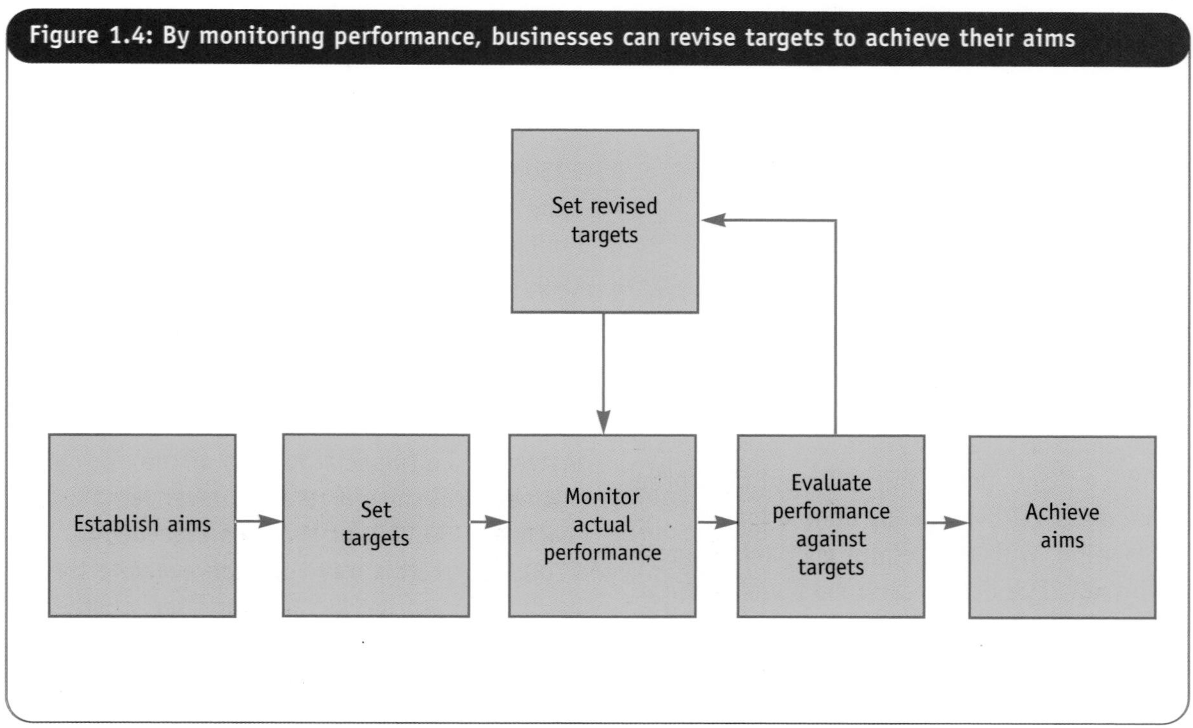

CASE STUDY

Lucy Sibanda's hairdressing business

Lucy Sibanda is a hairdresser who owns three salons in Birmingham. There are many other hairdressers in her area, but Lucy wants to expand and become the largest and most profitable hairdresser in her part of the city.

To fulfil this business aim, she realises that she must:

- increase the number of clients
- increase sales revenue so that her sales are higher than her competitors
- keep the costs of the business to a minimum.

Achieving each of these objectives involves setting targets and planning how she can achieve them. Lucy's targets for the coming year are to:

- attract (and keep) an additional 100 clients
- achieve a sales revenue of £750,000 (last year's revenue was £700,000 and her closest competitor has sales of around £730,000 a year)
- keep costs below £700,000.

'Meeting these targets is going to be a challenge,' Lucy admits. 'But I've got to do it if I'm going to achieve my aims. I can only become the largest hairdresser in the area if I have more clients and sell more than other hairdressers. I've already done a lot of planning, with the help of my bank manager, and now I've got to carry my plans through.

'I am going to advertise in the local paper and the cinema, and we will be offering some new services. We're starting to offer manicuring and facial treatments, so

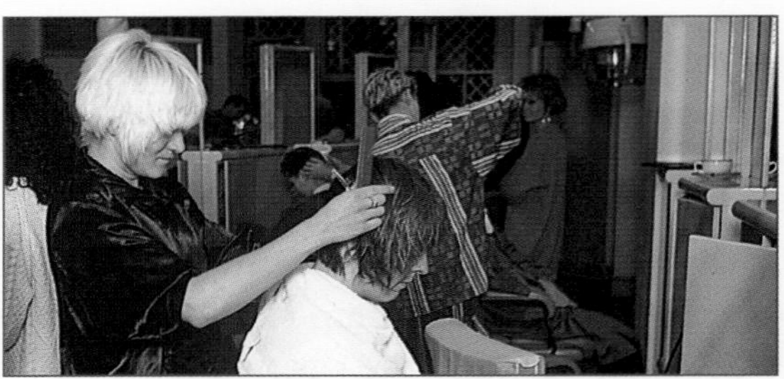

hopefully this will attract more clients. I've also been checking on other hairdressers' prices, and am going to reduce some of our prices to make them more competitive, although this will mean we'll have to generate more sales to make up for the loss of revenue.'

Each of Lucy's objectives is expressed in numerical terms: 100 additional customers, £750,000 sales revenue, and costs of no more than £700,000. She has also set a time limit of one year in which to achieve these targets. Lucy will therefore be able to check whether or not they have been achieved. Monitoring customer records will enable her to know if the business has attracted, and kept, 100 additional customers. Similarly a review of the financial records of the business will show if its sales revenue has reached £750,000, or its costs exceeded £700,000. In this way Lucy can evaluate the performance of her business and see whether it has achieved her objectives. If it hasn't, Lucy may have to set new or revised objectives to achieve her aims.

Aiming high

Read the case study about Lucy Sibanda carefully. Write notes analysing:

- how setting quantifiable objectives will help Lucy achieve her aims
- what action Lucy might take if after six months her salons had only gained an additional 30 regular clients, generating £355,000 revenue in the six-month period, with costs of £340,000.

Why do you think Lucy said that meeting her targets was going to be a challenge?

Build your learning

Summary points

- All businesses have aims and objectives.
- Aims are overall goals and purposes.
- Objectives are specific targets that help a business achieve its aims.
- Objectives should be measurable.
- Businesses evaluate their actual performance by comparing it with their objectives or targets.

Key words and phrases

You should know the meaning of the words and phrases listed below as they relate to the aims and objectives of businesses. Go back through the last 12 pages to check or refresh your understanding.

- **Achievable objectives**
- **Aims**
- **Charitable services**
- **Competitive service**
- **Environmentally friendly**
- **Evaluate**
- **Expanding**
- **Goods**
- **Improve quality**
- **Income**
- **Loss**
- **Maximise sales**
- **Monitor**
- **Profit**
- **Quantifiable objectives**
- **Revenue**
- **Services**
- **Services to the public**
- **Survival**
- **Targets**
- **Voluntary services**

Student questions

1 Explain in your own words what aims and objectives are, and how you would distinguish between them.

2 How can setting objectives help a business to achieve its aims?

3 Why can objectives sometimes include a challenge to the business?

4 Identify three objectives of a business and explain which areas of the business they affect.

5 How can monitoring and evaluating their performance help businesses meet their aims?

1 COLLECT THE EVIDENCE

All businesses have aims and objectives. This activity gives you an opportunity to produce work that demonstrates your knowledge and understanding of the aims and objectives of a business. The work that you complete for this activity will form part of your assessment evidence for this unit. You should refer to page 97 to see what you need to do to achieve a pass, merit or distinction.

What to do

1. **Identify a large or medium-sized business to investigate. Try to select a business that you can visit. Your tutor may be able to help you to find a suitable business.**
2. **Find out the name of the personnel officer, or somebody else in the business, to whom you can write for information about how the business works. If you telephone the business, explain that you are studying for GNVQ Intermediate Business, and ask for the name of someone you can write to for help with your assessment.**
3. **Write a letter asking for information about what the business does and its aims and objectives. You may like to arrange a meeting so that you can discuss this in greater detail. If you do arrange a meeting, you should write out some questions based on pages 19 to 27 of this unit. Be sure that you attend any meeting on time, and that you behave courteously. Make notes of the replies to your questions and be prepared to ask further questions that occur to you. Thank the other person for his or her time and help.**
4. **Write an account that clearly describes the main activity, aims and objectives of the business.**

You should note that there will be some confidential information that the business may be unwilling to give you in detail. This may include specific financial targets that the business is trying to achieve.

Functional areas within the business

All businesses perform various functions, or activities. Some are directly concerned with developing, producing and distributing the goods or services that the business provides, while others are concerned with making the business run smoothly. All functions and activities contribute in some way to achieving the aims of the business.

In small businesses, where there are only a few employees, one person often performs several functions. Let's look at an example. Jim Thomson and Davina Hillgrove are partners in Hillgrove Associates, a small business that develops and markets computer software. Besides Jim and Davina, Hillgrove employs Jessica Meadows, the clerk/receptionist, and Bob Simpson, who designs much of the software. Because it is a small organisation, Jim and Davina share the running of the business. Jim looks after the administration (including human resources) and finance, while Davina is responsible for marketing and sales, production of the software and customer service. These functions are described in detail on pages 54–74.

▶ Even small businesses can be organised into different functional areas

In larger organisations the amount of work involved in each function is much greater. Only four people work at Hillgrove Associates, including Davina and Jim, so Jim can easily deal with the human resources function. In a giant company such as ICI, however, with thousands of employees, the work involved in running human resources is too great for one person to undertake alone. As businesses grow, therefore, they tend to employ specialists to perform each function. As the work involved becomes too much for one person, others are employed to help them. In this way larger businesses become structured into **departments**, each dealing with a specific functional area.

The actual departments or functional areas found in any business depend on the type and purpose of the particular company or organisation. Businesses organise their functional areas in ways that help them achieve their aims and objectives. A newspaper, for example, has editorial and advertising functions, while a hospital will have a casualty department and a physiotherapy department. It is impossible, therefore, to describe every function that might be found in a business. However, functional areas that are typically found in business organisations include:

- **human resources**, which deals with the recruitment and welfare of people who work in the business
- **finance**, which deals with the management of the money coming into and going out of the business
- **administration**, which helps the business run smoothly
- **production**, which makes the goods that the business supplies
- **marketing** and **sales**, which ensures that the products of the business are what people want, and that customers know about them and buy them
- **customer service**, which tries to ensure that customers are happy, both with the goods or services of the business and with the way in which they have been served
- other areas such as **quality control** and **research and development**.

Although these functions are separate, and each involves specific activities, they are interdependent. This means that most departments cannot operate without the help of other departments. For example, the function of the production department is to produce goods. It cannot function, however, without the human resources department to ensure it has the right employees with the appropriate skills, the finance department to ensure that money is available to buy raw materials to produce the goods, and the sales department to sell the goods it produces.

Human resources

Human resources is one of the most important functions in any business. It covers:

- recruitment, retention and dismissal of employees
- working conditions
- health and safety
- training, development and promotion
- dealing with employee organisations and trade unions.

Figure 1.5: Recruitment

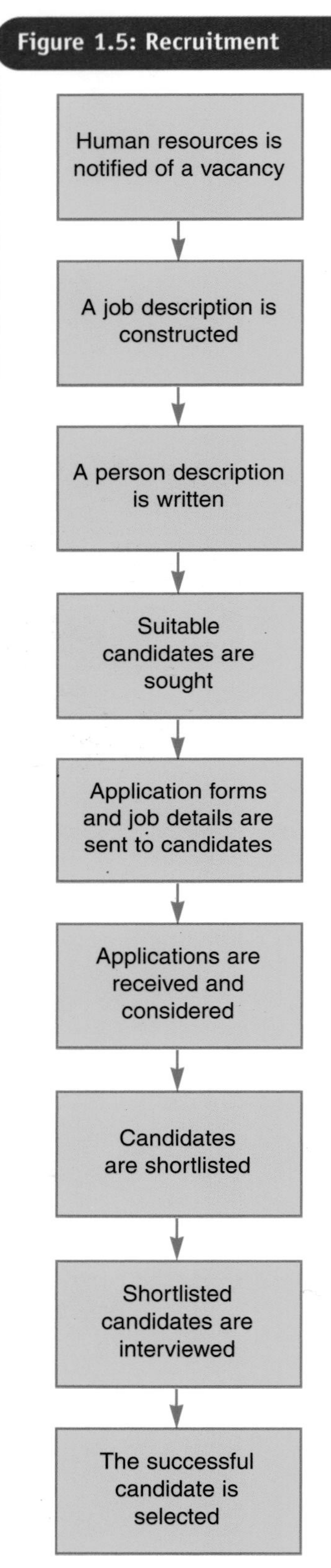

Typical job titles of people working in human resources are:

- human resources (or personnel) manager
- training officer
- health and safety officer
- personnel assistants.

No business can operate without people and an effective human resources function is therefore essential for a business to achieve its aims. Since people are employed in all areas of a business, some human resources functions may be carried out within other functional areas.

Recruitment

In any business, new employees need to be recruited from time to time in order to fill a vacancy created by an employee leaving the business or to fill a new vacancy, perhaps created because the business is expanding and needs more employees.

Recruitment is often a lengthy process and can be broken down into a number of separate stages.

1. **Notification of the vacancy** by the functional area in which the vacancy exists.
2. **Constructing a job description**, listing the tasks and responsibilities of the job. This is usually done in consultation with the functional area with the vacancy.
3. **Writing a person description**, identifying the personal attributes, skills, qualifications and experience that candidates (people applying for the job) must have.
4. **Finding candidates**, for example by advertising both within the business, perhaps on staff notice boards, and outside, in newspapers and in jobcentres and employment agencies.
5. **Sending out application forms and job details** to interested candidates so that they can apply for the job and give appropriate information about themselves. Many businesses ask applicants to send in a curriculum vitae (CV).
6. **Considering applications** when they are received to assess the suitability of the applicant.
7. **Shortlisting** – if a large number of applications are received, the most suitable are shortlisted for interview.
8. **Interviewing shortlisted candidates**, on a one-to-one basis or by a panel. The functional area in which the vacancy exists is usually involved in the interview. Candidates may also be given aptitude tests, such as intelligence tests, or practical tests such as using a computer.
9. **Selecting** the most suitable candidate, usually at a selection meeting following the interviews.

At all times, candidates and potential candidates must be treated fairly and equally. Once a business has selected a candidate, there are two further vital stages in the recruitment process.

- **Making an offer** of employment to the candidate selected.
- **Issuing a contract** outlining the terms and conditions of employment (title of job, hours to be worked, rate of pay, holiday entitlement) to the new employee. A contract of employment is a legal contract.

▼ Examples of job advertisements

IMMEDIATE PART-TIME VACANCIES

FULHAM BASED

1) WAREHOUSE AND DISTRIBUTION MANAGER experienced in stock management, packing and distribution. Computer literate and clean driving licence essential.

2) OFFICE ASSISTANT to help with general office duties and developing database system. Computer literate.

Both posts are from 10am to 3pm, Monday to Friday. Would suit persons returning to work or semi-retired.

Please fax CVs to 0171 731 3250

RECEPTIONIST

One of our top clients based in Hammersmith is seeking a well presented receptionist with an excellent telephone manner. Skills necessary include 40wpm typing and basic computer knowledge. GNVQ or equivalent preferred. Would suit a bright 2nd jobber. Excellent career prospects!

£12-14k aae

0181 883 8322

Keystone (Agy)

Assistant Accountant

We are a rapidly expanding publishing company based in N7 and need an individual with good all round experience to play an important part in a team. Exp in Peg Opera essential together with spreadsheets knowledge. Salary range £20-25,000.

Post CV to Box p6504, ES Classified, 1st floor, 2 Derry Street, London, W8 5EE (no agencies)

Retention

When a business has recruited good employees, it wants to keep them. Employees who continue to work for an employer develop a knowledge of the employer's business and of their own jobs. They also develop valuable skills and experience that help them to carry out their tasks more efficiently.

In order to keep the people it has recruited, a business must recognise its **rights and responsibilities** towards its employees and motivate them.

Rights and responsibilities

All employees have a right:

- to be paid at an agreed rate
- to be treated fairly
- to be provided with a workplace that is healthy and safe
- to be provided with equipment that is safe to use
- to receive appropriate training
- not to be asked to do anything that is dangerous, unethical or illegal.

Employers have a responsibility to their employees to fulfil these expectations, and the degree of cooperation between employers and employees depends on their fulfilment. In return, employers have a right to expect their employees to:

- work conscientiously in accordance with the agreed terms of their employment
- maintain standards of quality
- cooperate in trying to achieve the objectives of the business
- follow established procedures
- comply with health and safety regulations.

The rights and responsibilities of employers and employees is the subject of two major areas of law:

- employment legislation
- health and safety legislation.

An important aspect of rights and responsibilities concerns **equal opportunities**. All employees and prospective employees have a right to be treated fairly and without prejudice with regard to disability, religion, sex or sexual orientation, or race, by the employer and by other employees. There is no legal requirement for an employer to have a formal equal opportunities policy, but all employers must conform to the relevant **employment legislation**.

- **The Equal Pay Act 1970** states that women performing comparable tasks to men should be treated equally, including receiving the same rates of pay.
- **The Sex Discrimination Acts 1975 and 1986** rule against discrimination on the basis of sex or marital status.
- **The Race Relations Act 1976** makes it illegal to discriminate against employees or potential employees on the grounds of race or ethnic origin.
- **The Disability Discrimination Act 1995** gives additional rights to disabled people and provides for a code of practice aimed at ending discrimination.
- **The Employment Rights Act 1996** confirms the statutory (legal) rights of employees and covers the contract of employment, payslips, guarantee payments, Sunday working, time off work, suspension from work, maternity rights, termination of employment, unfair dismissal and remedies for unfair dismissal, redundancy, lay-offs and short time working, and the insolvency of an employer.

The Equal Opportunities Commission investigates complaints of discrimination on the grounds of sex or marital status. The Commission for Racial Equality investigates complaints of discrimination on the grounds of race or ethnic origin.

Motivation

In order to contribute fully to their work and to the success of their employer, employees must be motivated. People are motivated when they have an interest or drive that makes them want to do something. A motivator is something that gives them that interest or drive. Businesses use two types of motivators:

- financial, such as wages and salaries, overtime and bonuses
- non-financial, such as holidays, opportunities for promotion and a sense of achievement.

Non-financial motivators also include aspects of the job itself, such as interesting and stimulating tasks, opportunities to use initiative and take responsibility, and job security.

Dismissal

When an employer feels that the behaviour of an employee is unreasonable or breaks the terms of his or her contract, it may be necessary to enforce disciplinary procedures, or to take disciplinary action, which can ultimately lead to the dismissal (sacking) of the employee.

The disciplinary process has three stages (see Figure 1.6). The first stage is one of informal discussion, where the employer tries to resolve the matter by talking with the employee. If the matter can be resolved at this stage, no further action is necessary. The second stage is a formal procedure. This involves the following steps.

- A verbal warning that certain behaviour of the employee will not be tolerated and that unless the behaviour changes within a certain period further disciplinary action will be taken.
- A written warning detailing the offence for which the employee is being disciplined and explaining what is expected of the employee in the future and what action will be taken if the employee continues to offend. The employee must sign a copy to show that he or she has received and understands the written warning. There may be a first and a final written warning.

The third stage is disciplinary action. If an employee continues to commit an offence, despite receiving verbal and final written warnings, the employer may take disciplinary action consisting of dismissal, suspension, or in some cases transfer or demotion according to the severity of the offence.

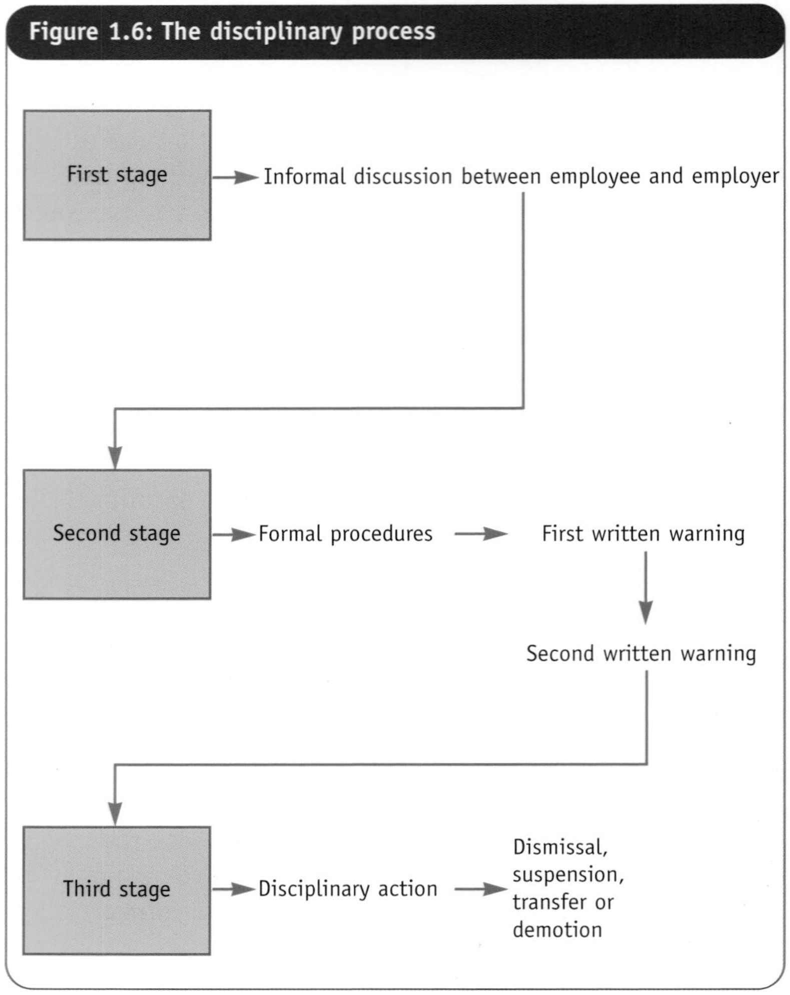

Working conditions

An employee's **working conditions** include both matters covered by his or her contract of employment, such as pay and hours of work, and other matters, such as type of working environment. Working conditions vary between businesses, and even between specific jobs within a business.

▶ Some working environments offer more freedom

Some working environments offer more comfort

Here are some of the most significant features of working conditions.

- **The working environment**. This is often connected with the nature of the job. Some environments, such as offices and hotels, are clean and comfortable, while others, such as iron foundries and oil rigs are less so.
- **Hours of work**. These vary between jobs. A traditional office job in a bank, for example, may be from 9.00 a.m. to 5.00 p.m., although this is becoming less the norm, with the trend towards flexible working hours. Senior managers often find themselves working considerably longer – perhaps even working at home in the evenings and at weekends. Other workers may have to work hours to suit their customers. For example, many shops have a late night opening at least once during the week and open on Saturdays and (in many cases) Sundays, as these are the times when most people are able to do their shopping.
- **Pay**. Employees are normally paid weekly, in the form of wages, or monthly, in the form of a salary. Extra payments, such as overtime, bonuses or commission, may also be made. Rates of pay vary enormously between different jobs in the same organisation, and between different organisations.
- **Job security**. A low level of job security is stressful for employees. If they are not sure how long their employment will last, people find it difficult to plan for the future or commit themselves financially by, for example, taking out a mortgage to buy a house.

CASE STUDY

Karen Harper

Karen Harper is the personnel manager of Western Distribution Services Limited in Bristol. She has a skilled job, calling for specific qualifications and experience. The position is full time and permanent. Karen feels her job is secure, and likes to know that a regular salary will be paid into her bank account each month.

Karen went into personnel work when she left college, because she likes working with people and she thought she would enjoy being in an office. She started with a large national company as a personnel assistant, in an office with four others. Obviously, since becoming personnel manager, her pay has increased, and she now has her own office, although she often works long hours and sometimes takes work home at weekends.

CASE STUDY

Michael Adobe

Michael is a college lecturer in business studies. He is a single parent and needs to be around for his young daughter, Katy, taking her to school and collecting her again at the end of the day. For this reason, Michael is unable to work full time, and has part-time positions at two nearby colleges of further education.

His hours of work vary from week to week, according to the needs of the colleges. This means that he has to do a considerable amount of lesson preparation and marking of students' work at home when Katy is in bed, but at least he is there for her. He used to work in an office, but could not find part-time office work to suit his needs.

The positions at each college are only temporary, and Michael has to renew his contract with each college at the beginning of the academic year. So far, the colleges he works for have wanted him back, but he knows that if the numbers of students on his courses drops significantly, he could lose his position with one or more of the colleges.

While he would like more job security, Michael needs the flexibility of the part-time position. The money he earns enables him to care for Katy as he wants to, and he enjoys the challenge of the classroom environment.

Health and safety

Health and safety at work is an important area that is being increasingly regulated by legislation from the United Kingdom and the European Union. The **Health and Safety at Work Act 1974** (HASAW) places responsibilities on employers to:

- provide a workplace that is safe and healthy
- carry out safety procedures such as fire drills, and to display safety notices and indicate fire exits
- provide machinery and equipment that is safe to operate and properly guarded
- provide trained safety staff
- have a written statement of health and safety policy which is available to all employees.

◀ The Health and Safety Executive publishes many useful information booklets

HASAW also places responsibilities on employees to:

- follow health and safety procedures
- use machinery and equipment in a safe manner, including using any safety devices and guards
- always act in ways that will not endanger themselves or others
- not misuse any safety equipment provided or deface safety notices.

The **Control of Substances Hazardous to Health Regulations 1988** (COSHH) covers the storage, handling and use of substances that are hazardous to health, such as chemicals and cleaning materials.

Training, development and promotion

Training helps employees to acquire the skills necessary both to do their current jobs to the best of their abilities and to progress to other types of employment in accordance with their career plans.

Most businesses provide some induction training for new employees, designed to help them settle in with their new employer. During induction, new employees are usually given information about staff welfare and other general matters as well as about the functional area or department in which they are to work.

Training is also provided when new developments in areas such as information technology mean that employees need to update their skills. Some employees may also be given training for promotion to supervisory or management positions.

The availability of training can be an important motivator to employees. Training provided by an employer may be internal or external.

- **Internal training** is provided within the business. This may be on the job, where the jobholder learns by doing the job under the supervision of a more experienced employee, or off the job, where the employee may receive specialist training, perhaps in specific skills such as report writing or supervisory techniques.
- **External training** is where employees receive training at outside centres, such as colleges of further education. This training may be job specific, such as computer-aided design (CAD), or more general.

Opportunities for promotion or career development can act as a strong motivator, especially when the chance for promotion is combined with appropriate training. Many people choose employment with the aim of improving their position as they progress in their job. A business that provides clear opportunities for career development will attract employees with a higher degree of loyalty and commitment than an organisation that does not.

Employee organisations and unions

The human resources personnel within a business sometimes negotiate with employee organisations such as staff associations and trade unions. Negotiations may be over disputes, such as the unfair treatment of employees, or over improvements to pay and other working conditions, such as health and safety, welfare, disciplinary procedures and the provision of training. Where an employer has to make a number of employees redundant, this also often calls for negotiation with the appropriate staff associations and trade unions.

- A **staff association** is a group of employees within a single business organisation. The association's officers are normally elected by the employees of the business to represent their interests in negotiations with the senior management. Negotiations might cover specific grievances or general matters, such as working conditions.
- A **trade union** is an organisation that is set up to represent the interests of employees in a particular trade or industry and to promote good relations and cooperation between employers and employees. In representing their members (that is employees who have joined the union), trade unions might negotiate with employers or employers' representatives over pay and conditions, act on behalf of members and provide legal advice and support in disputes. Agreements reached between trade unions, on behalf of their members, and employers are called **collective agreements**

Trade unions help to advise employees of their rights at work

Negotiations between employers and trade unions take place on two levels:

- nationally, where the trade union is trying to reach an agreement with all employers in an industry for all its members, or for all its members in a business which operates nationally
- locally, where the trade union negotiates on behalf of its members with employers in a specific part of the country, or with one employer on behalf of members at a particular factory or base.

CASE STUDY

The human resources function at DC Food Group Services

DC Food Group Services plc is a large national company that manufactures and distributes foodstuffs to the hotel and catering trade throughout the United Kingdom. The company has three factories and 40 distribution depots throughout the country.

The main aims of the company are to make a profit, to maximise sales and improve the quality of its products, and to provide a highly competitive service.

The human resources function in DC Food Group Services is given a high profile. The company recognises that its employees are its most valuable assets and wants to ensure that the best interests of its employees are considered at every level throughout the company. This means that while overall responsibility for human resources lies with the human resources department, which sets out policies and guidelines, all managers and supervisors in every other function of the company are expected to consider the welfare, motivation and discipline of the employees for whom they are responsible.

The human resources department is run by Angela Dube, the human resources manager. She is responsible for planning staffing levels to meet the needs of other departments, and she meets the managers of the other departments at weekly planning meetings. It is also Angela's responsibility to check that the company's human resources policies are applied throughout the organisation.

Angela frequently meets with representatives from the trade unions that represent different groups of employees at DC Food Group Services to negotiate wage levels or to discuss matters of employee welfare. If there is a dispute between employees and

management which she cannot resolve herself, she also meets with senior directors and managers of the company and representatives of the trade unions to try to resolve the matter.

A major part of the human resources function is the recruitment and employment of new staff. This is always done by Jatin Parmar, the employment officer, together with the manager of the department in which the vacancy exists. Most vacancies are advertised internally as well as in the local paper. They also interview all shortlisted candidates, unless the position is for a senior manager, in which case Angela conducts the interview.

Staff training is the responsibility of David Johnson, training officer. He has recently introduced an induction programme for all new employees in order that they learn about the company, what it does and their role within the company and the department in which they will be working. David also organises on-the-job training for employees wishing to improve their skills at work and arranges some courses in food technology and management skills, which are run by a nearby college of further education. When asked, he also tries to find training courses that suit the needs of individual employees who are seeking to develop their careers, or just looking for personal development.

In the human resources department, there is a personnel assistant, Lalit Nathanwi, who is responsible for keeping staff records and ensuring they are up to date, and a welfare officer, Hussan Malik, who works closely with people in all other departments concerning staff welfare and health and safety matters.

ACTIVITY

Recruitment and working conditions

Read the case study on DC Food Group Services and answer the following questions.

- Explain the procedure that would be followed by DC Food Group Services if there is a vacancy in the sales department.
- Who, apart from personnel in the human resources department at DC Food Group Services, is involved in the human resources function within the company?

Look at the job advertisements in your local paper. Select one that you think might be suitable for you when you have finished your studies. Write notes analysing the advertisement. For example:

- do you think the job advertisement is effective
- will it attract the type of candidates required
- does it adequately describe the job
- what other information do you think the advertisement should give
- how would you apply for the job?

Look back at the case studies on Karen Harper and Michael Adobe (see page 40). Explain the difference in their working conditions. Write a description of the working conditions of the job for which you selected the advertisement in the previous task.

Finance

Businesses receive money in return for the goods and services they sell. This is their revenue. From this, they must pay for those goods and services they use in running the business and producing the goods and services they supply.

When you buy a new pair of trainers from a shop such as Sports Division, for example, you have to pay the shop an amount of money, say £49, in return for the footwear. The shop then uses the £49 it has received from you, together with all the money it has received from other customers, to pay for:

- the wages and salaries of its staff
- the costs of running the business, including rent, light and heating, postage and advertising
- the trainers, which the shop has to buy from a manufacturer (such as Nike) so that it can sell them to you.

The money you pay for a pair of trainers contributes to the costs of running the shop as well as the manufacturing costs

It is the job of the finance function to manage the money coming into and going out of the business so that at any time there is enough money to pay the bills that are due. The business may also need money to pay for new machinery and equipment, vehicles, or even factories and offices. In addition, the finance function sets the financial targets the business must meet in order to make a profit.

Finance, therefore, affects all other functions of the business. For example, if a business fails to pay a supplier for raw materials it has received, the supplier will not want to make further deliveries. This means that the production department may run out of raw materials, and be unable to produce any more goods.

The main activities of the finance function are:

- preparing accounts
- paying wages and salaries
- obtaining capital and resources.

Preparing accounts

The financial targets of a business are set out, normally on a monthly basis, in a document called a **budget**. The accounts of the business show its actual financial performance. They can be regularly compared with the budget and any significant variation can be analysed. In this way, appropriate action can be taken to ensure that the business meets its targets.

Figure 1.7: The accounting process

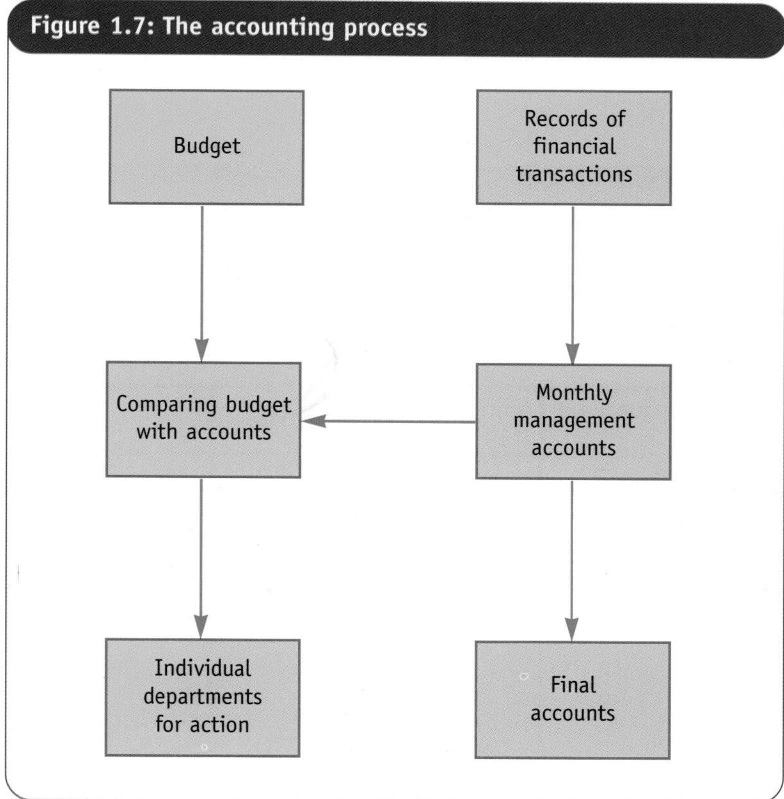

Accounts are usually prepared by accounts clerks or assistants under the supervision of the company accountant or financial manager, who may be at the head of an accounts or finance department. **Management accounts** contain a detailed analysis of revenue and expenditure. **Financial accounts** show a summary of the profit or loss and the financial position of the business. Financial accounts are submitted to the Inland Revenue each year.

Paying wages and salaries

The finance function is responsible for paying the wages and salaries of employees. A **wage** is a payment that is calculated on an hourly rate. Wages are usually paid weekly. The hourly rate is shown on the contract of employment and this is multiplied by the number of hours the employee actually works each week in order to arrive at the wage to be paid for that week. For example, an employee who is paid at a rate of £8.56 per hour, and who works 40 hours in one week, will receive wages of £342.40 (£8.56 × 40) for that week.

A **salary** is a payment based on an annual, or yearly, rate. This is known as the rate per annum. The annual rate is shown on the contract of employment. Salaries are usually paid monthly. The amount of salary paid each month is found by dividing the annual salary by 12 monthly payments. For example, an employee whose annual salary is £12,000 will be paid £1,000 (£12,000 ÷ 12) per month.

Figure 1.8: A pay slip

Employee Name					Pay Period	
National Insurance Number					Tax Code	
Hours	Rate	Total	Deductions	Amount	Year to date	
			Tax NI Pension Other		Gross Pay Tax NI	Amount
Gross Pay			Total Deductions		Net Pay	

Although an employee's contract of employment states that he or she will be paid a wage or salary at a certain rate, this is not the actual amount the employee receives. Before an employer makes a wage or salary payment to an employee, the following must be deducted from the total amount:

- income tax, which is paid to the government through the Inland Revenue
- national insurance, which is paid to the government to pay for the National Health Service and state pensions
- pension deductions, which are paid if the employee is in a private pension scheme and this is stated in the contract of employment.

Obtaining capital and resources

All businesses need money to purchase **capital** items such as buildings and land, machinery and equipment. These are items that often last for a number of years. They also need money to buy **resources** such as raw materials and power. These are items that are used up in the production process: the more a business produces, the more resources it uses.

◀ Banks are one source of capital for businesses

A business requires capital and resources whether it is just starting up, continuing production or expanding. Part of the finance function is to obtain the money for, or finance the purchase of, these items. There are various sources of finance available to a business.

- Owners' resources – the owners of the business may be able to provide the finance required from their own resources; this may require them to take out a personal loan, such as a mortgage on their house.
- Banks and finance houses – these provide loans to new and existing businesses. Interest is charged on the loan, and this becomes an ongoing expense that the business has to pay.
- Profits – a successful business may be able to fund expansion and pay for additional or replacement machinery out of the profits it makes from its present operation.
- Other sources – these include sources specifically designed for small start-up businesses, such as the Prince's Youth Business Trust, established by the Prince of Wales, and training and enterprise councils (TECs).

CASE STUDY

The finance function at DC Food Group Services

The finance function of DC Food Group Services is carried out by the finance department. The department is run by Mary Tilly, the chief accountant.

Mary's job involves coordinating the work of the other members of the department, reviewing the financial information produced, such as budgets, cash flow forecasts and management accounts, and making recommendations. Sometimes this involves liaising with the managers of other departments over cutting costs in different areas, or perhaps increasing sales or production levels in order to meet the financial targets of the company. This is not always popular – nobody likes to be told they must spend less or do more. Mary also prepares the financial accounts when necessary and arranges with the company's bank, or elsewhere, for additional finance, perhaps to purchase a new office building or factory, or an expensive item of machinery.

Bianca Read, the management accountant, is responsible to Mary. She prepares monthly management accounts, presenting detailed information on the expenses and income of each department of the company. These are compared with the budget to show where there are differences between planned and actual performance. Each department is asked to carry out a variance analysis to explain any major differences. By identifying and highlighting variances in this way, departments can take action to ensure that the company achieves its overall targets.

Information for the management accounts is produced by Chris Nugent, who obtains the appropriate financial information from each department and records it on computer so that the management accounts can be produced quickly following each month end. Chris also produces other information, such as weekly sales figures, which is required by senior managers for their weekly planning meetings, and carries out the credit control function. This involves checking credit references of customers who want to purchase goods on credit, and chasing overdue accounts. Only rarely does Chris take a customer to court over an unpaid bill.

There are four wages clerks and a cost clerk in the finance department. The wages clerks prepare the wages and salaries for all employees, calculating the wages of hourly paid employees and arranging for the money to be transferred from the company's bank account to the bank accounts of individual employees, weekly or monthly as appropriate. The cost clerk is responsible for checking the costings of all the company's products to ensure that the margin between the selling price and the cost of producing the product – the profit margin – is maintained.

The finance department

Make a list of the job titles of the personnel in the finance department at DC Food Group Services who:

- prepare the management accounts
- produce the final accounts
- pay wages and salaries
- obtain capital and resources.

How does the work of the finance department at DC Food Group Services affect the work of other functional areas in the company and which functional areas are affected?

Administration

No organisation can operate effectively without an efficient administration system. In larger organisations this will comprise an administration department, whose job is to provide back-up for all the other functions and departments of the organisation.

Figure 1.9: The administration function

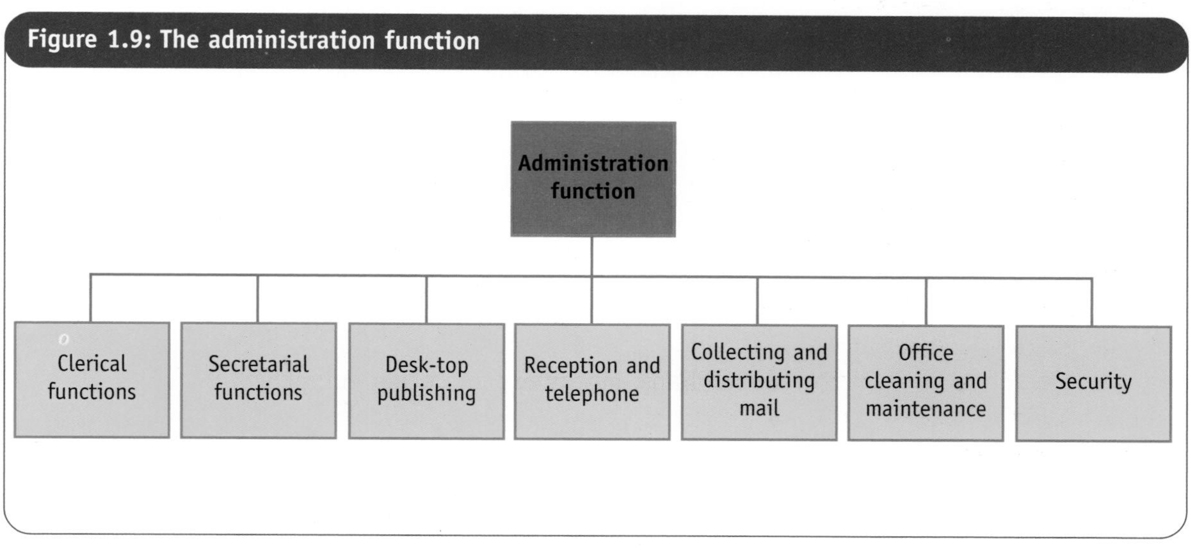

The administration department (sometimes called the office services department) provides services such as:

- clerical work, including filing and keeping records
- typing and secretarial services
- organising meetings
- desk-top publishing
- photocopying
- design and production of forms
- reception and telephone
- dealing with queries
- collecting and distributing mail.

The actual services provided depend on the type and size of the organisation. The administration function is both involved with and crosses every other function in the business. For example, some employees in finance or human resources will be responsible for the administration of their functional area, performing tasks such as photocopying and filing.

In addition to providing services such as those listed, the administration function also covers services such as cleaning, security and the maintenance of offices and buildings.

The cleanliness of premises where people work is an aspect of the working environment that is emphasised by both health and safety and employment legislation. It includes keeping work areas free from dirt and debris that could cause a health hazard, and cleaning floors, walls and ceilings in factories and offices. Where food production or preparation is involved, or in hospitals, doctors' surgeries and elsewhere where there is a danger of contamination, the need for cleanliness is even more critical. If hazardous substances are involved, as in the case of a chemical spillage, it may be necessary to obtain the services of a specialist cleaner with particular knowledge and skills for dealing with the hazardous material.

Security is also a consideration of increasing importance for many businesses. A business may need to ensure the security of:

- buildings, machinery and other equipment
- stocks of raw materials and finished goods
- money
- employees
- customers.

Some organisations need particular types of security staff, for example, leisure centres need lifeguards. In certain areas, the need for security has grown with technological and other developments. Hi-tech products such as mobile phones, computers and computer peripherals (such as modems and zip drives) have become targets for theft, as have products in some other fields, such as drugs. A particularly disturbing development is the need for hospitals and similar establishments to provide security to protect their staff from assault.

CASE STUDY

The administration function at DC Food Group Services

All departments in DC Food Group Services carry out their own basic administration, producing letters, documents and information on computer, filing and keeping records. There is, however, an administration department that coordinates the administrative systems of the company and that deals with general matters that affect all departments.

The head of the administration department is Brendan O'Reilly, the company secretary. He is responsible for all legal matters and matters affecting shareholders. Together with the office manager, May Heatherington, Brendan deals with all insurance matters and organises meetings of the board of directors and other important meetings such as the weekly planning meetings. He frequently contacts managers of other departments.

May's duties involve overseeing the planning and running of the administration department. She is also responsible for the administrative systems of the whole company. For example, if there is any problem with a photocopier or computer in the human resources department, they will contact May to sort the problem out and keep the department running smoothly.

There is a post room with three members of staff (a supervisor and two clerks), who receive the mail delivery from the post

office, sort it and deliver it to the appropriate member of staff or department. The post room also arranges collection of mail from individual departments and delivers it either within the company in the case of internal mail, or to the post office for posting in the case of external mail.

Rachael Jones, the receptionist, is also part of the administration department. She is the first contact most people have with the company, either greeting them as they enter the offices, or answering their telephone call before connecting them to the appropriate member of staff and department.

Administration

Using the case study on the administration function in DC Food Group Services as an example, show how administration can be a function both of an administration department and every other department within a business.

To what extent does the administration department at DC Food Group Services support other functions within the company, and to what extent are its functions separate from other functional areas?

Explain how the administrative function helps a business to achieve its aims.

Figure 1.10: The production process

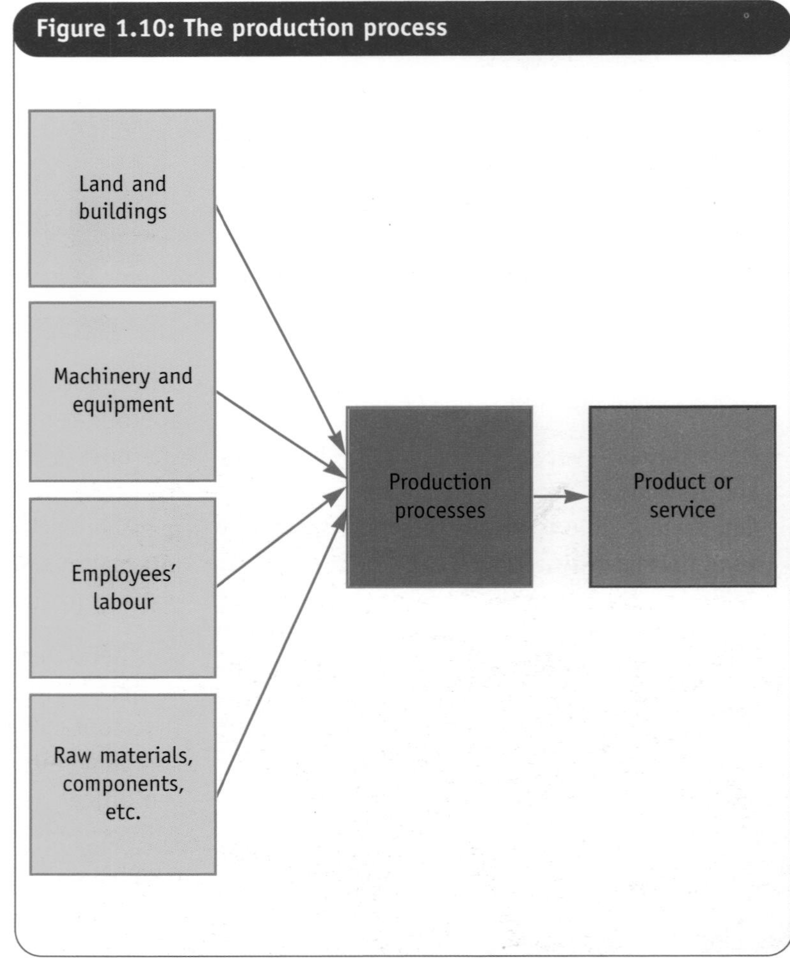

Production

The production function is responsible for making the goods or services that are provided by the business. This involves the use of capital and resources including:

- buildings and land, such as offices, factories, shops, farmland
- equipment, such as vehicles, computers, machinery
- people, such as operatives, managers, support staff, specialists
- materials, such as products for retailing, raw materials.

There are two essential aspects to managing production. The first is planning production to ensure that there are enough raw materials, components, personnel with the right skills, and machines or other equipment available to make the product in sufficient quantities and at the right time to meet the needs of customers.

The second aspect is controlling production to ensure that there are no delays or problems in the production process, so that customers' orders are filled on time and as planned. It is also important to monitor the cost, use and waste of raw materials and components.

Planning and controlling production involves the finance function in purchasing the raw materials and components, machinery and equipment, and the human resources function in recruiting and training employees. There must also be close liaison with marketing and sales, who inform production how many units of production customers are expected to want.

◀ Controlling production ensures that products are delivered to customers in the right quantities at the right time and to the right quality

CASE STUDY

The production function at DC Food Group Services

Each of DC Food Group Services' three factories has its own production department, which is responsible for actually producing the goods.

At the Stratford-upon-Avon factory, which produces canned vegetables, the operations manager, Simon Branston, is responsible for ensuring that all the necessary resources – machinery and equipment, personnel and raw materials including empty cans, vegetables and labels – are available in the right quantities and at the right time.

Simon works to a production budget calculated in consultation with the marketing department and the sales department. This ensures that production levels of each line are sufficient to meet anticipated customer needs, but not so high as to result in unsold stock – and questions from the chief accountant!

The works manager, James Marston, actually controls the production of the factory on a day-to-day basis, allocating work to factory operatives and the machines they operate. This is normally done in response to production requests, which are completed according to Simon's instructions the day before by the production control clerk.

James is also responsible for quality and stock levels. There is a quality controller who keeps a regular check on the quality of the product, but James favours the Japanese *Kaizen* approach to quality – organising the production operatives and supervisors into quality circles so that they can oversee the quality of their own part of the production process and, when they see a problem, make recommendations or take action without waiting for someone else to step in when it may be too late.

Maintenance of the equipment is undertaken by the maintenance engineer, John Newcombe.

Production

Make a list of the different resources needed by the production department at DC Food Group Services' Stratford-upon-Avon factory.

Explain the different roles of and Simon Branston and James Marston.

In what way do the activities of the production department affect other functional areas of a business and help the business achieve its aims?

Marketing and sales

Although they are often considered aspects of the same function, marketing and sales are in fact separate activities.

Marketing

The marketing activities of a business are designed to ensure that there are potential customers who know about the business and its goods or services, and who want to buy those products.

For customers to want to buy an organisation's products, the products must be:

- the right product (the product the customers want)
- at the right price (a price customers are happy to pay)
- in the right place (where customers want and expect to be able to buy the product)
- at the right time (available when customers want it).

Marketing activities consist of market research and promotion. We look at these next.

Market research

Businesses undertake **market research** in order to find out:

- what goods and services customers want
- what customers think of the products already being supplied – both by the business itself and by its competitors
- the existing and potential sales of a product
- the attitudes of customers to a product
- the strengths and weakness of competitors
- expected trends in the market and in demand for a product.

A market researcher interviewing a member of the public in the street

By finding out what customers want, a business can supply a product that will satisfy them. This may be an improvement to an existing product or a new product that more closely meets customers' requirements. Other market research information will enable the business to respond to changes in demand and to meet challenges presented by the activities of competitors.

Primary research involves a direct investigation of potential and existing customers' attitudes and behaviour. This is undertaken by the business itself or a market research organisation, and may be done by observation or interview. An example of observation is where a market researcher watches the behaviour of customers in a supermarket, recording how many choose a certain product or a packet of a certain colour. Interviews are usually carried out using a questionnaire. They may be conducted face to face (for example by market researchers who call at your front door or stop you in the street), over the telephone or by post. A postal questionnaire is the cheapest method but has the lowest response rate. Questionnaires are usually designed so that the results obtained can be analysed quickly and easily by computer.

Secondary research (sometimes called desk research) is carried out using existing records and sources of information. These include the business's own sales and customer records, government publications such as *Social Trends* and the *Annual Abstract of Statistics*, and reports and sets of statistics published by private organisations including *The Economist*, the *Financial Times*, the Bank of England and other banks, accountants and marketing organisations such as Mintel.

The main problem with using secondary sources is that the information they contain has usually been gathered for purposes other than that for which the market researcher requires it. It may therefore be less useful or trustworthy than primary information.

Promotion

All businesses must promote themselves and the goods or services they provide if they are to sell them in sufficient quantities. By promoting its goods or services a business organisation aims to create:

- awareness in customers and consumers both of the business and of the goods or services it provides
- demand for those goods or services by persuading customers and consumers that they want the product or service being promoted.

There are four main types of **promotion** which businesses use to market their goods and services:

- **point of sale** promotions, which include displays of books, videos and perfumes in stores and supermarkets and other promotional material on display where the product is sold such as details about special offers and free gifts
- **advertisements**, for example on television and radio, in newspapers and magazines and on billboard posters
- **sponsorship**, of sporting, arts and other events and of personalities
- **competitions**, often through the post, such as those regularly run by *Reader's Digest, Which?* and home shopping catalogue companies.

▼ Business promotion takes many forms

CASE STUDY

The marketing function at DC Food Group Services

DC Food Group Services considers marketing to be vital to its success. It is a long-established and well-known company in the trade, but unless it produces the type of goods that its customers want and lets them know about new lines and special offers, it will lose out to its competitors.

Adrian Burgess, the marketing manager, plans the marketing strategy of the company. He makes sure that the company is kept aware of the current requirements of its customers and potential customers through regular market research. Jill Bryant is the market researcher who actually designs questionnaires and talks to customers either on the phone or in person.

The company's sales representatives, who regularly visit and talk to their customers, also gather much important information about the requirements of customers and their attitudes towards DC Food Group Services and its products. Much of the information, especially about changes in the requirements of customers, is passed to the production department. For example, in recent years, customers have started to demand foods that have fewer additives such as artificial flavourings and colourings.

Although the products and services of the company are well known in the catering trade, DC Food Group Services still sees the need for advertising and maintaining good public relations. The advertising manager, Tara Ellison, who also issues press releases about new products and other company matters, arranges advertising, mainly in trade magazines and by direct mail.

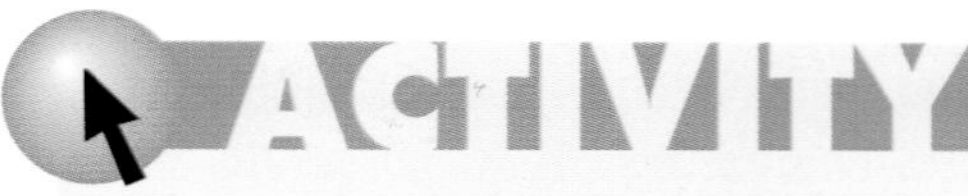

Marketing

DC Food Group Services is planning to produce a new line of low calorie, organic, tinned vegetables. What market research should the company carry out? Your answer should cover:

- primary research
- secondary research.

Once a decision to produce the new line has been taken, the company must promote the product to existing and potential customers. Describe the methods of promotion that you think DC Food Group Services should undertake.

Choose one promotional method that you described in your answer to the last task. Produce a draft of that promotion. If possible, you should use a desk-top publishing package for this task.

Sales

Any business that provides goods or services must sell them in order to make enough revenue to cover its costs. Every other functional area of a business therefore relies on the sales function to obtain the revenue to pay for the resources required. The methods used, and the type of employees involved in the selling process depend on the type of organisation, the goods or services it produces and its customers.

A shop, for example, uses sales assistants to sell goods to customers who come into the store. A manufacturer which supplies the shop with goods for resale probably has a team of sales executives, or representatives, who visit shops to persuade them to buy its goods. Each sales executive may have an exclusive area – all the shops in a certain area are considered to be (potential) customers of one sales executive.

Similarly, businesses which produce machinery, raw materials and goods that are used by other businesses to produce their own goods have sales teams which visit customers and potential customers in order to persuade them to buy their product.

Some businesses that sell to the general public use teams of sales executives to visit potential customers at their homes. The sales executive normally makes an appointment with the potential customer before the visit. This method of selling is used extensively by insurance companies, financial services and double glazing manufacturers. Other businesses use sales people who sell door to door, either from a catalogue of goods which may have been previously delivered through the letter box (such as Avon and Betterwear) or from a mobile shop.

Avon employs sales teams to sell door to door

Whichever method is used, selling is a skilled job that is usually done by employees who have been specially trained. It is essential that any employee selling products to customers is thoroughly familiar with the business and its products and is able to communicate effectively with the customers. Many larger companies have a sales department whose sole activity is to sell to the organisation's customers.

It is not only profit-making businesses in the private sector that need to sell their products. Many public sector organisations, such as schools and hospitals receive funds from local and national government according to the number of clients (pupils or patients) they serve. These organisations, therefore, also have to sell their services. A head teacher showing his or her school to parents considering a new school for their child, is in fact selling the services of the school to potential customers.

CASE STUDY

The sales function at DC Food Group Services

At DC Food Group Services most sales are achieved by sales representatives, who regularly visit customers and potential customers within a specified area.

Mary Duffy's area covers the highlands and islands of Scotland, and she frequently has to spend two or three nights away from home – especially when she is visiting customers on some of the islands and is constrained by the timing of the ferry services.

Mary is one of the representatives attached to the northern England and Scotland region, which is controlled by a regional sales manager. In all, there are six regional sales managers responsible for the activities of sales representatives throughout the United Kingdom. The regional sales managers are in turn responsible to the sales manager, Ken Gooderham, who sets the individual sales targets according to the sales budget. Any changes in expected sales levels are reported by the sales representatives through the regional sales managers to Ken, who liaises with the production department over production levels. It is Ken's responsibility to ensure that sales are maintained at the level necessary to produce the profit required by the company.

In addition to the sales representatives, sales orders are obtained by a team of six telephone sales staff based at the company's head office. As orders are received, either from the representatives or telephone sales staff, order forms are completed and faxed to the customer's nearest DC Food Group Services distribution depot where the order is made up and dispatched. It is up to each distribution depot to make sure it has enough stock to meet customers' demands. When stocks of a particular product are running low, the distribution depot sends a request for more stocks through to the production department at the appropriate factory.

Sales

Basing your answer on the marketing and sales departments of DC Food Group Services, explain the difference between marketing and sales to someone with no knowledge of business studies.

What types of business aims and objectives do you think are supported by the activities of that sales department?

Customer service

All businesses need customers to buy their products and services. In today's increasingly competitive world, businesses must ensure that they provide what their customers want, so that they do not go elsewhere. This means that businesses must not only provide a high-quality product or service that is safe and reliable, does what it is supposed to, and offers good value for money, but they must also ensure a high standard of service in dealing with customers.

A customer is likely to shop elsewhere if he or she has received poor service, perhaps because the store's staff are rude or unhelpful, even if the product itself is satisfactory. This aspect of customer relations is so important that many larger organisations have established dedicated customer service departments to deal with customers' enquiries, complaints and requests and, if necessary, to pass these on to the appropriate department. A customer service department can also be a valuable source of market research information.

All organisations must strive to meet their customers' needs by:

- providing information
- giving advice
- providing credit facilities
- delivering goods
- providing after-sales service.

A business that meets these needs provides a high standard of customer service, sometimes called **best practice** customer service. The benefit is customer satisfaction and this is reflected in a high level of sales and repeat business.

The individual needs of customers and the methods of providing customer service vary between different types of business. In fact, the methods of providing customer service even vary between organisations providing the same goods and services. These methods range from simple notices in shop windows giving information about opening hours, to customer service staff specially trained to deal with customers' enquiries, requests for refunds and complaints. Other methods of providing good customer service include:

- taking action to reduce the time taken for customers to be served
- producing leaflets and information about products, their effects on health or the environment, and about the business itself
- providing improved access to premises and facilities for customers with special needs
- training staff to greet customers with a smile and a friendly gesture, making them feel welcome and valued by the business.

Businesses must keep various aspects of customer service under review.

- **Reliability.** A reputation for reliability helps businesses to increase sales by retaining existing customers and attracting new ones.
- **Friendliness.** Most customers appreciate being made to feel welcome. They like the sense that the business, represented by the person serving them, values them as a customer. A smile and a friendly word cost nothing but, as many businesses have found out, are aspects of customer service which customers rate highly. Many businesses, such as major supermarkets and restaurants, give special training in greeting and serving people to their staff who have direct contact with customers.
- **Availability of goods and services.** Customers are more likely to go to a business if they know that the goods or services they want will be easily available when they require them.
- **Speed of delivery.** In the same way, customers expect goods which they have purchased, but which may be too heavy or bulky to take away themselves, to be delivered promptly. If you buy a new computer system, you want it delivered in a few days so that you can start using it. If a retailer is unable to deliver it until next month, you will probably look to buy it somewhere else. You also want it delivered on the day it is promised.

▼ Using leaflets to keep customers informed

- **Care for the environment.** Customers expect manufacturers and suppliers to help maintain the environment by avoiding pollution and waste. When McDonald's began a programme of rapid expansion during the 1960s and 1970s, there was a considerable public outcry about the amount of rubbish dropped outside its restaurants littering the roads and pavements. McDonald's soon responded by employing people to clear up the rubbish and keep the environment around its restaurants litter-free – even though the rubbish was dropped by McDonald's customers and not McDonald's employees. McDonald's now has clear, well-publicised environmental policies, which are considered to contribute to its success.

McDonald's sponsors anti-litter campaigns

- **Customer safety.** Customer safety must be paramount. All customers have a right to expect any business organisation supplying them with goods or services to take all reasonable precautions to ensure their safety and well being. This applies on the premises of the business, in the customer's home and elsewhere. Even when there is an element of danger involved, a business must take all reasonable measures to safeguard the customer. For example, many sports, such as motor racing, are inevitably dangerous – this is part of their attraction. However, the organisers of a motor racing meeting have a duty to take reasonable precautions to ensure the safety of spectators.

- **Published policy for exchanges or refunds.** Many businesses have a policy of exchanging goods if they are faulty or do not meet the needs of the customer. Customers are encouraged to buy, confident in the knowledge that if their purchase turns out to be unsatisfactory in any way, they can exchange it or obtain a refund. Marks and Spencer, for example, has a well-publicised policy of exchanging goods or giving refunds. Obviously the policy is open to abuse; for example, some people take back their Christmas and birthday presents, preferring the money instead. However, the option of being able to return goods for exchange and refund encourages more sales, which more than offsets the number of people who return goods.

PLEASE KEEP YOUR RECEIPT
Next is happy to exchange / refund any perfect merchandise returned within 28 days of purchase upon production of your receipt except items cut or made to customer order, pierced earrings or grooming products.

This does not affect your statutory rights.

The proprietor of Next is
Next Retail Limited
Desford Road
Enderby
Leicester LE9 5AT

Next's refund policy

- **Access to buildings.** Ease of access to buildings is an aspect of customer service which businesses often overlook. People in wheelchairs, and parents with children in pushchairs particularly need ease of access. Steps can be difficult to negotiate for many customers, and handrails can provide ease of access for the elderly or infirm. Business premises are increasingly being provided with ramps for customers in wheelchairs, or with pushchairs. Wide doors and lifts also assist people in wheelchairs. Many supermarkets now have specially widened checkouts for customers in wheelchairs or pushing prams.

CASE STUDY

The customer service function at DC Food Group Services

The directors of DC Food Group Services believe that good customer service is the responsibility of everybody in the company. Every employee has a part to play in providing customers with a service that can compare with the best practice found anywhere in the trade.

Nevertheless, the directors are aware that there are some matters that require special attention, and the company has established a dedicated customer service department consisting of Sue Proctor, the customer services manager, and two administration staff. Her department keeps in contact with customers at all times. She wants to know that customers are satisfied, both with the company's products and the service that it provides.

Part of her job is to monitor customer satisfaction and report on any improvements to service that should be made. She often discusses levels of customer satisfaction with the marketing department. Recently, Sue arranged with David Johnson, the training officer, for all customer service staff and telephone sales staff to attend a course on good telephone communications.

The customer services department also deals with requests from customers and prospective customers for information about the company or its products. Usually, any complaints are referred to Sue at an early stage, so that she can help the customer sort matters out to their satisfaction. Fortunately, there are not many of these, but Sue knows they are an important part of her job, as a satisfied customer remains a customer.

Sue is always looking for ways in which the company can improve the service it provides to its customers. She often visits the distribution depots checking on all aspect of customer service, from access to buildings to aspects of customer safety and care for the environment.

Customer service

How do the activities of customer service involve and affect other functional areas in DC Food Group Services?

Imagine you work in the customer service department of DC Food Group Services. Sue Proctor wants to overhaul the provision of customer service throughout the company to ensure that the standards provided by DC Food Group Services fulfil the ideals of best practice. Sue has asked you to write her a report outlining the aspects of customer service that together make up best practice. Write the report to Sue.

Some other functions of businesses

Quality control

Businesses must carefully monitor the quality of their products to ensure that they meet both the requirements of customers and the expected standards of the organisation. Quality assurance means having an effective system of checking the

Figure 1.11: The quality control process

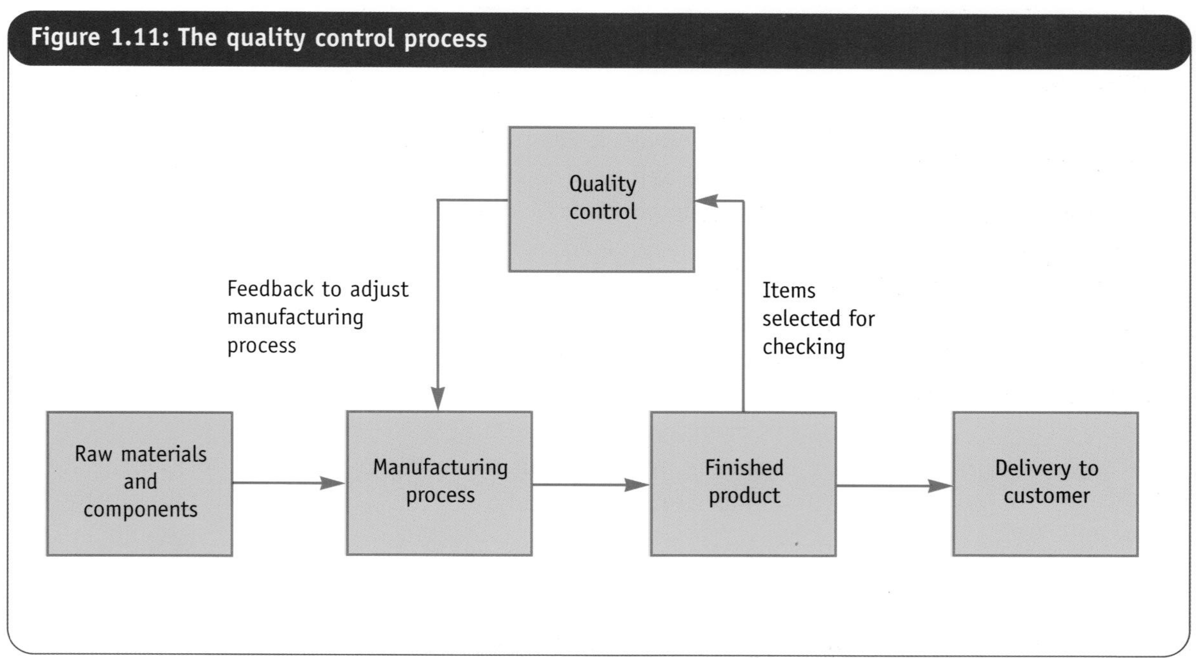

quality of goods and services that a business produces. It involves:

- specifying the standard of quality that customers require
- ensuring that the required quality can be achieved by, for example, controlling the standard of raw materials and components used in the production process and training production operatives
- checking for errors in production and correcting any problems
- reducing waste.

Some businesses adopt a zero defects approach to quality assurance. This means that employees are encouraged to ensure that the goods they produce are right first time, reducing waste and scrap to a minimum. To achieve this, employees involved in the same stage of production are sometimes formed into quality circles, identifying potential problems and finding solutions. In this way, a consistently high standard of quality can be achieved.

Research and development

The work of the research and development department involves designing new products and improving existing products. New products and improvements to existing products are needed to meet the requirements of customers, taking into consideration changes in consumer demand and the availability of new materials and technology. The marketing department collects this information about changes in consumer demand and the requirements of customers. The research and development department must also be aware of new materials, technology and products that affect customer requirements. For example, the development of multimedia computer technology has led to the availability of interactive encyclopaedias and other materials on CD-ROM.

New technology can also enable an organisation to manufacture a product that meets a consumer need more fully. Research into methods of improving safety in cars, for example, coupled with technological advances, has enabled many cars to be fitted with front and side impact airbags as standard.

Many large companies spend millions of pounds every year on research and development to try to stay ahead of their competitors in providing the latest products for their customers.

Distribution (logistics)

For many organisations, a sale is not complete until the product has been delivered to the customer. For example, if a

A distribution depot

farmer wants to sell eggs to a supermarket, the eggs must be delivered to the supermarket before it will buy them.

When this is the case, arrangements must be made to distribute the product to customers. This is the function of the distribution department. Depending on the product and its destination, distribution may be made by:

- post
- the organisation's own vehicles
- an outside haulier's vehicles
- rail, sea or air.

Obviously, if an organisation has to distribute its goods to its customers, by whatever method, the customer must receive them on time and in good condition. The method of distribution chosen must also be cost-effective, as distribution can be a major expense to an organisation.

Computer services

In smaller organisations, computer services (and information technology) may be part of the administration function. Nowadays, however, the importance of computers and information technology is so vital to the success and efficiency of an organisation, and the work involved is so complex, that it frequently requires a separate department.

The computer services department works closely with other functions, obtaining data and entering them onto the computer network. The data are then processed and information is produced in a form that is useful and easily understood by senior management. The speed with which this can be done, enabling decisions on future courses of action to be taken quickly and based on timely and accurate information, has meant that computers are now accepted tools in most business organisations.

The computer services department may also be involved in:

- raising sales invoices
- processing purchase invoices for payment
- compiling budgets and accounts
- planning production
- checking and maintaining stock levels
- keeping records (including employee records)
- developing specialised software.

Build your learning

Summary points

- Businesses carry out a range of functions including human resources, finance, administration, production, marketing and sales, and customer services.
- The functions of a business help it to achieve its aims and objectives.
- The functional areas of business are interdependent.
- Human resources staff are involved with recruitment, retention and dismissal, working conditions, health and safety, training, development and promotion, employee organisations and trade unions.
- Employers and employees have both responsibilities and rights, some of which are safeguarded by law.
- The finance function manages the money coming into and going out of the business.
- Finance personnel deal with preparing accounts, paying wages and salaries, and obtaining capital and resources.
- Administration is concerned with the smooth day-to-day running of the business.
- The production function uses resources such as land and buildings, machinery and equipment, labour and raw materials to produce the product of the business.
- Marketing and sales are concerned with finding out the needs of customers, promoting the products of the business and selling the products to customers.
- Businesses also have other functional areas such as quality control and research and development.

Key words and phrases

You should know the meaning of the words and phrases listed below as they relate to the functional areas and activities of businesses. Go back through the last 41 pages of the unit to check or refresh your understanding.

- **Administration**
- **Best practice**
- **Budget**
- **Capital**
- **Customer service**
- **Employment legislation**
- **Equal opportunities**
- **Finance**
- **Financial accounts**
- **Health and safety**
- **Human resources**
- **Management accounts**
- **Market research**
- **Marketing**
- **Production**
- **Promotion**
- **Quality control**
- **Research and development**
- **Resources**
- **Rights and responsibilities**
- **Salary**
- **Sales**
- **Wage**
- **Working conditions**

Student questions

1. Name and describe the activities of four functional areas typically found in businesses.
2. What are the rights and responsibilities of employers and employees and how are these protected by legislation and by employee organisations and unions?
3. What are the key issues relating to equal opportunities in employment?
4. What accounts are prepared within the finance function and what is their purpose?
5. Explain, with examples, the interdependence of functional areas in a business.

2 COLLECT THE EVIDENCE

For this activity you will investigate some of the functional activities of the business you selected for the 'Collect the evidence' activity on page 31. It gives you an opportunity to produce work that demonstrates your knowledge and understanding of the functional areas and activities of a business. The work that you complete for this activity will form part of your assessment evidence for this unit. You should refer to the grid on page 97 to see what you need to do to achieve a pass, merit or distinction.

Remember, if you carry out the following activities now, you will have completed part of the work needed for your end of unit assessment. You are advised to do this now, to avoid overload at the end of the unit.

What to do

1. **Select four functional areas of your chosen business to investigate. One of the functional areas must be human resources and you must choose three others, excluding customer services.**

2. **Obtain information from your chosen business about the functional areas you have selected. You will find the best way to do this is to arrange one or more visits to the business, and if possible talk to personnel, possibly the manager, involved in each functional area. You must find out the main activities of each area and how it contributes to the activity of the business. You also need to identify job roles within each area, and understand how the different functional areas interact to achieve the aims and objectives of the business.**

3. **Concerning human resources, you need to find out how equal opportunities are applied in the business, and how the rights of employees are safeguarded.**

4. **In addition to four functional areas of your selected business you must also investigate the forms of customer service provided by the business.**

5 **When you have obtained your information, you should write a description of the purposes and activities of the functional areas you have investigated and how they contribute to the activity of the business and help it to achieve its aims. You must give examples of job roles associated with each area you have described. You should also explain and give examples of how employees are safeguarded by employment law.**

6 **Prepare an oral presentation that compares the customer service of your selected business with best practice. Suggest any improvements that you consider can be made. You should make your presentation in front of your class and tutor, who will give you a written assessment of your presentation.**

Organisational structure

A business consists of people working together in different departments or functional areas to achieve common overall goals. In order to achieve these goals, and to ensure that employees are working together effectively, the goals must be communicated to employees, jobs must be allocated and the individual activities of employees must be coordinated.

If employees are unsure of what they are working towards, jobs are not allocated, or their individual activities are not coordinated, the employees will not know what they are supposed to do or what is expected of them. This can result in:

- duplication of effort, with some jobs being done twice by different people
- jobs being left undone, because everybody thought someone else was doing the work
- poor quality, with work not being done to the appropriate standard.

A business must plan and organise the work and functional activities of its workforce. Even a sole trader, working on his or her own, must plan and organise his or her work, just as you have to plan and organise your work when doing an assignment for GNVQ Intermediate Business.

When more than one person works in a business, the business develops an organisational structure that establishes:

- **job roles**, so that all employees know what they are supposed to do and what is expected of them
- **levels of authority**, so that employees know who they are responsible to (and what for), and who makes the plans and takes the decisions which affect the way the business is run and the jobs the employees do
- **channels of communication**, so that all employees know what the business is trying to achieve (and therefore what they are working towards) and are aware of decisions that have been taken which affect their work – good channels of communication also allow employees to feed back information to their colleagues about any problems that may occur, and suggestions how about performance could be improved.

Types of organisational structure

The way a business is structured depends on the specific functional areas and needs of the business. Some functional areas such as production will be focused on a single department while others such as administration may be spread across several departments. There are some characteristics of organisational structure, however, that are common to all businesses.

Hierarchical structures

Figure 1.12: A hierarchical structure

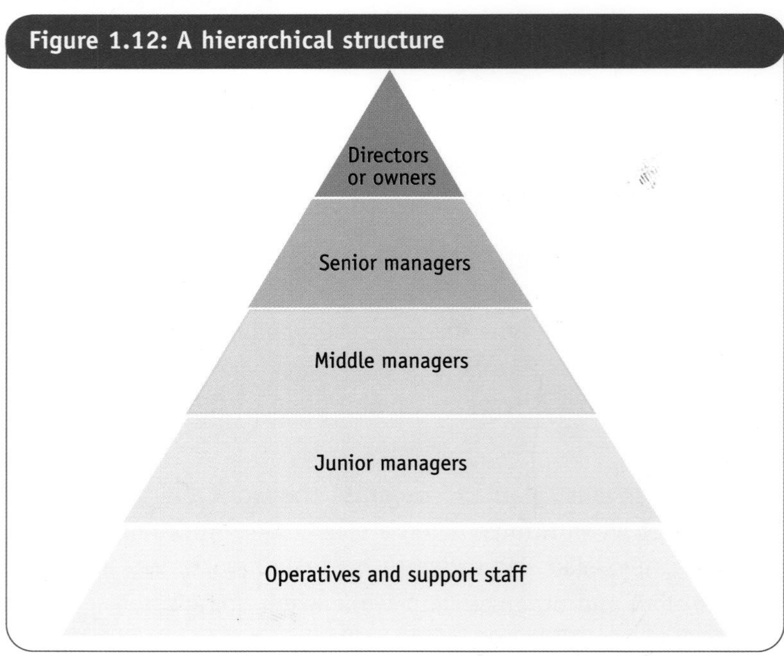

Traditionally, business organisations in the UK have been given **hierarchical structures**. An hierarchical structure is based on levels of authority and responsibility, with each person in the organisation having a clearly defined position that sets limits on the amount of authority and responsibility they have. Hierarchical structures are usually shown in the form of a pyramid (see Figure 1.12).

At the top of the structure is the most senior manager of the business; this is usually the owner or the managing director. Below this are levels of less senior managers, middle managers, junior managers, supervisors, operatives and support staff.

Employees at each level, except the top and the bottom, are responsible to a supervisor or manager at the level above and have authority over a number of employees at the level below. For example, a middle manager reports to a senior manager and may have authority over three junior managers. The number of employees a manager or supervisor has authority over is called their **span of control**. The span of control of the sales manager in Figure 1.13 is, therefore, three.

Figure 1.13: The span of control

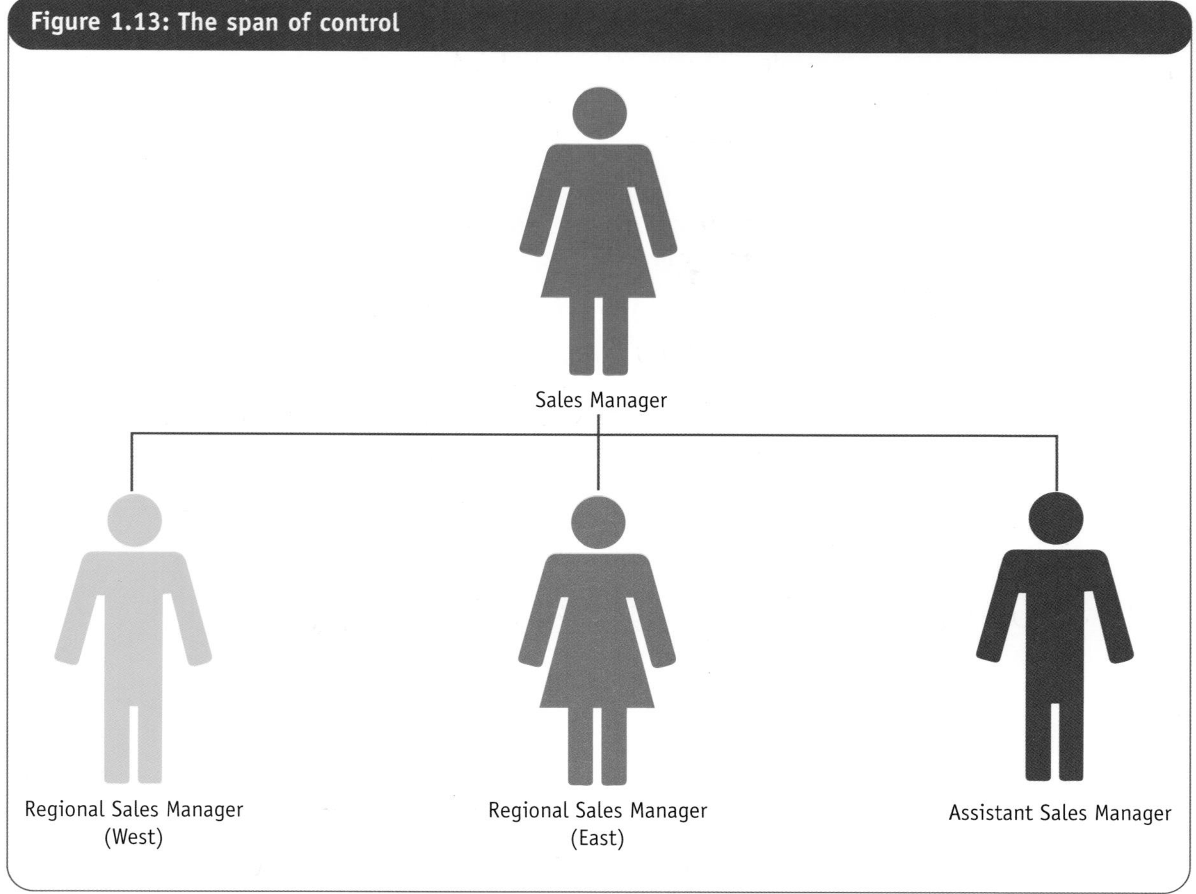

The advantages of hierarchical structures are that:

- control of the organisation is kept in the hands of the person at the top of the organisation
- it is easy to maintain a particular identity or standard of service and quality in a large organisation, which is especially important in large service organisations with several branches such as major banks, building societies, hotel chains and supermarkets
- there is a clearly defined chain of command, with instructions flowing downward through all employees, and information about performance and problems flowing upwards
- everyone in the organisation knows their role within the organisation, who they are responsible to and who they have authority over.

The main disadvantages of hierarchical structures are that:

- there is no limit to the number of levels of management between the top decision-maker and the shop floor operatives or other support staff
- decision making can be slow or delayed as it takes a long time for information to flow upwards, for decisions to be taken at the top and communicated downwards again and implemented by production operatives or support staff
- at each level, information and instructions may be interpreted differently so that information passed on, or action taken, may be biased by the attitudes of individual managers.

Flat structures

In order to overcome the disadvantages of hierarchical structures while retaining the advantages, many large organisations have reduced the number of levels of management, so bringing the most senior managers closer to operatives and support staff. As you can see in Figure 1.14, the removal of levels of management gives a flatter organisational structure.

The advantages of **flat organisational structures** are that:

- the flow of information between upper and lower levels is much faster, enabling quicker decision making and faster response to problems
- with fewer levels of management, many managers and operatives feel they have more responsibility for their own work, increasing motivation and job satisfaction.

Figure 1.14: A flat organisational structure

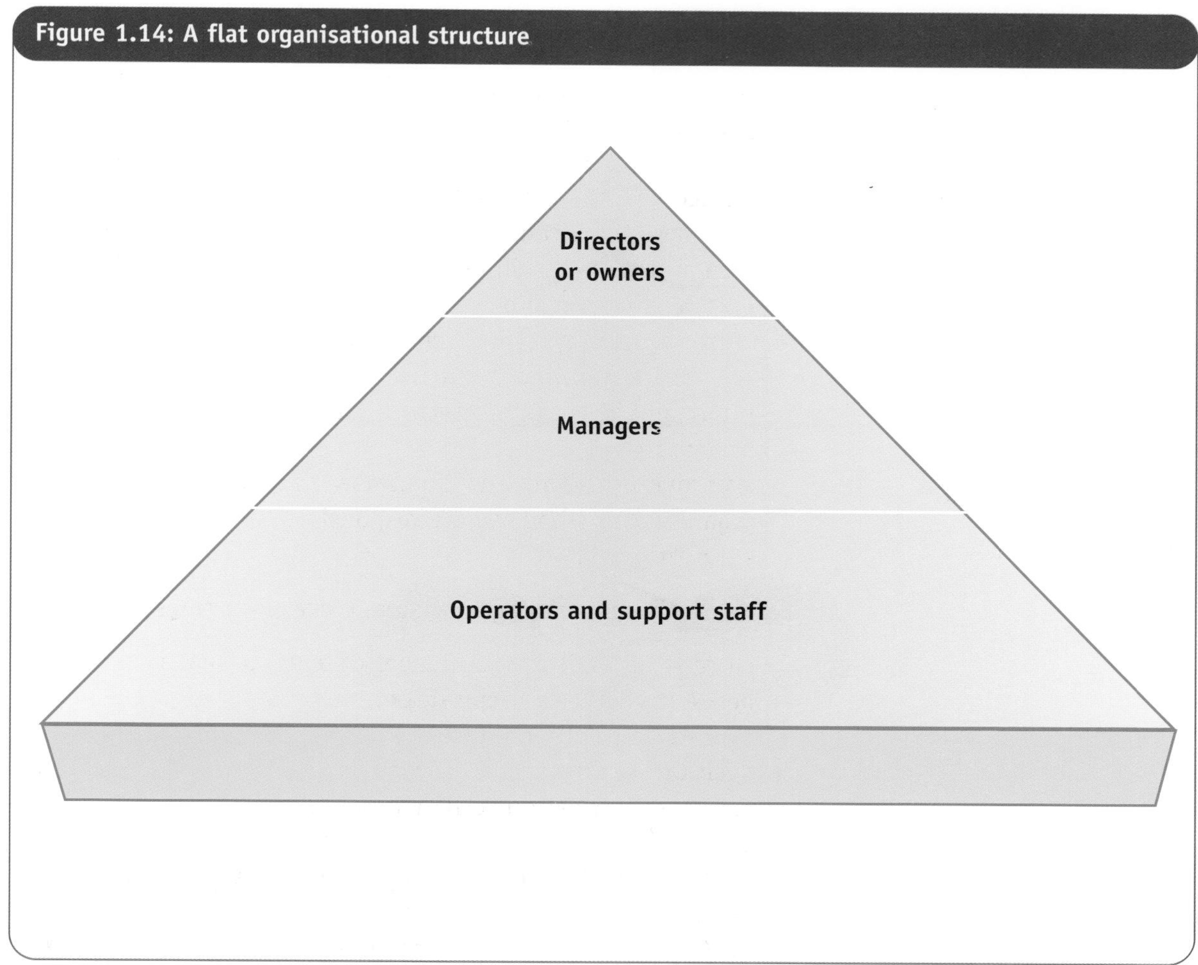

In recent years, more and more business organisations in both the public and private sectors have developed flatter structures by cutting out layers of middle management. This has enabled them to save money, and has been helped by an increased use of information technology.

Matrix structures

A third type of organisational structure, which is more flexible than the hierarchical structures described, is known as a **matrix structure**. This type of structure is often used for running specific projects, such as developing a new product.

In a matrix structure, specialists are brought together from different functions or departments within the organisation, to share their knowledge and give advice about various aspects of the project. Matrix structures therefore tend to be based on functions or key processes that may cross the more traditional departmental boundaries of hierarchical organisations.

Figure 1.15: A matrix structure

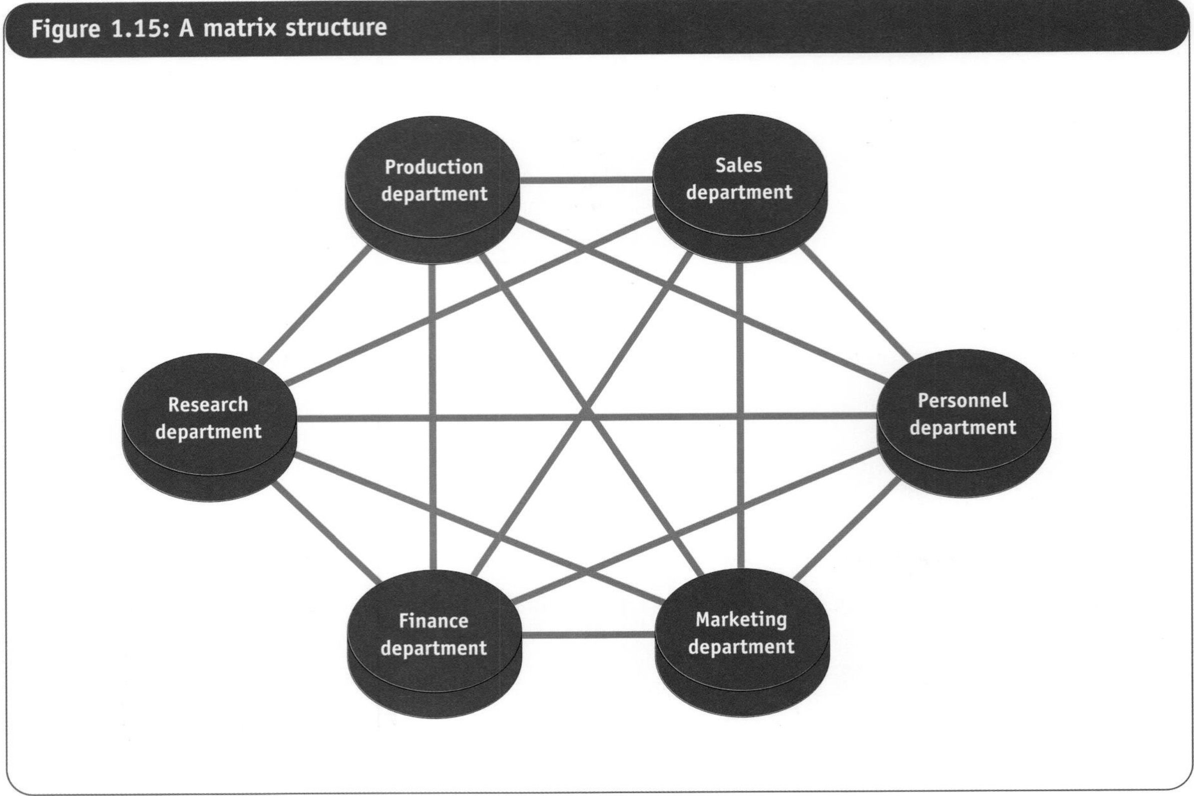

For example, when Firenze Holdings plc wanted to develop a new type of aircraft engine, it formed a project group consisting of people from the research and development, production, marketing and finance departments. In this way the company made sure that all aspects of the development and production of the new engine were considered, including costs, production needs and what the customers wanted.

A group organised on a matrix structure is usually disbanded once the project for which it has been formed is finished.

Organisational charts

The structure of an organisation is usually shown on an **organisational chart**. These charts are normally constructed in the form of a tree diagram, although this is not suitable for matrix structures. An organisational chart for a small company may show the names and job titles of employees(see Figure 1.16). An organisational chart for a large business, however, perhaps with thousands of employees, normally shows the departments in the organisation (see Figure 1.17).

Organisational charts are useful because they show the relationships between people and departments within the organisation, and lines of formal communication.

Figure 1.16: An organisational chart

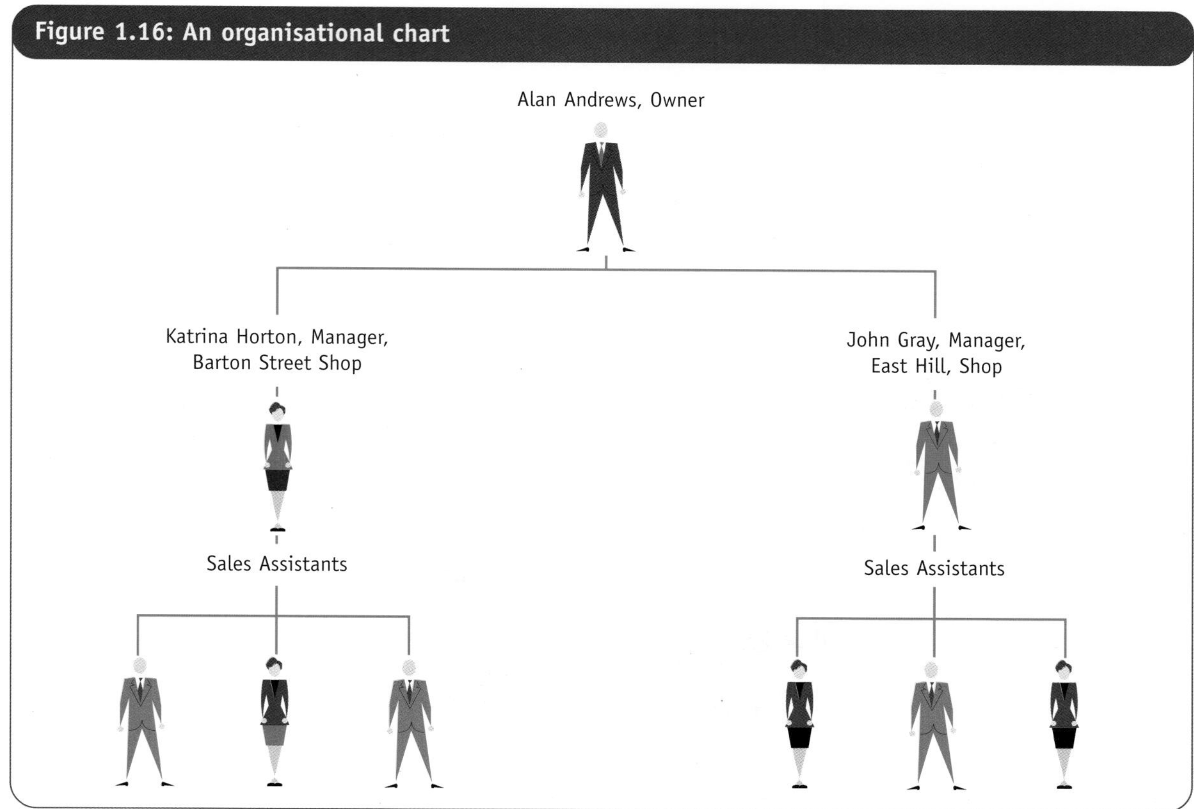

ACTIVITY

Organisational charts

Investigate the structure of your school or college, or your employer if you are employed. Write notes identifying the type of structure, and explaining how this affects:

- communications within the organisation
- how well the organisation is able to achieve its aims and objectives.

Construct an organisational chart for the organisation you have selected. Your chart should show departments and functional areas and the different job roles within them.

Centralised and decentralised organisations

A **centralised organisation** is characterised by the traditional hierarchical structure (see page 76). It has set channels of communication and levels of authority. Control of the organisation is kept in the hands of a few senior managers or directors at the top of the pyramid. Some advantages of a centralised structure are:

- greater control of the organisation
- uniform standards can be more easily maintained
- planning and decision making is in the interests of organisation as a whole, rather than of individual centres
- managers at the top of the pyramid usually have more experience on which to base decisions.

In a **decentralised organisation**, authority and control is delegated to the managers of individual centres of activity or operation, such as divisions, factories or branches. This brings decision making in large and complex organisations closer to customers and workforce, helping the organisation to respond quickly to their needs and so foster good customer and employee relations.

Figure 1.17: A decentralised organisational structure

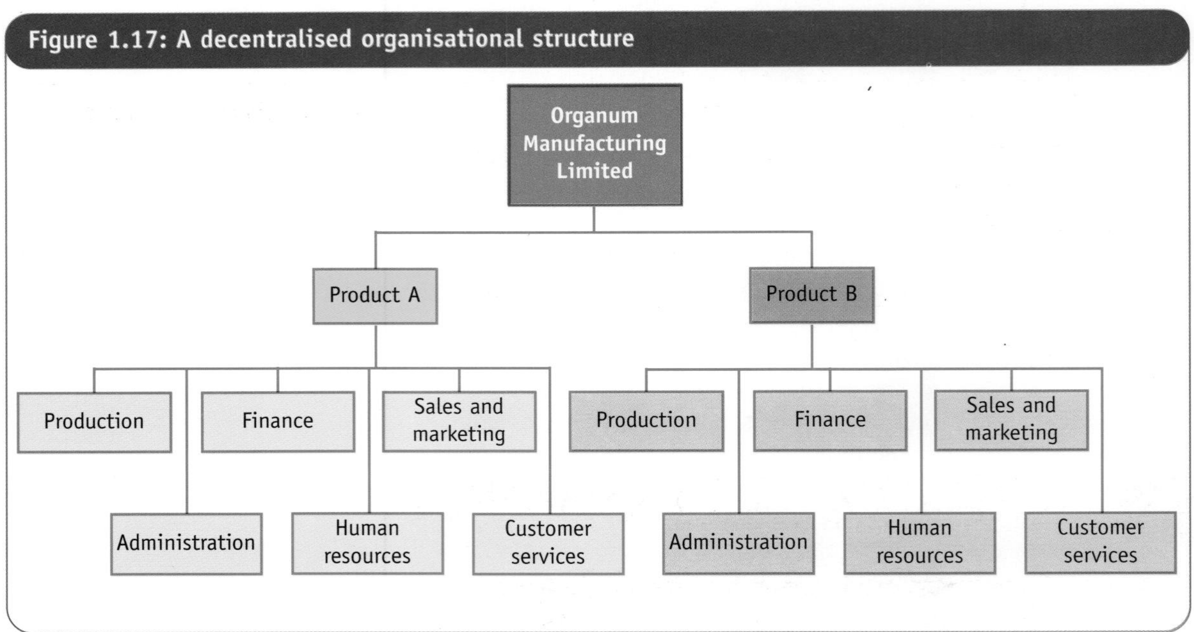

Some advantages of a decentralised structure are:

- faster response to the needs of customers and employees
- greater flexibility and faster decision making based on the needs of the centre of activity or operation
- the involvement of junior managers and their teams in the decision-making process (leading to increased motivation)
- increased responsibility for junior managers and their teams and opportunities for junior staff to develop their careers
- reduced involvement of top managers in daily operations, resulting in less stress and increased effectiveness.

Build your learning

Summary points

- The structure of a business shows how the employees of the business are organised. This can be shown on an organisational chart.
- Businesses may have a hierarchical, flat or matrix structure and may be centralised or decentralised.
- The type of organisational structure affects how a business communicates and achieves its aims.

Key words and phrases

You should know the meanings of the words and phrases listed below as they relate to the organisational structures of businesses. Go back through the last eight pages of the unit to check or refresh your understanding.

- **Centralised organisation**
- **Decentralised organisation**
- **Flat structure**
- **Hierarchical structure**
- **Matrix structure**
- **Organisational chart**
- **Span of control**

Student questions

1 Explain the difference between hierarchical, flat and matrix structures.

2 How does the organisational structure of a business influence the activities and success of the business?

3 What is a decentralised organisation?

4 How can the organisational structure of a business affect communications within the business?

5 What is an organisational chart and what does it show?

3 COLLECT THE EVIDENCE

All businesses develop structures to help them organise their employees and what they do, take decisions and carry them out. This activity gives you an opportunity to produce work that demonstrates your knowledge and understanding of organisational structures. Again this activity is based on the business you have been investigating in the previous 'Collect the evidence' activities (see pages 31 and 74).

The work that you complete for this activity will form part of your assessment evidence for this unit. You should refer to the grid on page 97 to see what you need to do to achieve a pass, merit or distinction.

Remember, if you carry out the following activities now, you will have completed part of the work needed for your end-of-unit assessment. You are advised to do this now to avoid overload at the end of the unit.

What to do

1. **Describe the organisational structure of your selected business.**
2. **Compare the structure of your selected business with a contrasting structure described on pages 76–80, explaining the difference in communication flows.**
3. **Identify and evaluate the strengths and weaknesses in the organisational structure of your chosen business, explaining how these may affect the success of the business in achieving its aims and objectives.**

Working together: business communications

During your GNVQ Intermediate Business course you will communicate with others for many reasons. For example, you might communicate with:

- your tutor, so that he or she can pass information to you and also check that you have understood the information
- fellow students, so that you can discuss any problems with assignments or other matters
- your school or college administration, so that you can receive instructions about school or college procedures.

Without communications you would be unable to pass your course, because both your portfolio evidence and the external assessment are forms of communication designed to provide feedback on the knowledge and skills you have acquired. Even this book is a form of communication.

Communication is an essential part of life. The basic purposes of communication are to:

- pass on information
- give instructions
- check and receive feedback on activities
- discuss matters of concern.

In business, effective communication is vital. Without it, employees would not know what to do, the owners and managers of the business would not know whether the business was achieving its targets or what goods and services customers wanted; and the customers themselves would not know about or be able to purchase the goods and services that the business provides.

Communications between people within a single business organisation are called **internal communications**; those between someone in a business organisation and someone outside – perhaps a customer or a supplier in another business organisation – are called **external communications**. While there are many types of communications that can be used for internal or external communications, all types fall into two basic categories: oral or written. Both oral and written communications can take many forms, and the actual form of communication used depends on the purpose of the communication.

Oral communications

Whenever you speak to someone, or someone speaks to you, you are using **oral communication**. This is the most common form of communication, and the one with which the majority of people are most familiar. Most oral communication is either **face to face** or using the telephone.

For example, when you go into a shop and ask the sales assistant for a pair of jeans you are using oral communication. If, when you get home, you find the jeans are faulty, you may telephone and speak to the sales assistant to let the shop know that you will bring the jeans back next week and expect to exchange them for a perfect pair. This again is oral communication, although this time you are not speaking to the assistant face to face. Because you are not present with the person you are speaking to, but using the telephone, this form of oral communication is said to be **at a distance**

Although we talk to people every day, being able to communicate orally is a skill that must be learned and practised. Here are some points about effective oral communication that you should bear in mind.

- Always speak clearly and without rushing.
- Check that your listener understands what you are saying.
- Use words that are appropriate to the listener and the situation. Do not use slang and do not swear, particularly in front of customers.
- Be polite, but not cold. Try to put the listener at ease.
- Watch carefully for any non-verbal clues to what the other person is thinking, such as facial expressions and posture. These can sometimes be different from what they are saying!
- Listen carefully to what the other person says to you and allow him or her time to say it.
- Be confident and helpful.
- If you cannot answer someone, or deal with a query, say so. Do not waffle or make excuses: pass the problem on to someone who can deal with it.

Using the telephone is more difficult than speaking face to face, and many people are uncomfortable about making telephone calls, although this is becoming less so through the widespread use of mobile phones.

One of the main problems with telephone communications is that when you talk to people on the telephone, you cannot see their response or facial expressions. It is important, therefore, to listen carefully to what the other person is saying and the way it is said; the tone of voice and the words they use.

◀ Oral communication

The telephone can be an important tool in communicating quickly with others, but as with all forms of communications, you need to know how to use it effectively.

- When the telephone rings, answer it promptly and efficiently.
- Be polite and helpful, even if the person on the other end is angry or annoyed.
- Tell callers your name, so that they know who they are talking to.
- Write down the important points of the conversation as you talk, so that you can refer to them later (it is useful to keep a pen and paper near the telephone).
- If you cannot deal with the call, pass it to someone who can (make sure you know how the telephone system works, and how to transfer calls).
- When you cannot deal with a call then and there, or cannot transfer it, write down the caller's name and telephone number and promise to call back. If possible, arrange a time for this.
- When you do promise to call someone back, or arrange for someone else to do so, make sure the call is actually made.

A major problem with communicating by telephone is that the caller can only speak to the person they are calling if that person is able to get to the telephone. Imagine, for example, that you want to speak to a colleague in another office about some information she has sent you. You may decide to telephone her using the internal telephone system. However, if she is away from her office, you obviously will not be able to speak to her. You will either have to wait and try to telephone again later, or (if somebody else answers your call and takes a message) wait for her to telephone you and hope that you will be there when she calls.

Two developments in information technology are designed to avoid the delays in communication that are caused in this way.

- Mobile phones are small, portable telephones that transmit and receive using radio waves and an aerial. They can easily be carried around and enable people to make and receive telephone calls almost anywhere that radio waves can be received.
- Pagers are small electronic devices that can receive short messages, but not transmit. Messages are displayed on a small screen. They cannot be used to make calls, but are useful for people who need to be contacted urgently.

Oral communications are quick and direct. They also offer an opportunity for discussion and for instant feedback to check that the content of the communication (the message) has been communicated effectively and understood.

Meetings

While most oral communications are between individuals on a one-to-one basis, either face to face or at a distance, there are times when it is appropriate for several people to communicate with each other at a meeting. A **meeting** involves an identifiable group of people with a common purpose that may be to:

- discuss matters of concern to all members of the group
- plan a course of action to accomplish specific objectives
- pass information
- negotiate.

Sometimes all members of the group take an equal part in the meeting, for example, when employees from different functional areas of a business meet to discuss the implications of meeting customer demands for improved quality. The purpose of other meetings may be for one person to pass information to a group, as in a team briefing meeting or a sales

A business meeting

presentation to a group of clients. Meetings may also take place between two groups, or representatives of two groups, as in negotiations between representatives of an employer and a trade union (representing the employees).

The main problem with oral communications is that there is no permanent record, unless one is made either in writing or on tape. The record of what was said and decided at a meeting is called the **minutes** of the meeting.

Oral communication

Make a list of the different types of oral communications you use in your GNVQ Intermediate Business course. You should write down:

- the method of communication used
- the person or people you are communicating with
- the purpose of the communication
- the effectiveness of the method of communication for the purpose
- what, if any, written record of the communication is made or desirable.

Written communications

The most common types of **written communications** are letters and memos. Recently, businesses are also increasingly using information technology, such as e-mail and fax, for written communication (see page 92–3).

Letters are written for external communications, in other words communications with people and organisations outside the business. **Memos** (short for memoranda) are used for written communications between people within the same business, perhaps working in different functional areas. Business letters and memos are more formal than the letters you write to your friends, although they serve the same basic purpose – to communicate a message.

An advantage of written communications is that they are permanent records of the communication and can be referred to later if required. Since they are permanent, they can also be read at leisure, which means that they can contain information that may take longer to digest and understand, such as figures and technical data. Pictures, tables, graphs and diagrams can also be included in written communications.

Figure 1.18: The main types of written business communications

Type of communication	Typical purpose	Appearance
Memos (memoranda)	Used internally to communicate with colleagues within the organisation: giving instructions, requesting information, asking for guidance, etc.	Usually written or typed on printed forms. More informal than a business letter, although this will depend on the relationship between the sender and the recipient.
Letters	Used to communicate with people outside the organisation (customers, suppliers, etc.): answering enquiries, dealing with complaints, confirming meetings and orders, and so on.	Business letters should be typed or word-processed on printed, headed letter paper. Business letters are formal documents and should follow certain conventions. For example, if the letter is addressed Dear Sir/ Madam, the closing should be 'Yours faithfully'; if the letter is addressed to a recipient by name, the closing should be 'Yours sincerely'.
Financial documents	Financial documents may be used internally or externally. External financial documents are used to communicate information, confirm orders or request payment, etc. Internal financial documents are mainly used to communicate information, particularly for accounting purposes.	Financial documents are normally preprinted forms (invoices, purchase orders, delivery notes, cheques, etc.). They may be completed by computer. Accuracy in completing financial documents is vital.
Advertisements	Advertisements are used to tell potential customers about the goods or services provided by an organisation.	Range from advertisements on television and in magazines to posters on hoardings and in shops. A good advertisement follows the **AIDA** principles: it **A**ttracts attention, stimulates **I**nterest, creates a **D**esire for the product; and prompts **A**ction to buy the product.
Notices	Notices are used to communicate with groups of people, giving general information, warning of hazards, giving general instructions, etc. They may be used internally, to communicate with employees, or externally to communicate with customers and suppliers, etc.	Notices have to attract the attention of the intended readership, convey the message and persuade readers to take appropriate action. Notices may be placed on noticeboards, where everybody can see them, displayed in a public place, or sent to individual members of the group to whom the notice applies.

Other forms of written communications are used in business for various purposes. These are often printed, or on pre-printed forms. Such communications include:

- financial documents
- advertisements
- notices
- customer and product information such as price lists and specifications
- guarantees and warranties which explain the rights of customers after the goods or services have been sold.

The appearance and quality of the documents produced by a business is very important. This is so whether they are for internal or external use. An organisation's documents reflect the image of the organisation itself: shoddy documents give the impression of a shoddy organisation. Most organisations have specially designed headed paper for letters, and the same design may be used on other printed documents. This gives an instantly recognisable identity and house style.

You must take care with any business documents you produce and check that each one is as attractive and easy to read as possible, paying particular attention to spelling, grammar and punctuation. Good documents should be:

- **accurate:** everything in the document should be checked, including all facts; a dictionary or computer spellchecker should be used to check spelling if necessary
- **clear:** the person reading the document should be able to understand its content immediately; the person writing the document must have the message clear in his or her mind before he or she begins to write it down
- **simple:** short words and sentences are more effective and have more impact than long ones; they also save time and are easily understood
- **complete:** a document which leaves a message unfinished or which leaves out a vital piece of information will fail in its purpose.

It is a good idea always to do a draft (rough copy) of a business document you are producing, so that you can check this carefully before you produce the final copy. A second copy should also be made of every business document produced so that it can be filed by the sender and retrieved later in case of any query or need for further action.

Written communication

What methods of written and oral communication do you think should be used in DC Food Group Services (see the case studies on pages 44, 50, 53, 56, 60, 63 and 68)? Make a list of:

- the method
- the purpose for which it should be used
- the advantages and disadvantages of your chosen method for the purpose you have identified.

Write a letter to DC Food Group Services asking for information about its new line of low calorie tinned vegetables. You should identify the person to whom you should address your letter from the earlier case studies.

In the role of the person to whom you have addressed your letter, write:

- a memo to Jo Lancer, sales representative, asking her to visit the writer of the letter as soon as possible
- a reply to your original letter of enquiry, stating that Jo Lancer will get in touch to arrange a meeting.

You should use a computer word processing package to produce both letters and the memo. You will need to design a letterhead for DC Food Group Services and the address of the company should be made up. Be polite and pay particular attention to spelling (always use the computer spellchecker) and grammar.

Communications and information technology

The rapid advances in **information technology** over recent years have led to radical new forms of communication. These have largely been made possible by the continual development and growth in use of personal computers (PCs) both in business and in people's homes.

The major developments include fax machines, which can be used to transmit text, graphics, charts and photographs quickly anywhere in the world, and mobile phones which (as we saw on page 88) can be carried away from the place of work.

Personal computers with modem and software are transforming business communications. E-mail, or **electronic mail** is a system whereby messages produced on a personal computer can be transmitted to another personal computer. Electronic mail uses a mailbox system, in which the message is held in the mailbox until collected by the recipient. E-mails can consist of text, graphics and even sounds, depending on the capabilities of the sender's and receiver's computers. It is possible to send entire computer files in this way. The sender and the receiver of an e-mail may be anywhere in the world.

Businesses with several computer terminals can link these to a network or **intranet**, so that each computer on the network can exchange information with the other computers and can even access information held on their hard drives, although some files may have restricted access. Employees working at home who have personal computers that are networked to their employer's intranet can also communicate with and access information stored on computers at their workplace, using a modem and telephone line.

The **internet** is a worldwide network of high-speed computers permanently linked up to provide and exchange information. Anyone with a personal computer and a modem connected to a telephone line can connect to the internet via an internet service provider, such as Freeserve. The number of computers connected to the internet is vast and growing daily, as is the amount and variety of information that can be obtained. The internet allows users to shop all over the world, listen to new music, find out about the latest products, visit art galleries, read the latest news, play games, and undertake research into almost anything.

The internet is also an invaluable tool for businesses which can use it for communications, marketing their products, providing customer and technical support and inviting customer feedback. In fact, the internet has become such an integral part of modern business, that the term e-commerce has been coined to refer to the marketing, buying and selling of products on the internet.

Rapid developments in information technology are likely to continue for the foreseeable future. The effects on business will be considerable, especially in the areas of international marketing and selling on the internet, and of employees increasingly working from home, being linked by computer to their employers.

▲ Barclays are one of a large number of companies that can advise on modern business communications

Build your learning

Summary points

- People in businesses have to communicate with each other (internally) and with people outside the business, such as customers and suppliers (externally).
- Communications may be oral, such as face to face or by telephone, or written, such as letters, memos, financial documents, advertisements, and notices.
- Communications may involve the use of information technology, such as personal computers, e-mail, mobile phones, pagers, and fax machines.

Key words and phrases

You should know the meanings of the words and phrases listed below as the relate to business communications. Go back through the last nine pages of the unit to check or refresh your understanding.

- **Electronic mail**
- **External communications**
- **Face-to-face communications**
- **Information technology**
- **Internal communications**
- **Internet**
- **Intranet**
- **Letters**
- **Meetings**
- **Memos**
- **Minutes**
- **Oral communications**
- **Written communications**

Student questions

1. Describe three different types of oral communication.
2. Describe four different methods of written communications.
3. What are the comparative advantages and disadvantages of oral and written communications?
4. How can oral and written communications be made easier and more effective by the use of information technology?
5. Identify four different types of information technology used in communications and explain what they are used for.

People in business have to communicate with each other and with people outside the business, for example customers and suppliers. This activity gives you an opportunity to produce work that demonstrates your knowledge and understanding of business communications. The work that you complete for this activity will form part of your assessment evidence for this unit. You should refer to the grid on page 97 to see what you need to do to achieve a pass, merit or distinction.

Remember, if you carry out the following activities now, you will have completed part of the work needed for your end-of-unit assessment. You are advised to do this now to avoid overload at the end of the unit.

What to do

1. **For this activity you need to investigate the methods of business communication used by your chosen business. You will probably therefore need to contact and visit your chosen business again.**

2. **When you have investigated the types of communications used by the business, write an account explaining how people in different functional areas of the business communicate with each other and with people outside the business. Explain how effective communications can help the business achieve its aims and objectives. Identify how the business uses information technology and, if appropriate, how this could be developed to improve the communications of the business.**

Assessment check list

This unit is assessed on the basis of your portfolio. If you have completed the 'Collect the evidence' activities in this unit, you will have produced sufficient evidence to meet the requirements of assessment. The evidence you have collected will be:

- a description of what your chosen business does, its aims and objectives (page 31)
- a description of the purposes and activities of human resources and three other functional areas, excluding customer services (page 74)
- a record of your oral presentation comparing the customer service provided by your chosen business with best practice (page 75)
- a description of the organisational structure of the business and how this differs from another organisational structure (page 84)
- a description of how effectively different areas of the business communicate with each other and with people outside the business (page 95).

You should check that you have all these items of evidence in your portfolio and that they have been completed to the best of your ability and to your satisfaction. When you are confident that you have completed everything, you should write a record of all the sources of information you have used, including books, notes from your tutor, information from your chosen business and so on. You should identify the information obtained and how you have used it.

The table below shows the grading criteria for this unit, which will be used to determine whether you receive a pass, merit or distinction for this unit.

Assessment grid

Section	To achieve a pass you must	To achieve a merit you must also	To achieve a distinction you must also
Aims and objectives	Describe clearly the aims and objectives of your chosen business.		
Functional areas within the business	Describe four functional areas of the business, including human resources, explaining fully how each contributes to business activity and giving examples of job role associated with each area. Describe how the equal opportunities of employees are protected by legislation. Explain orally how the customer service of your chosen business meets customers' expectations and suggest any necessary improvements based on best practice.	Explain clearly how different functional areas interact to achieve the aims and objectives of your chosen business. Explain and give examples of how employees are safeguarded by employment law.	Demonstrate a coherent understanding of how your chosen business works.
Organisational structure	Compare the organisational structure of your chosen business with a contrasting structure and explain the different communication flows.		Evaluate any strengths and weakness in the organisational structure and communications flows of your chosen business, explaining how these may affect its success in achieving its aims and objectives.
Working together: business communications	Explain, using examples, how different functional areas communicate with each other and external contacts. List the sources of evidence you used in your research. Speak clearly during your presentation, keeping to the subject and using an image to illustrate your main point(s).	Explain how effective communications are helping the business to achieve its aims and objectives.	

How businesses develop 2

In this unit we examine different types of business organisations, their main activities and some of the influences that affect the way they develop. You will see that businesses can be classified according to their type of ownership and the goods or services they produce. Classifying businesses in this way helps us to understand where an individual business fits into the wider business world and relates to other businesses. You will examine some of the external influences on businesses and find out how, while they cannot control these, they must respond to them. In particular, you will investigate the importance and influence of location and different stakeholders on businesses.

This unit will be assessed through your portfolio work. In order to gather evidence for your portfolio you need to investigate two contrasting businesses. You will have to describe how they are owned, show which industrial sector each business operates in, describe their business activities, explain the reasons for the location of each business and identify the different stakeholders in the business.

Completing the 'Collect the evidence' activities in this unit will help you gather the evidence you require.

Ownership

Whose business is it anyway?

All businesses are owned by individuals or groups of people. There are, however, many different types of business organisation and types of business ownership. We examine the main types of business organisation and ownership in this section.

Private or public

Business can be divided into two main categories, those in the private sector and those in the public sector.

- The **private sector** consists of organisations that are owned and operated by one or more private individuals or other private organisations.
- The **public sector** consists of organisations wholly owned and operated by the national or local government.

The private sector includes a wide variety of businesses ranging from giant companies, such as Marks and Spencer, which is owned by almost 310,000 individuals and organisations, to small businesses such as a local plumber, who owns his own business, and may even work on his own.

Figure 2.1: Types of private sector businesses

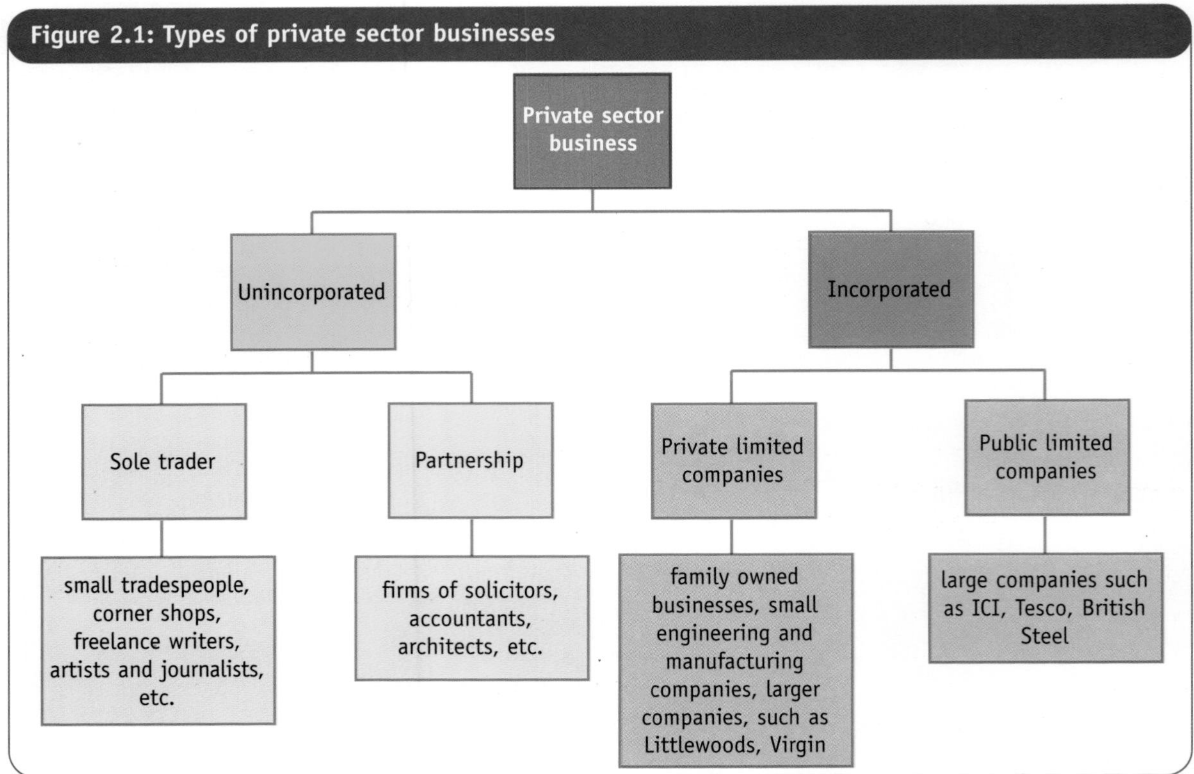

The public sector includes organisations such as the Post Office, the Department of Social Security, libraries and leisure centres. These are all owned and operated by local or national government. The Post Office and the Department of Social Security are owned by national government; libraries and leisure centres are owned by local governments.

Some types of organisation are found in both the private and the public sectors. Most schools and hospitals, for example, are owned and run by a local government authority and are therefore in the public sector. However, some schools, such as Eton and Harrow, and hospitals, such as The Cromwell and The Portland, are privately owned.

Figure 2.2: Types of public sector businesses

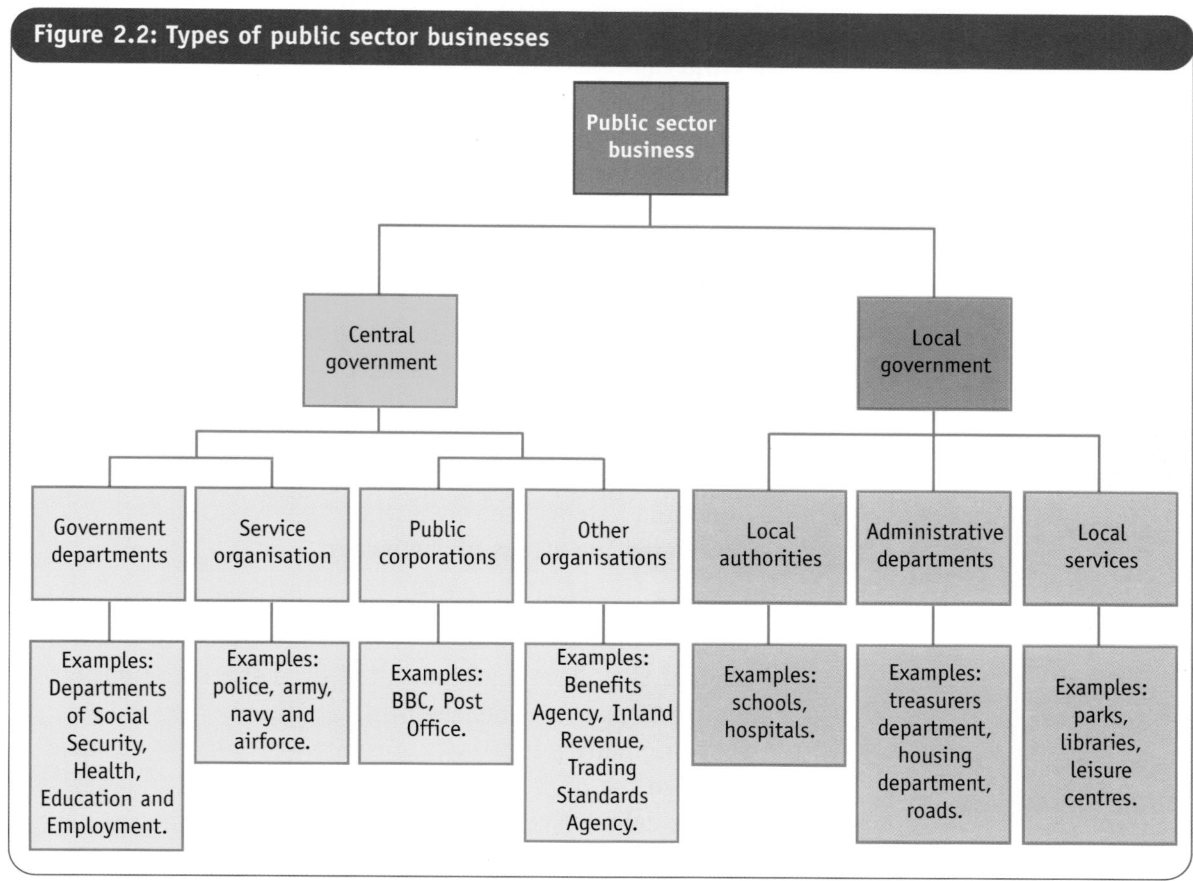

Incorporated or unincorporated

Businesses in the private sector may be unincorporated or incorporated.

- **Unincorporated businesses** are legally considered to be the same as their owners.
- **Incorporated businesses** exist as legal entities in their own right, with identities quite separate from those of their owners.

Since they are legal entities, incorporated businesses are able to employ people, own property such as factories and offices, machinery and equipment, and borrow money. In the case of unincorporated businesses on the other hand, it is the owner or owners of the business who employ people, own the property of the business and borrow the money that the business needs.

Liability

An important aspect of business ownership, which is related to whether the business in unincorporated or incorporated, is liability. The owners of a business establish the business, and put their money into it, because they expect to get a return on it. In other words they expect to get something back. However, they will only get a return if the business is successful. If the business is not successful, they may lose everything they have put into it. They may also be personally liable (that is held responsible) for any debts the business has incurred. Such liability may be unlimited or limited.

- **Unlimited liability** means that the owners of the business are personally responsible for all the debts the business incurs. If the business is unable to pay its debts because it has insufficient funds available, the debts must be paid in full by the owners, even if they have to sell the business and all their personal possessions – including their house and car – to do so. The owners of unincorporated businesses have unlimited liability, since the affairs of the business are considered the affairs of the owners.
- **Limited liability** means that the owners of the business are only responsible for the debts of the business up to the amount they have invested in the business. If the business is unable to pay its debts the owners will only lose the amount they originally put into the business (they may of course also lose the business itself, if it has to be sold in order to pay its debts). The owners of incorporated businesses have limited liability, since the business is a legal entity and therefore responsible for its own affairs.

Profits and dividends

Obviously, there are risks attached to owning a business. Liability is only one aspect of owning a business, however. Perhaps a more important aspect to most people who start or invest in a business is profit. They expect to get a return on the money they have put into (or invested in) the business. This return is paid out of the profits of the business.

The owners of unincorporated businesses who have unlimited liability are considered to own the full profit of the business. They can choose how to use the profit of the business: draw it for their own personal use or retain it in the business in order to buy new equipment or fund expansion.

The owners of incorporated companies receive a **dividend** on their investment. A dividend is a proportion of profits set aside by the company for distributing to the owners of the business. Dividends are distributed according to the proportion of the business owned (see page 112).

Types of ownership

There are several different types of business ownership. In the public sector, businesses are simply owned by local or national government. In the private sector, however, there are several different types of ownership (see Figure 2.3). We now look at some of these business structures in the private sector in more detail.

Figure 2.3: Types of business ownership in the private sector

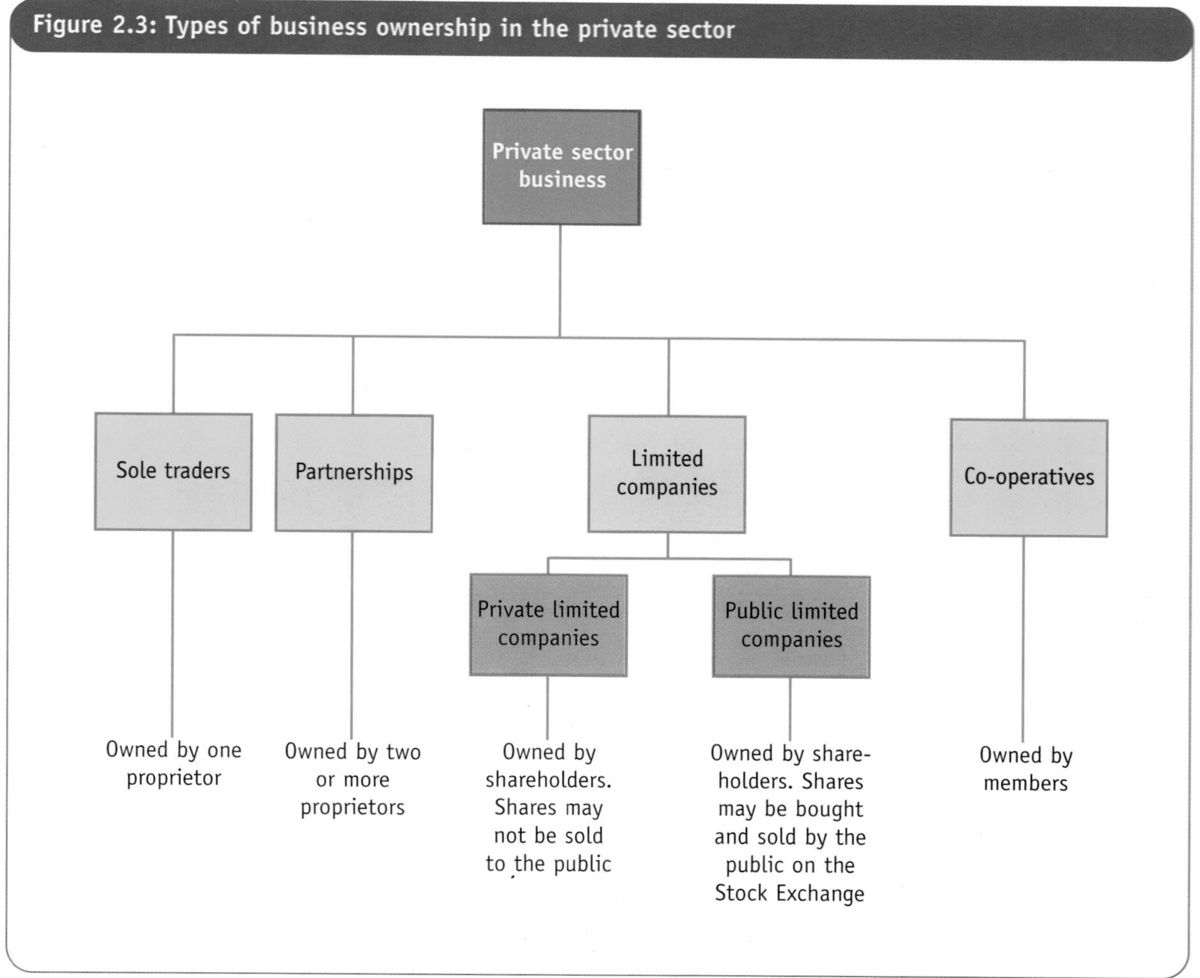

Unincorporated businesses

Sole traders

A sole trader is the simplest form of business organisation. There is one owner (the **sole trader**), who has complete control over the decision making and running of the business. While many sole traders are indeed people working on their own, a sole trader can employ others to help run the business. Since a sole trader business is unincorporated, any people working in the business, apart from the owner, are actually employed by the owner. The owner is **self-employed**

Setting up as a sole trader is very easy, as there are few legal formalities to go through. The sole trader must tell the Inland Revenue that he or she has set up a business and is self-employed. Details of any profit or loss made by the sole trader during the financial year must be given to the Inland Revenue annually, together with the balance sheet, if there is one. This is so that the Inland Revenue can charge income tax on the sole trader's profits, adjusted by certain items. A sole trader must also keep employment records in respect of any employees.

▶ Sole traders often use their own names for their businesses

Any business name used by the sole trader has to comply with the **Business Names Act 1985**. This allows a business to trade under any name, as long as the name is not intended to mislead customers into thinking that it has a connection with any other business or government department if no such connection exists. It is also illegal to use terms such as 'royal' or 'international' without the permission of the Secretary of State for Trade and Industry.

Many sole trader businesses adopt the name of the sole trader. For example, if Sally Beaumont established an estate agency business she might call it Sally Beaumont, Estate Agent. Others may adopt a name that describes their product or service. Instead of calling her estate agency Sally Beaumont, Estate Agent, Sally could call it something like The Property Shop. In this case, Sally Beaumont would be trading as The Property Shop, which would be her business name.

CASE STUDY

The case of Day and Martin

Day and Martin was a well-known and respected firm of boot polish manufacturers with a business in Holborn. Two other people, whose real names were Mr Day and Mr Martin, decided to set up a boot polish business under the name of Day and Martin. Their intention was to gain customers by getting them to think they were actually buying from the well-known firm.

The original firm applied to the courts to stop the new business trading under the name of Day and Martin. The firm's application was granted, since although Day and Martin were the actual names of the people who had set up the new business, in doing so they were attempting to deceive the public into thinking that they were dealing with the well-known and established firm.

Setting up as a sole trader can be the least expensive way of starting a business. Many sole traders start with a minimum of capital or finance. They often begin by operating from small premises, such as a shop, small workshop or office unit, or even from the home of the owner of the business. Starting out as a sole trader is the most common way of setting up in business. There are more sole traders than any other type of business in Britain today.

On the other hand, there are few sources of finance available to sole traders, apart from the personal funds of the owner and any profits the business makes. This is partly because sole traders are usually small businesses and partly because they have unlimited liability. Many sole traders take out a bank loan to help finance the start-up costs of the business. These include the costs of premises and equipment, and also raw materials, labour and other running costs that have to be paid before the business starts receiving sufficient revenue from sales of its goods or services.

Because the business affairs of a sole trader are legally the same as his or her personal affairs, however, any loan is in effect a personal loan to the owner of the business. The lender will probably require the loan to be secured on the owner's personal property, for example, in the form of a mortgage on his or her house. Obviously there is a limit to the amount of money a sole trader can raise in this way, and the lack of availability of other sources of funds means that sole traders usually start as small businesses and do not have real opportunities for growth.

▼ An original Marks and Spencer Penny Bazaar

Not all sole traders are destined to remain small companies, however. The beginnings of Marks and Spencer were in 1882 when Michael Marks, a young Russian refugee, arrived in north east England and started selling haberdashery in the villages around Leeds, from a tray hung around his neck. By 1894, Marks had a chain of stalls in markets throughout north east England. It was at this time that he formed the famous partnership with Tom Spencer. Marks and Spencer registered the business as a limited company in 1903, becoming a public limited company in 1926 with 125 stores. Today, Marks and Spencer is an internationally known and respected company, with almost 700 outlets worldwide, as well as large interests in financial services.

▼ Marks and Spencer has diversified into financial services

There is an advantage to being a sole trader, however, which can often give a competitive edge over a larger business. In a small business, the owner and decision maker usually maintains close and direct contact with customers. He or she is aware of any changes in customer needs and demand and can respond quickly, whereas in larger organisations it can take longer for the decision makers to become aware of and respond to these changes. For example, the owner or manager of a small corner shop is probably much more in touch with what his or her customers want and is able to respond much more quickly than the senior managers and buyers of major supermarket chains like Tesco or Sainsbury.

Typical sole trader businesses are local independent shops, plumbers and similar tradespeople, freelance artists and other self-employed people.

CASE STUDY

The village store

When Delyth Evans was made redundant from her job as a floor manager at a local supermarket, she decided to use her redundancy money to realise her dream and buy her own shop.

She found that a small corner confectioner and newsagents was for sale in a nearby village, although her redundancy would only pay the deposit she needed. Still, there was a flat above the shop, and she decided that if she sold her house and took out a mortgage on the shop she would have enough to buy the shop and the stock she needed, with a little left over to help her through the first few months. Since the shop had well-established trade, Delyth believed that the existing level of sales would continue when she took over.

'It's exciting,' Delyth told her sister Megan when she had decided that she would buy the shop. 'It's what I've always wanted to do, own my own village shop. I'll be my own boss, and rise or fall on my own efforts. All the profits will be mine; they will not go to a big company with a head office somewhere in London.'

Megan was not so sure. 'But you'll also be on your own,' she said. 'You'll be working on your own – think of the long hours you'll have to put in. Even after the shop shuts, you'll have to do the books, take stock, place orders and things like that. You've never run a business yourself before. What about the accounts and paperwork? You may not find that as much fun as serving in the shop – but you've got to do it, because there won't be anybody else to do it for you. And supposing it all goes wrong? Supposing you don't get as many sales as you hope, for whatever reason? You could lose everything – not just the shop but your home and livelihood as well.'

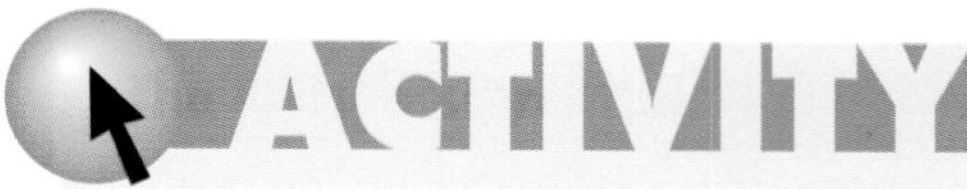

The village store

1 What are the advantages Delyth has put forward for running her own business?

2 What are the disadvantages Megan has raised?

3 Do you think that Delyth should buy the shop? Give your reasons.

Partnerships

Unlike a sole trader, a **partnership** has two or more owners. These are the partners themselves. Generally a partnership has between two and twenty partners. In certain cases, such as large firms of accountants, there may be more than twenty partners.

The partners share both control of the business and its profits. Sometimes a 'senior' partner has overall authority for decision making. There are a few legal formalities that must be followed in setting up a partnership; the legal requirements are the same as those for sole traders. However, most partnerships are established with a legally drawn up **deed of partnership** This sets out the role each partner is to play in running the business and how any profits will be distributed between partners – this is usually on the basis of the amount of capital each partner originally put into the business. Any dispute arising at a later date can be settled by referring to the deed of partnership. In the absence of such a deed, all partnerships are governed by the **Partnership Act 1890**

One advantage of forming a partnership is that responsibility for the business is shared between the partners. This means that no single partner has to oversee the whole business, but each partner is able to concentrate on that part of the business in which he or she excels. For example, Jim Peters and Mary Lloyd have a business manufacturing wooden toys. They run the business as a partnership: Jim makes and packages the toys while Mary concentrates on selling them to local shops. Mary also does the paperwork, which Jim admits is not his strong point. In this way, Jim and Mary are able to run the business much more efficiently and successfully than either of them could do on their own.

The sources of finance available to partnerships are similar to those available to sole traders: these are the personal funds of the owners, profits retained within the business and bank loans. Like sole traders, the owners of a partnership have unlimited liability and they are likely to have to use their personal property as security for any loan. Since there is more than one partner, however, it is usually possible for a partnership to obtain larger amounts of capital in this way.

Typical partnerships include professional firms such as doctors, solicitors, accountants and consultants, as well as small traders such as shops, garages and small manufacturing firms in which two or more people have joined together to set up in business.

The John Lewis Partnership is Britain's largest partnership. With stores in every major town, including the Waitrose supermarket chain, every one of its employees is a partner in the company. This means that John Lewis has around 40,000 partners. While all partners are led by the store's managers and do not have shares in the company, they do elect five members to the board. They also share in the profits made by John Lewis Partnership, which are used to finance investment in the business and to make a bonus payment to staff.

The partnership

Read the case study on page 111 about the Paterson, Severn and Goodly Partnership and then answer these questions.

1 What do you think are the advantages and disadvantages for Steve Goodly of being a partner in the firm Paterson, Severn and Goodly rather than an employee in the large firm of accountants?

2 Instead of joining Allan Paterson and Janine Severn, Steve could have decided to set up on his own as a sole trader. In view of the problems the partnership seems to be having at the moment, do you think Steve would have been better off on his own?

CASE STUDY

The Paterson, Severn and Goodly Partnership

Steve Goodly is a partner in the firm of Paterson, Severn and Goodly Accountants. He joined the firm three years ago.

Steve became a partner when invited by the two original partners. He had to put an amount of capital into the business in order to become a partner.

Before joining the firm, Steve had worked for ten years for a large firm of accountants with a network of offices throughout the UK. He always felt that he had little scope for developing his career with the larger firm. As a partner in a small firm, Steve feels that he has much more control of his life and career. But he also has much more responsibility.

Together with the other two partners, he is responsible for making sure that the firm has enough clients and business to pay its expenses – including the salaries of three assistants and a receptionist – and to make a profit. Like the two other partners, the money he earns now is based on the firm's profit.

Recently, there have been one or two disagreements between the partners at their weekly meetings. Business has been harder to get over the last few months and this has caused a drop in the firm's revenue. Steve feels that they should plan a marketing campaign to try to win more clients among local businesses. He wants to produce a new brochure, but Janine Severn believes that the firm's clients are more likely to come through personal contact. She wants the partners to spend more time making contact and socialising with prospective clients through organisations such as the Rotary Club and chambers of trade and commerce.

Allan Paterson, the third director, caused an argument last week when he bought an expensive new company car without consulting the others. He pointed out that he was the senior partner, with overall decision making powers, and since he was the one who would probably spend most time at meetings and social events with prospective clients, he ought to have a decent car. 'Clients often judge an accountant by the car he drives,' Allan says.

Incorporated businesses

We have seen (page 101) that incorporated businesses are legal entities in their own right. The entire capital of an incorporated business contributed by its owners (the capital of the business, excluding loans) is divided into shares. Each owner therefore becomes a **shareholder**.

Shares have a nominal (face) value which is set when the shares are first issued (normally when the company is set up or becomes an incorporated business). The cost to the purchaser of actually buying these shares, however, depends on how well the company is expected to perform, the anticipated level of profits and how many people want to buy the shares.

▼ A share certificate

0450-01

Reference

Certificate number	Account number	Transfer number	Date	Number of shares
123456	06543212	4321	01 JAN 1999	**1000**

of 25p each

BT

British Telecommunications plc
Ordinary Shares of 25p each

THE ATTACHED CERTIFICATE IS VALUABLE.
PLEASE KEEP IT IN A SAFE PLACE.

The BT shares shown in the attached share certificate have been entered in your name(s) in the Company's Register of Members.

Your address is currently recorded in the Register of Members. You should notify any change to your address to the Registrar either by completing and returning the change of address form on the reverse of this counterfoil or by writing, quoting your share account number, to the Registrar, Lloyds TSB Registrars, The Causeway, Worthing, West Sussex, BN99 6DA.
Please ensure that the notification is signed.

In the case of a joint shareholding, changes of address of the first-named holder only should be notified to the Registrar. The notification should be signed by the first-named holder only.

Please do NOT return your share certificate with a change of address notification.

MR A N OTHER
1 ANYWHERE
ANYTOWN
SUNSHIRE
XX1 2YY

Please do not detach this counterfoil unless you wish to notify the Registrar of a change of address.

BT

Ordinary Shares

British Telecommunications plc

Incorporated under the Companies Acts 1948 to 1981
Registered in England No 1800000

This is to certify that the undermentioned is/are the Registered Holder(s) of fully paid Ordinary Shares of 25p each in the above Company as shown herein subject to the Memorandum and Articles of Association of the Company.

Name(s) of Member(s)
MR A N OTHER

Number of Ordinary Shares of 25p each
**ONE THOUSAND SHARES

Given under the Seal of the Company

SPECIMEN

This certificate should be kept in a safe place. It will be needed when you sell or transfer the shares.
The registrar's address is Lloyds TSB Registrars, The Causeway, Worthing, West Sussex BN99 6DA and the relevant reference for correspondence is No. 0450.

2656662

There are two types of shares, ordinary shares and preference shares. **Ordinary shares** entitle the shareholder to a share of the profits of the company, after all other costs and investors have been paid, and to vote at general meetings of the company, including on the appointment of directors. The directors of a company are responsible to its shareholders for the performance and profits of the company. The capital raised by the issue of ordinary shares is called **equity capital**

Preference shares entitle the shareholder to a dividend out of profits before any payment is made to ordinary shareholders (thus possibly limiting the amount available for distribution to ordinary shareholders).

Businesses that are owned by shareholders are commonly called companies.

Companies

A company must have at least two shareholders. It must be legally established (incorporated) and have a written constitution (called Memoranda and Articles of Association) which sets out:

- what the company has been established to do
- the name and address of the company
- the amount of shares that have been issued and who owns them
- the names and addresses of the directors of the company.

A company must also send annual accounts to the Inland Revenue and an annual return to the Registrar of Companies, notifying any changes in directors, number of shares issued or mortgage debts.

◀ Companies House in Cardiff holds records about all legally established companies in the United Kingdom

Although the shareholders are the owners of the company, they appoint a board of directors to actually run the company on their behalf. This is normally done at the annual general meeting of shareholders. The directors are responsible for running the company and also for setting, and achieving, its aims and objectives (see Unit 1). Much of the day-to-day running of the company is delegated to the managers of each functional area. The shareholders, however, retain ultimate control and can vote to have a director removed if they feel that he or she is not doing a good job.

A company raises capital initially through the sale of shares. As a legal entity, however, a company is also able to take out loans from banks and other financial institutions. Being a company is no guarantee of profitability or success, but companies do tend to be larger than other forms of business and find it easier to raise the capital they need to operate and grow.

There are two types of companies:

- private limited companies
- public limited companies.

Private limited companies

Private limited companies have the word 'limited' after their name, indicating that the company is owned by shareholders who have limited liability (see page 102). This is usually abbreviated to Ltd: for example, the Lincoln Bus Company Ltd.

The shareholders of a private limited company can only buy or sell their shares with the agreement of the other shareholders – the shares cannot be freely bought by members of the public. The shareholders of a private limited company are usually closely involved with the running of the company. In fact, the shareholders are often also the directors of the company, so that they are responsible for the day-to-day management of the company and also have ultimate control.

This is not always the case, however. For example, when Anita Roddick first started up The Body Shop as a private limited company, she obtained capital from a businessman in return for a substantial shareholding in the new company. As The Body Shop became successful, and eventually The Body Shop International, that businessman has seen his shareholding increase in value from a few thousand pounds to several millions. This shareholder retains his shareholding but has never played any active part in running the company.

Tarsett Foods

Read the case study on page 115 about Tarsett Foods and then answer these questions.

What are the advantages and disadvantages to Mary of forming a private limited company?

Do you think that a private limited company is a more suitable form of business for Mary :

- now
- when she had a tearoom?

Give your reasons.

CASE STUDY

Tarsett Foods

Mary Tarsett has a tearoom on the farm near Yeovil that her uncle left to her. When the business ran into difficulties, she had to find a new source of customers.

For some time Mary has been producing her own sausages, pasties and pies, made to a traditional recipe. She sold these in her tea shop and they proved very popular with customers. Mary contacted several local supermarkets and other food retailers in Yeovil and they agreed to sell her foods.

Gradually, Mary found that she was having to produce more and more in order to satisfy a growing demand. If she is going to continue selling her food products through local outlets, she needs to rethink her business structure. When she opened her tea shop, she did so as a sole trader. Now, however, she needs larger, purpose-built premises with the right equipment and people to operate it.

Mary does not have the money she needs for the kind of expansion she is planning. She could raise a loan on the farm but that will not be sufficient on its own, and in any case she doesn't want to risk losing the farm if her plans don't work out. She is also unsure about employing people and running the business herself.

She decides to talk over her worries with Darren Campbell, a friend who has some knowledge of business. He says he would like to start his own business and suggests they join forces to form a limited company. Mary will be the major shareholder, as it is her business, but he will buy a substantial shareholding to provide the company with more capital. He can attend to all the administration of the business.

However, even with the money Darren is contributing, they do not have enough to find new premises, buy the equipment they need and employ people. They need cash to tide them over until they are receiving sufficient revenue from sales to cover all their outgoings, and this might take some time. They need to ask the bank for a loan.

When Mary goes to see her bank manager, she is surprised that he seems quite prepared to lend the money they need – not to her but to the company. So Tarsett Foods is born, with a loan from the bank and capital from Mary and Darren. Mary knows that if the company fails, and the bank sells the new industrial unit and equipment to recover its loan, she would not lose the farm and she can always start again in the tearoom.

The Abbey National Group

WOOLWORTHS

▲ Two well-known public limited companies

Public limited companies

The main difference between private and public limited companies is that **public limited companies** have no restriction on the number of shareholders or on the freedom to buy and sell shares. Shares in public limited companies can be bought and sold on the stock market at any time by individual members of the public, other companies or organisations. Public limited companies have 'plc' (meaning public limited company) after their name, as for example ICI plc.

The government actually owns shares in some major public limited companies, such as BP, but since the majority of shares in these companies are owned by private individuals and organisations, the companies themselves remain in the private sector.

Figure 2.4: The share prices of some well-known UK companies

Company	Share price	Change from previous day's trading
Abbey National	945.00	–16.00
Alliance and Leicester	763.00	– 6.50
BAA	448.50	+ 12.50
BG Group	374.00	+ 10.25
British Airways	407.25	+ 1.00
British Energy	353.75	
British Telecom	1339.00	– 84.00
Centrica	184.00	+5.75
Corus	174.00	+ 6.25
Glaxo Wellcome	1687.00	– 3.00
Granada	596.00	– 34.00
Halifax	669.50	+ 12.50
ICI	632.00	– 19.00
Marks and Spencer	312.75	+ 2.25
National Grid	466.50	+ 2.50
Northern Rock	381.50	+ 2.75
Norwich Union	439.50	– 3.25
Railtrack	972.00	+ 17.00
Tesco	184.75	+ 3.00
Thomson Travel	105.50	+ 0.50
Woolwich	327.75	+ 9.25

Source: *The Guardian*, Metro, 6 January 2000

By selling shares to the general public as well as to other companies and organisations, public limited companies can raise vast amounts of capital in ways that are inaccessible to private limited companies. Additional shares can be issued and sold to raise further capital. In this way, a public limited company can finance costly expansion, development and research programmes which are often beyond the means of other types of business. For example, retail chains such as Sainsbury and Marks and Spencer can purchase prime trading sites in order to attract more customers, and major companies like Unilever can spend huge amounts on research to keep its products ahead of its competitors.

One potential drawback of the freedom to buy or sell shares in a public limited company, however, is that it is possible for all the shares in one plc to be bought by another company. In this way, the company buying the shares would take over the company whose shares it had bought. Although not all take-overs are unwelcome or hostile, they do mean that control of the company whose shares have been bought passes entirely into the hands of the company that bought them.

Public limited companies are generally the largest UK companies, although some private limited companies rival even the largest public ones. Virgin and Littlewoods are both major well-known private limited companies. As companies grow in size, they frequently become difficult to manage as single organisations. It is not unusual, therefore, for a public limited company to split its operations into several private limited companies, each of which is wholly owned by the public limited company (the parent company).

Figure 2.5: A public limited company may split its holdings into several private limited companies

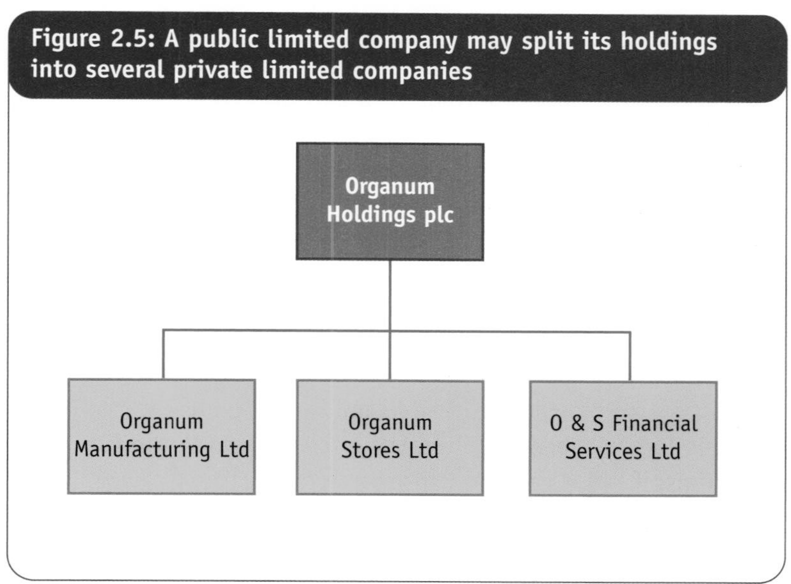

CASE STUDY

The Virgin Group

Virgin is one of the best known business names in Britain today. The Virgin Group of companies is led by its founder, head and prime mover, Richard Branson.

Richard Branson's first business venture, publishing a student magazine, started in 1968 while he was still a student. When the magazine ran into financial difficulties in 1970 he looked for a way to save it, and he started selling cut-price records by mail order. So successful was the mail order operation that by 1971 Richard Branson was able to open his first Virgin record shop in Oxford Street, London. Now Virgin Megastores are familiar in most large towns in Britain.

Over the years, the activities of Richard Branson have multiplied, many in conjunction with other major businesses. The Virgin Group has interests that include air travel, stores, financial services, music, rail travel, entertainment, cosmetics, cola and the internet. These are grouped into five major divisions:

- Virgin Travel
- Virgin Retail
- Voyager Investments
- Virgin Communications
- Virgin Hotels.

Virgin remained a private limited company, one of the most successful the UK has ever seen, until 1986. Then, Branson floated the major part of the group on the London Stock Exchange. He hoped to obtain a huge injection of capital to finance his plans for developing the businesses. Branson himself remained the major shareholder in the new public limited company, but 35 per cent of the shares issued were bought by a total of 87,000 individuals and institutions.

While floating Virgin as a public limited company gave Branson the capital he required, he soon saw that there were drawbacks. The shares soon became concentrated in the hands of major shareholders. Branson's control of the Virgin Group became diluted as the major shareholders sought to influence his decisions and the decisions of the board. He also saw that, to a certain extent, the success of the group was linked to the vagaries of the Stock Exchange and the value put on the business by financial institutions.

In 1988, therefore, following a stock market crash the previous year, Richard Branson led a management buyout. He offered the shareholders £1.40 per share, valuing the business at £248 million. The offer was accepted, and the whole of the Virgin Group once again became a group of private limited companies, with Branson firmly in control.

The Virgin Group

1 Why did the Virgin Group become a public limited company?

2 Why did Richard Branson lead a management buyout of the company?

3 What are the advantages and disadvantages of becoming a plc? Look at the case study to prepare your answer.

Businesses in public ownership

Many business organisations are owned and run by national or local government on behalf of the state, or society as a whole. These organisations are in **public ownership** – in the public sector. The purpose of these organisations is to provide a service to the public. National or local government provides the finance for state-owned organisations out of taxes or government borrowing. Public organisations owned and run by national government include the National Health Service, the police force and the Benefits Agency. Public organisations owned and run by local government include state-run hospitals, schools and libraries.

A public library, a state-owned asset

Although their purpose is not to make a profit, organisations in public ownership have to operate within tight financial budgets. They are run by a chief executive and directors who are accountable to Parliament or to local authorities for their performance. They are increasingly being made responsible for managing their own affairs in the same way as businesses in the private sector.

Many publicly owned organisations do not make a charge for the services they provide. These include schools, government departments, such as the Department of Social Security, and libraries (unless you are late returning your books). Other publicly owned organisations, such as leisure centres and the National Health Service (which charges for prescriptions), make a nominal charge to generate additional income – on top of that provided by government – to cover the full cost of providing services. Some hospitals also accept private patients, and schools and colleges often increase their revenue by providing services to private business and by accepting fee-paying students for certain courses.

Figure 2.6: Privatisation since 1979

Business	Nationalised	Privatised	Proceeds (£m)
Associated British Ports	1963	1983, 1985	139
British Aerospace	1977	1981	556
British Airports Authority	1966	1987	1,590
British Airways	1939, 1946	1987	1,400
British Coal	1947	1995	1,280
British Gas	1949	1986	12,930
British Petroleum	1913	1979, 1981	8,570
British Railways	1948	1996	3,185
British Steel	1951, 1967	1988	4,150
British Telecom	Before 1900	1984	21,990
Britoil	1976	1982, 1985	1,513
Cable & Wireless	Before 1900	1983, 1985	1,466
Jaguar Cars	1975	1984	425
National Freight	1969	1982	9
Regional Electricity Boards	1948	1990	n/a
Royal Ordnance	Before 1800	1986	305
Rolls Royce	1971	1987	1,770
Water Authorities	1983	1989	7,150

Source: H Stephen Gardner, *Comparative Economic Systems* (Dryden Press Series (US) *1997)*

Another type of organisation in public ownership is the public corporation. Public corporations are industrial organisations, such as the Post Office and the BBC, which are considered to provide essential products or services. The belief is that they should be owned by the government, on behalf of everyone in society, rather than by a few profit-motivated individuals. Organisations brought into public ownership in this way are called **nationalised industries**.

Public corporations charge an economic rate for their products or services (a rate at which income should cover costs). For example, the Post Office charges for postal and other services, while the BBC charges a licence fee. The government, however, makes good any losses incurred by a public corporation and ensures that sufficient funds are available out of taxes to cover necessary expenditure.

As a result of government economic policy, many public corporations have been sold to the private sector in the last 20 years. This process is called **privatisation**. Figure 2.6 lists some of the nationalised industries that were privatised in the 1980s and 1990s following the Conservative Party's general election victory in 1979 which saw Mrs Thatcher become Prime Minister.

Other types of business

Cooperatives

Cooperatives are business organisations that are owned by members. Each member has a share in the cooperative. Members are entitled to one vote each in decisions concerning the running of the cooperative, thus ensuring members have complete control. Cooperatives exist for the mutual benefit of the members. Finance is raised by members, who normally receive a fixed rate of interest on the capital they contribute. The members also decide how the profits of the cooperative

A Co-op store

should be used or distributed. A cooperative may be set up as a limited company.

There are four types of cooperative:

- **cooperative retail societies**, which buy goods in bulk at a discount and sell them as cheaply as possible to members
- **cooperative trading societies,** which are formed to distribute and sell the products or services of their members (usually small businesses)
- **worker cooperatives**, which are business organisations that are owned by their employees
- **housing cooperatives**, which develop, maintain and manage (usually low-cost) rented housing.

The best known cooperative is, of course, the high street Co-op, which is an organisation comprising around 40 retail cooperative societies. Other cooperatives may be set up by groups of farmers or small craftspeople who are able to buy in bulk through the cooperative, and so gain greater discounts, and also sell their products in larger quantities.

CASE STUDY

Suma Wholefoods

Suma Wholefoods is based in Halifax, West Yorkshire. It is the UK's largest independent wholesaler and distributor of vegetarian, organic and natural foods.

Suma is owned entirely by its employees. Its mission statement is 'to provide a high quality service to customers and a rewarding environment for the members, within a sustainable, ethical, cooperative business structure'. Today, Suma is a multi-million pound enterprise, with around 70 employees.

The business began in the early 1970s, when its founder started selling rice and lentils from his front room in Leeds. Demand was strong, and Suma was quickly established as a business with seven employees or members. In 1977, it registered as a common ownership workers' cooperative.

In the early days, members showed little discipline. They worked the hours they wanted, and in return took the wages they wanted. They often also took stock. Any questioning of each other's behaviour was considered unethical. Meetings 'just happened'. The wholefoods business was very profitable, however, and the business grew at around 12 per cent per year.

In 1979, the cooperative moved into a three-storey warehouse in the Leeds riverside area. It purchased vehicles and distribution management became the first functional area of the business to be organised on a formal basis.

Management meetings at this time were held weekly. All employees were present – the business closed for the afternoon. Decisions were taken by general consensus. The meetings became long discussions: individual members could block any decision of the majority, and decisions taken one week were frequently reversed the next. In practice, most decisions were taken on the job, by individual job holders, with little coordination.

In the mid-1980s, Suma moved to a mill shed in Halifax. Separated from the alternative culture of Leeds, customers and workers drifted away. The cooperative recognised that if it was to survive and grow it needed a new approach to business. A new management structure was designed. Sectors, groups of members with common interests, met weekly. Each sector then sent a delegate to the 'hub' committee to agree corporate decisions. However, it still took a long time to reach decisions and hub delegates tried to force through decisions only to find them constitutionally challenged.

In the early 1990s, sales stagnated and Suma was under threat. It was decided to elect a management committee from among the membership. Strategic policy was to be decided at quarterly general meetings of all members. The management committee would then use its delegated powers to carry the policy out through the company officers (personnel, finance, training, information and operations) and departmental coordinators.

The management committee now meets weekly to review progress and take appropriate action. After the weekly meetings, management committee members return to their normal jobs as ordinary members. This is to safeguard against the development of a clique of full-time managers pursuing their own interests rather than those of its members

Suma remains a cooperative. All workers are paid the same daily wage plus allowances and time in lieu to reduce any imbalance in hours. Suma also has a profit-related pay scheme and pension scheme. Wage costs overall are the industry average, but they are shared equally among workers. Other benefits are better than average and include six months maternity leave on full pay.

Job variety is considered important. For example, drivers only drive for a maximum of three days, working the remainder of the week in the warehouse or office. Office workers do manual work for at least one day a week. Members are encouraged to develop new skills and take on different jobs. This enables Suma to use labour and skills more efficiently in coping with the peaks and troughs of the business. Employees also stay fresh and enthusiastic for longer.

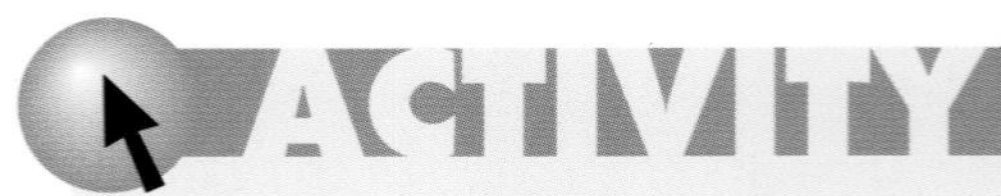

Suma Wholefoods

1 What type of co-operative is Suma?

2 What problems did Suma encounter in its early development, and why do you think they arose?

3 What action has Suma taken to overcome its problems? Do you think Suma's actions will be effective?

4 What are the benefits of the co-operative for (a) the business and (b) the workers?

Franchises

Instead of starting an entirely new business, some people prefer to trade under the name of a well-known company and sell its products. Some companies sell the right to do this, usually granting the right for an exclusive area or a specific location. The person or business buying this right, or **franchise**, is known as a franchisee. Franchises are often run by sole traders who put their money into setting up the business (perhaps with the help of a bank loan). In addition to the original purchase price of the franchise, the purchaser usually has to pay the franchisor – the company selling the franchise – an annual fee. This is often calculated as a percentage of turnover or profits.

In return, the purchaser of the franchise not only gets the right to trade under a well-known name (such as McDonald's) and sell a well-known product (such as Big Macs), but may also get help purchasing premises and equipment. In addition, many companies that operate franchise systems offer purchasers of their franchises training in administration, marketing and other areas of business. Franchisees can also benefit from bulk discounts on supplies not normally available to a sole trader and any national marketing campaigns undertaken by the company.

Running a franchise is often seen as a good compromise between being a small trader with complete control of your own business and being part of a large limited company. The franchisor benefits from its outlets being operated as independent businesses, each with a strong interest in ensuring that the main company is a success. The employees and capital of the franchisor company can be concentrated on core business, such as manufacturing and developing the product.

◀ Individual Pizza Hut restaurants are operated as franchises

Franchising is a growing sector of business, with major national and international companies such as Benetton, The Body Shop and Tie Rack operating in this way. By producing the goods that are sold through their franchises, these companies are able to protect their reputations and ensure the quality of their products. There are, however, many smaller businesses offering rather risky franchises based on less well-developed business ideas.

Which business?

With so many different types of business ownership, how do you decide which type to choose? This is an important question for anybody starting a business, and it should be answered at the outset. Figure 2.7 (see page 126) outlines the advantages and disadvantages of each type of ownership.

The type of product or service being provided should also influence the final choice of business ownership. For example, it obviously makes sense that services which are available equally to all members of society – such as national security, health and education – should be provided by publicly owned business organisations. For someone setting up in business, however, the choice is less clear. The choice should be made on the basis of:

- the amount of capital required and available
- the anticipated size of the business
- the skills of the business owner.

A person setting up as a mobile hairdresser, for example, requires less capital than someone opening a factory to manufacture cars. The hairdresser will probably only need a

Figure 2.7: Advantages and disadvantages of different types of business ownership

Type of ownership	Advantages	Disadvantages
Sole trader	Owner has full control of business and profits. Low start up costs and minimum of legal requirements.	Unlimited liability for the owner. Difficult for business to find sources of finance for expansion.
Partnership	Owners have full control over the business and profits. Few legal requirements, but a deed of partnership is desirable.	As with a sole trader, although as there is more than one owner more finance may be available.
Cooperative	May have limited liability. Members have control over the business and profits.	Finance must be provided by members. Other sources are often reluctant to lend to cooperatives. All members have equal say in running the cooperative. Disagreements can be difficult and time-consuming to resolve before action can be taken.
Private limited company	Owned by shareholders who have limited liability. Shareholders are often closely involved in running the business. Banks and other finance houses are often happier to lend to limited companies, which therefore have access to greater sources of funds.	Shares can only be sold or transferred with the agreement of all other shareholders. Shares cannot be freely sold to the general public.
Public limited company	Owned by shareholders who have limited liability. Shares may be bought and sold by the public. The issue of additional shares can provide a vast source of finance for plcs.	Since shares can be openly traded on the stock market, public limited companies are open to take over. Most shareholders will have no interest or involvement in the running of the company.
Public ownership	Ensures continued supply and delivery of goods and services, as well as continuation of employment. Any profits claimed by the state can be used to provide other services.	The efficiency of the organisation depends on the government's commitment to invest sufficiently in, for example, new and up-to-date equipment. Changing government policies and attitudes may lead to a lack of commitment from employees and poor management of the organisation. The absence of competition may result in a product-led rather than customer-led approach to business.

small bank loan, which is usually available to a sole trader, but the car manufacturer may need access to far greater funds which are usually only accessible to companies, perhaps from the issue of shares. The hairdresser is also likely to be a small business, appropriate to a sole trader, while the car manufacturer is likely to be a much larger concern and more suited to a company.

As a small business, the hairdresser will probably be able to run the business him or herself. If, however, he or she thinks she lacks the necessary administrative skills to run a business, it may be better to involve someone else who has these skills as a partner. The car manufacturer, on the other hand, being a larger business, will probably need to employ specialists in various aspects of running the company.

Build your learning

Summary points

- There are several different types of business ownership.
- A sole trader has full control over the business and its profits, but unlimited liability.
- In a partnership, the partners have full control over the business and profits as set out in a partnership agreement, but unlimited liability.
- A company is owned by shareholders who have limited liability and who receive a share of the profits called a dividend.
- Business organisations in public ownership are owned and run by central or local government.
- Cooperatives are businesses that have been set up for mutual benefit by groups of members.
- A franchise is a small business operating in the name of a larger business, selling the products or services of the larger business and benefiting from the advantages of being part of a large organisation.

Key words and phrases

You should know the meaning of the words and phrases listed below as they relate to the ownership of businesses. Go back through the last 28 pages of the unit to check or refresh your understanding.

- **Cooperative**
- **Deed of partnership**
- **Dividend**
- **Equity capital**
- **Franchise**
- **Incorporated**
- **Limited liability**
- **Nationalised industry**
- **Ordinary shares**
- **Partnership**
- **Preference shares**
- **Private limited company**
- **Private sector**
- **Privatisation**
- **Public limited company**
- **Public ownership**
- **Public sector**
- **Self-employed**
- **Shareholder**
- **Sole trader**
- **Unincorporated**
- **Unlimited liability**

Student questions

1 Distinguish between unlimited and limited liability, using examples of different types of business ownership.

2 The shares of what type of company are bought and sold on the stock market?

3 What are the advantages of a franchise?

4 Name three different types of cooperative.

1 COLLECT THE EVIDENCE

The assessment evidence for this unit must be based on your investigation of two contrasting businesses, based on types of ownership. For example, you may choose to investigate:

- a sole trader and a limited company
- a partnership and a public limited company (plc)
- a private limited company and a publicly owned organisation such as a hospital or your school or college.

Your first job is to select two contrasting local business organisations to investigate. If you are unsure about which businesses are suitable, or how to contact them, your tutor will be able to help you. You may be able to use the business you investigated for your assessment evidence for Unit 1 as your first business, and your school or college (or your employer if you are employed) as your second.

Once you have chosen your two organisations, you should write a description of each business, by undertaking the following tasks.

What to do

1. **Clearly describe the type of ownership and the liabilities of the owners of your two organisations.**
2. **Explain, in each case, how the type of ownership suits the activities of the business.**

The work that you complete for this activity will form part of your assessment evidence for this unit. You should therefore keep this work in your portfolio. Refer to the grid on page 171 to see what you need to do to achieve a pass, merit or distinction.

Industrial sectors

All businesses – regardless of whether they are in the public or private sector – operate in three broad industrial sectors.

- The **primary sector** includes those businesses involved with growing or extracting raw materials from natural resources.
- The **secondary sector** includes businesses involved in manufacturing and construction, using the products of the primary sector.
- The **tertiary sector** includes businesses involved in providing services.

Primary sector industries obtain the basic raw materials, secondary sector industries use these to produce finished goods, and tertiary sector industries distribute the goods, sell them to customers and provide other services to business and to private individuals. Figure 2.8 shows how organisations in the three sectors form a chain of production and distribution to get goods and services to customers.

Primary sector

Industries in the primary sector include:

- farming and fishing, producing the basic foodstuffs needed by society
- forestry, producing the timber that is used in making houses, furniture, paper and other items
- mining and allied industries, producing coal, oil and gas for heating and power, metals for construction and manufacturing goods, and stone for building.

Many firms in the farming, fishing and forestry industries are small, and run by farmers, the owners of fishing vessels, landowners, etc. They often form cooperatives (see page 121) to give themselves more influence and to protect their interests. Large firms, however, tend to predominate in mining (for example, RJB Mining) and fuel extraction (for example, BP, Esso, British Gas and Powergen), mainly because of the huge investment in plant and machinery necessary to operate in these industries.

Overall, employment in the primary sector in Britain has been declining for many years as industries such as mining and agriculture have contracted. One reason for the decline in employment is that many primary industries are becoming more efficient. New technology means that one employee can now do the work that was previously undertaken by several

Figure 2.8: The chain of production

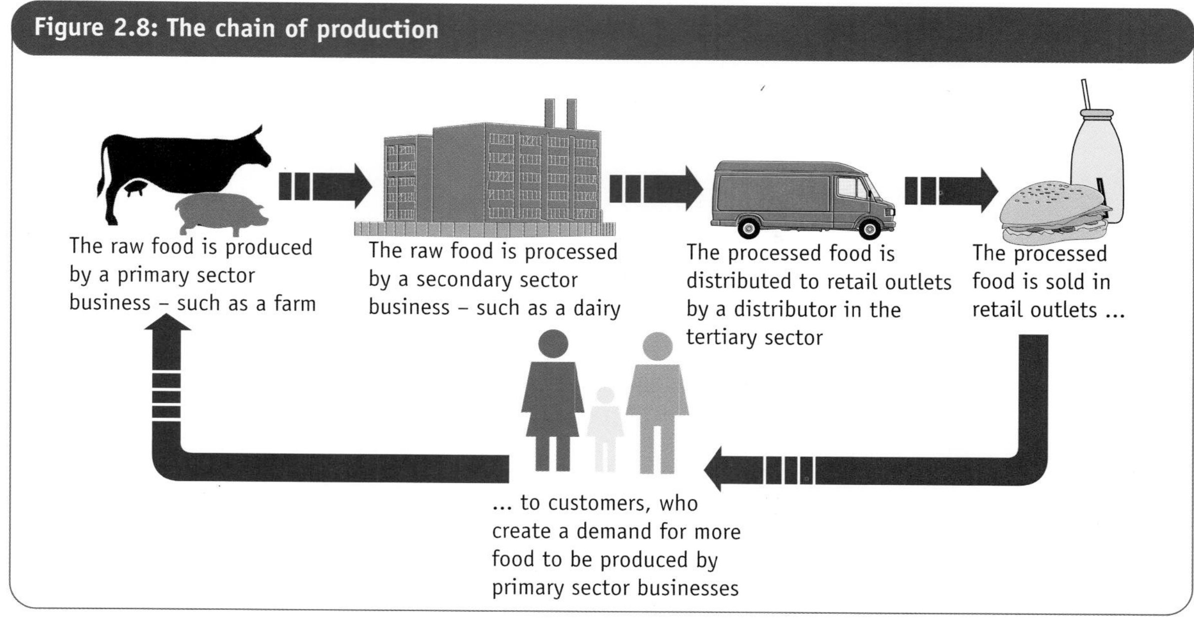

employees. For example, developments in farm machinery, as well as new methods of agriculture and animal husbandry, have led to greater productivity; this means that one person can now carry out tasks that used to require several farmhands.

In other industries, however, the reduction in employment is due to a general decline in the industry. There are many reasons why an industry goes into decline. Consider the coal industry as an example. In, 1991 coal accounted for 64 per cent of electricity generation. Now, electricity generators are increasingly being powered by gas and nuclear fuel rather than coal. This change is partly due to environmental concerns, but it is mainly due to the falling price of gas since competition was introduced into the gas industry. The effect on the coal industry has been devastating, since electricity generation has always been its main market. By 1997, coal accounted for just 37 per cent of electricity generation. Because of the lower demand for coal, there are lower levels of production and employment in the coal industry.

Modern farm machinery has reduced the need for farm workers

In other industries, the reason for decline may be due to increased competition from abroad, a fall in demand for manufactured products, or a change in general economic conditions. Thus the demand for basic metals is linked to the demand for engineering and construction products, cars and other vehicles, household goods such as washing machines and so on. Demand for these products has fallen since 1989 resulting in output of base metals being around 11 per cent lower in 1998 than in 1989. Demand has also been weakened by an increase in imports, as the strength of sterling has made imports relatively cheaper. In fact, the greatest challenge for UK metals producers is competition from abroad, which has been helped by falls in the value of currencies in Asia and Russia. UK producers have responded by trying to reduce costs and become more efficient. Employment in the base metals industry fell by 2 per cent in the year to June 1998 in an attempt to cut costs, and more reductions are likely.

These trends in the primary sector are expected to continue for the foreseeable future.

CASE STUDY

Fuel extraction

The fuel extraction sector accounts for 8.9 per cent of UK industrial production. Oil and gas extraction – on the UK mainland and the continental shelf – accounts for 93 per cent of the output of fuel extraction industries, with coal mining and other solid fuels accounting for the remaining 7 per cent.

In 1998, there were 170 firms involved in mining coal and other solid fuels registered for VAT. Of these, 24 per cent had a turnover of less than £100,000, and 59 per cent had a turnover of less than £1 million. There were 255 firms involved in the extraction of oil and gas registered for VAT, of which 27 per cent had a turnover below £100,000 and 47 per cent had a turnover below £1 million (again 1998 figures). There are very few small firms in these industries compared with most other industries. There were 42,800 employees in the fuel extraction industries in June 1998.

The demand for output from fuel extraction industries is a derived demand, which means it is determined by levels of demand in other industries. Demand for oil, coal and gas are affected by the demand for electricity generation and demand from the manufacturing sector, since fuel is required for the production process. The level of economic activity overseas is also important, particularly for oil, as the UK produces more oil than it uses. UK manufacturing output is expected to show only weak growth in the early years of the twenty-first century. Growth in industrial demand for fuel will also therefore be weak.

The UK coal industry was privatised on 1 January 1995, when most English mines were bought by RJB Mining. Costs were cut, improving competitiveness with other fuels, but the volume of output continued to fall as electricity generators moved away from coal and oil towards cleaner gas. Demand for coal was partly protected until April 1998 by contracts agreed with the electricity generators before privatisation, but output of coal declined by about 18 per cent in 1998 once the contracts expired.

The government has intervened to stem the decline of the coal mining industry by placing severe restrictions on new gas-fired generation plants and on open-cast coal mining, which produces coal at a lower cost than deep mining. In addition, generators are being required to sell underused coal-fired plants, to stimulate competition in electricity generation and boost the demand for coal. However, in the long term, the cost and environmental consequences of using coal will continue to cause output to shrink. Although generators will continue to source some coal from UK mines to guarantee continuity of supply, it is likely that an increasing proportion will be imported, particularly while sterling is strong. Imports accounted for 31 per cent of inland consumption of coal in 1997 compared with 18–20 per cent in the years just before privatisation and less than 10 per cent ten years earlier.

Output of the oil and gas extraction industries in 1998 was barely unchanged from 1997. Output growth has halted as the prospects for growth in demand have deteriorated. Growth in demand for gas is declining as the fuel switch by generators is stemmed. However, gas-fuelled plants already under construction will continue to come on stream, suggesting that gas is likely to remain the best performing of the fuel extraction industries. The demand for oil is mainly affected by world developments – since late 1997, the oil price has fallen significantly from over $20 a barrel to around $10 at the end of 1998. This is the result of a large oil stockpiles due to weak growth in south-east Asia, and prospects of weak growth in other developing economies.

Source: Lloyds TSB Industrial Prospects

Fuel extraction

Explain in your own words the trends in the fuel extraction industry reported in the case study. You should consider the causes of the trends and whether they are expected to continue.

What are the implications of the trends in the fuel extraction industry for employment:

- in the fuel extraction industry
- within the UK generally?

Secondary sector

Industries in the secondary sector take raw materials, such as metals, timber and foodstuffs, produced by primary sector industries and turn them into finished goods such as cars, houses and fishfingers. The goods that are produced by secondary sector businesses fall broadly into two categories:

- **consumer goods**, that are bought by members of society for their own use, such as washing machines, televisions and bread
- **producer goods**, that are used in the production of other goods, such as machinery and commercial vehicles.

A carpentry workshop, a secondary sector business

As individual customers we are more familiar with manufacturers that supply consumer goods than with those companies that supply producer goods. For example, most of us are familiar with the products of companies such as Hotpoint which manufactures household goods like washing machines and refrigerators, Sony which manufactures hi-fi equipment (like the original Walkman), and Raleigh which manufactures bikes. Yet, by buying the products of these companies, we are also buying products that have been manufactured using machines supplied by manufacturers of producer goods.

Secondary sector industries include those involved in manufacturing and construction. Manufacturing covers:

- the refining and processing of metals, minerals and mineral products
- the production of chemicals and artificial fibres
- engineering and allied trades
- food and drink processing, and tobacco products
- the making of textiles, footwear, clothing and leather goods.

Construction covers:

- building, including domestic and commercial projects
- civil engineering, such as road and bridge construction.

Businesses in the construction industries mainly produce **capital goods**, that is, goods that are expected to last and not be used up, such as roads, houses and hospitals.

Some industries operate in both the primary and secondary sectors. These are called **production industries**. Esso UK, for example, extracts crude oil from the North Sea oilfields, which is a primary sector activity, and also refines the crude oil into petroleum products such as petrol, diesel and lubricants. which is a secondary sector activity.

Despite a slight overall increase in manufacturing output each year since 1992, employment in UK manufacturing is declining, especially in textiles, shipbuilding, clothing and footwear. Manufacturing costs are high in the UK compared to other industrialised countries. Competition from abroad is fierce, particularly from within the European Union, and from some newly industrialised countries such as South Korea, Malaysia, Taiwan and Singapore.

New technology has also transformed manufacturing. By enabling mass production methods to be used, improving efficiency and allowing production plants to be run with fewer employees, new technology has contributed to the fall in employment in the secondary sector.

Manufacturing industries are expected to show significant growth in the future. There is a high level of foreign investment – that is, overseas money coming into the UK to purchase or set up businesses. Investment by foreign companies such as Nissan, Toyota, BMW and Samsung, is creating many new jobs in this sector. However, UK manufacturing industries will continue to face fierce competition from abroad, and this will limit the extent to which this sector can develop. In addition, new technology will continue to increase productivity, further limiting opportunities for new employment.

Modern automated car manufacture – the Rover 75 production line

ACTIVITY

Food and drink manufacturing

Read the case study on page 137 about the food and drink manufacturing industry and then answer these questions.

1 Is food and drink manufacturing in the UK declining or increasing?

2 How does this affect industries in the primary and tertiary sectors?

CASE STUDY

Food and drink manufacturing

Food and drink manufacturing accounts for around 2.8 per cent of the net output of the whole UK economy, and 13 per cent of net output of manufacturing industries.

In 1996, there were 7,670 firms currently registered for VAT in the food and drink manufacturing sector, of which 30 per cent had a turnover below £100,000 and 72 per cent below £100 million.

There were 375,300 employees in employment in food manufacturing in September 1997, a 0.2 per cent decline from a year earlier. Employment figures for drink manufacturing are combined with tobacco manufacturing, and together there were 53,100 employees in employment in these industries in September 1997, a 2.7 per cent decline from a year earlier.

Exports account for around 18 per cent of total sales in the sector, and imports account for 23 per cent of home sales (1995).

The sector is more stable than many other manufacturing industries since most of its output consists of necessary commodities. Therefore, although output from the sector declined less than that of other industries during the recession of the early and mid-1990s, future growth in the sector is likely to be below average in an upturn.

However, there are also other trends that indicate that long-term output growth in the sector will be below average. First, consumer preferences are increasingly shifting towards more exotic foods, particularly fruit and vegetables, leading to rising imports. Consumption of fresh meat, potatoes, milk, eggs, butter and sugar is declining.

Second, increased health awareness means that people are drinking less alcohol. There is some movement away from beer and towards other alcohol products like wine, but the overall share of expenditure on alcoholic drink is declining faster than the share of expenditure on food.

With these long-term trends in the market for traditional products, food manufacturers must concentrate on the production of items such as convenience meals and health products. Brewers are increasing their range of products, by developing alcopops and new types of lagers. Spirits producers are trying to expand sales in emerging markets such as eastern Europe.

Although some of the long-term weaknesses in domestic (UK) markets can be addressed, overall the food and drink manufacturing industry will remain a slow growing sector.

Source: Lloyds TSB Industrial Prospects

Tertiary sector

The tertiary sector is the widest ranging industrial sector in the United Kingdom. It contains major public limited companies such as Granada plc, sole traders and small partnerships such as small estate agents, decorators and personal trainers, large partnerships such as Arthur Andersen Consulting, and public sector organisations such as doctors' surgeries, universities and the BBC. Figure 2.9 shows main types of industry in the tertiary sector.

Figure 2.9: Industries in the tertiary sector

Type of industry	Examples
Banking and other financial services	Lloyds TSB plc, Nationwide Building Society
Insurance	Eagle Star Group, Norwich Union
Leisure	Leisure centres, theatres, cinemas, hotels
Transport	Virgin Atlantic, Stagecoach
Wholesaling and retailing	Nurdin and Peacock, Bookers, Tesco, Harrods, WH Smith
Public services	Libraries, museums, the BBC
Distribution	British Airways, P&O, Virgin Rail, Excel Logistics, DHL
Post and telecommunications	The Post Office, British Telecom, Hutchinson Telecommunications, Vodaphone
Education	Schools, colleges, correspondence colleges, private language schools
Health services	Doctors' surgeries, hospitals, health screening services, alternative therapists

The tertiary sector is the fastest growing and most diverse sector of the UK economy. Unlike the primary and secondary sectors, employment in the tertiary sector is increasing. In some areas, however, notably in banking and public administration, increased efficiency and productivity resulting from the introduction of new technology has led to reductions in employment. Overall growth in areas such as banking, insurance and other financial services, business consultancy, leisure and tourism and health services is expected to continue for the foreseeable future.

CASE STUDY

Health services

Health services include hospital and consultant services, local authority health services, general medical, dental and other medical services, and nursing homes.

There were 3,820 businesses registered for VAT in 1998, although this figure understates the true number of firms in the health services industry due to VAT exemptions. Of those registered, 49 per cent had a turnover below £100,000, and 95 per cent below £1 million, similar to other service industries.

There are 1.5 million people employed in the health service industries (this definition includes veterinary services, however), of which 44 per cent are part-time (June 1998).

Fast growing consumer expectations and demographic trends (the size, structure and distribution of the population in terms of factors such as sex and age) are resulting in growth of demand for healthcare services of around 3–4 per cent per year. This demand growth puts pressure on government plans to maintain levels of overall public spending and refrain from rising taxes or borrowing.

The NHS was granted an additional £21 billion for 1998–2001 in a comprehensive spending review. Although this increase sounds significant, it equates to real growth in health spending of 4.7 per cent per year over the three years, which is only slightly higher than the demand growth. The increase is therefore unlikely to result in a great improvement in service quality; it will merely prevent the service worsening.

Demand for private medical and dentistry services will be boosted by demographic trends and the increasing disparity between the ease of obtaining treatment privately compared with under the NHS. However, the removal of tax relief on private insurance for the over 60s may price some people out of the private health market, increasing the burden on the NHS.

Since the care in the community reforms were introduced in 1993, nursing home occupancy rates have fallen to below 90 per cent. As a result, the private nursing home sector has undergone significant consolidation to cut costs, and many providers are diversifying into services such as drug and alcohol rehabilitation centres, and psychiatric and physical rehabilitation.

Private institutions now claim to provide 55 per cent of UK hospital beds, although half of these are in long-term nursing care. In 1997, the NHS and local authorities supplied around 355,000 care beds; independent healthcare providers supplied around 450,000. Reports suggest that a third of psychiatric treatment is already carried out in the private sector.

Source: Lloyds TSB Industrial Prospects

Health services

1 Describe the trends in the provision of health services in the UK.

2 What are the causes of these trends?

3 Are current trends in the provision of health services in the UK likely to continue? Justify your answer.

Employment by industrial sector

The service sector accounts for an increasing proportion of total business activity. This has led to widely differing trends in employment across industrial sectors. As Figure 2.10 shows, the two largest sectors in terms of employment were public services (which includes administration, defence, health and education activities) and distribution, hotels and catering. The two smallest sectors, agriculture and mining and utilities, accounted for under 3 per cent of total employment.

Financial and business services saw the fastest employment growth of the ten broad industrial sectors between 1981 and 1997. Employment in this sector increased at an average rate of almost 4 per cent per year, creating over two million additional jobs. In regional terms, growth in this sector was particularly strong in the south east.

Business services, which include advertising, accountancy and law, saw particularly strong employment growth over the period. Financial services saw fast growth in the 1980s, but fell victim to the recession. Deregulation also contributed to the fall in employment in financial services between 1991 and 1993, as mergers led to downsizing in many companies.

Between 1981 and 1997, a total of 1.3 million additional jobs were created in public services. The only other sector to see significant employment growth between 1981 and 1997 was distribution, hotels and catering, which benefited from increased demand due to rising personal disposable incomes.

Falls in employment in the years 1981–97 were heavily concentrated in manufacturing. Employment losses were particularly severe in metals, minerals and chemicals, and engineering, but less so in other manufacturing. Greater London lost a particularly large number of manufacturing jobs. In 1997, there were around 170,000 fewer manufacturing jobs in London than in 1987.

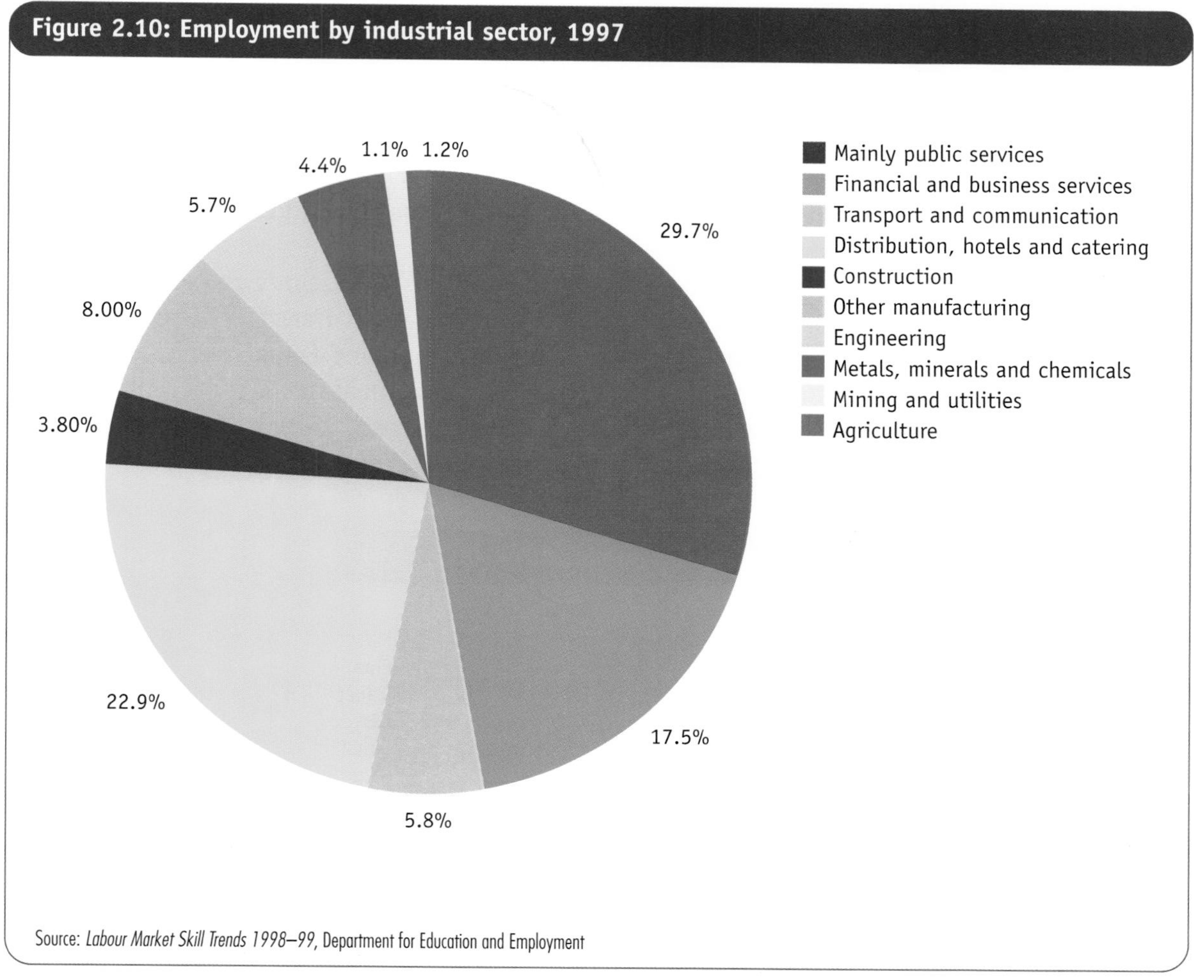

Figure 2.10: Employment by industrial sector, 1997

Source: *Labour Market Skill Trends 1998–99*, Department for Education and Employment

Engineering saw a temporary slowdown in the rate of job losses due to inward investment in electronics and some periods of employment growth in other parts of the sector, such as the motor industry.

Generally, the sectors which are forecast to show increased employment between 1997 and 2007 (see Figure 2.11) are those which have grown since 1981. The exception is construction, where employment is forecast to fall by 4.2 per cent between 1997 and 2007.

Financial and business services are expected to show the fastest proportionate growth over the forecast period, although growth is set to slow down to a relatively modest 1.5 per cent per year. Business services are expected to be the strongest performer in this sector with employment growth of 2.5 per cent per year, while a fall in employment is forecast in financial services.

The largest absolute increase in employment is expected to be in public services. The majority of new jobs are expected to be in education and health, an area which has already seen significant employment growth since 1981.

Manufacturing is set to see further productivity gains between 1997 and 2007. This will mean further falls in employment, although if employers fail to achieve productivity gains, then competitive pressures could lead to even greater job losses in many firms.

All the information, analysis and figures quoted above are taken from *Labour Market and Skills Trends 1998–99*, published by the Department for Education and Employment. *Labour Market and Skills Trends* is an annual publication containing information on employment across industrial sectors, and analysis of future employment trends.

Figure 2.11: Projected change in total employment 1997–2007

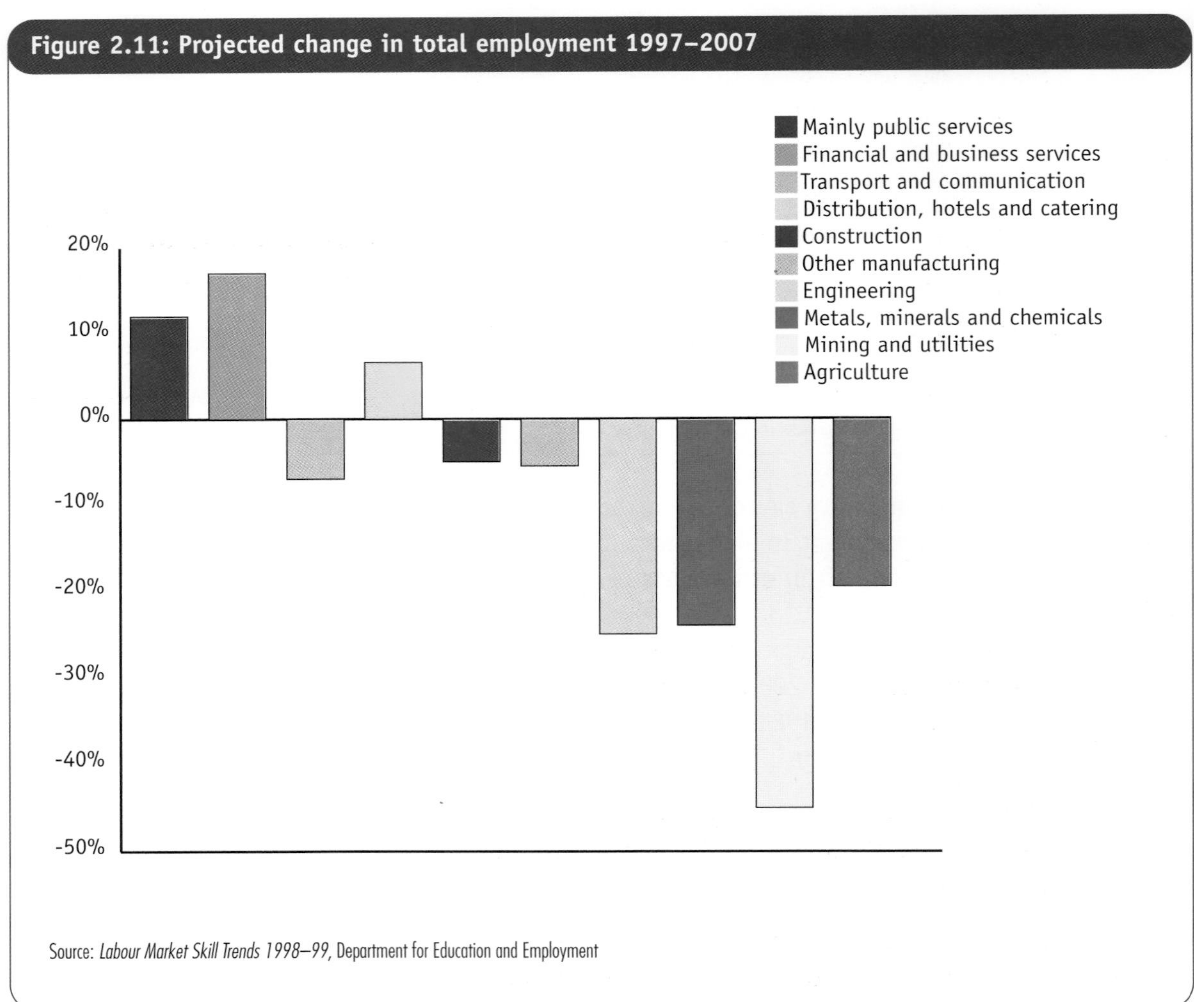

Source: *Labour Market Skill Trends 1998–99*, Department for Education and Employment

Build your learning

Summary points

- Businesses operate in the primary, secondary or tertiary industrial sectors.
- Primary sector businesses produce raw materials.
- Secondary sector businesses manufacture goods from raw materials and components.
- Tertiary sector businesses provide services to other businesses and individuals.

Key words and phrases

You should know the meaning of the words and phrases listed below, as they relate to industrial sectors. Go back through the last 13 pages of the unit to check or refresh your understanding.

- **Capital goods**
- **Consumer goods**
- **Industrial sector**
- **Primary sector**
- **Producer goods**
- **Production industries**
- **Secondary sector**
- **Tertiary sector**

Student questions

1 Identify the main activities of industries in the primary sector, the secondary sector and the tertiary sector.

2 Explain briefly the trends in each sector. Think about how levels of demand for each sector's goods have changed, and how levels of employment in each sector have been affected by changes in demand, technology and competition.

3 Use the production and sale of a loaf of bread as an example to show how all three industrial sectors are involved and relate to each other.

② COLLECT THE EVIDENCE

The work that you complete for this activity will form part of your assessment evidence for this unit. You should refer to the grid on page 171 to see what you need to do to achieve a pass, merit or distinction. Remember, if you carry out the following activities now, you will have completed part of the work needed for your end-of-unit assessment. You are advised to do this now, to avoid overload at the end of the unit.

What to do

Write a description of the industrial sectors, in which each of the businesses you selected for the 'Collect the evidence' activity on page 129 operate by completing the following tasks.

1. **Are the sectors growing or declining? Identify current UK business trends in the industrial sectors in which your businesses operate.**
2. **Explain how these trends are affecting at least one of the businesses you are investigating.**
3. **Support your account with appropriate diagrams, tables or charts.**

Business activity

The **main activity** (or **core activity**) of a business is closely connected with the industrial sector in which it operates.

- The main activity of WH Smith is retailing – selling books, magazines and stationery. This is a tertiary sector activity.
- The main activity of Abbey National plc is providing financial services, a tertiary sector activity.
- The main activity of Hoover is manufacturing vacuum cleaners and vacuum cleaner bags, which are consumer goods, although it also manufactures some industrial vacuum cleaners which are capital goods (see page 134 for the definitions of capital goods and consumer goods). Manufacturing is a secondary sector activity.
- The main activity of British Airways is transport, a tertiary sector activity.
- The main activity of British Telecommunications is communications, a tertiary sector activity.
- The main activity of RJB Mining is mining, a primary sector activity.

Some businesses, such as Hoover and RJB Mining, deal with products, while others, such as WH Smith, Abbey National and British Telecommunications, provide services.

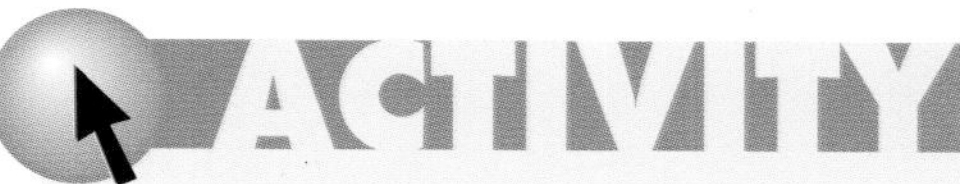

Main activities

Look at the list of businesses below. Some are well known, others less well known. Describe the main activity of each business and identify whether the business provides goods or services and whether it operates in the primary, secondary or tertiary industrial sector. If the business manufactures goods, does it produce consumer goods or capital goods?

- **Microsoft**
- **Sainsbury**
- **Ford**
- **Belvoir Fruit Farms**
- **Wimpy Homes**
- **McDonald's**
- **Lloyds TSB Bank**
- **Express Newspapers**
- **Harrods**
- **Raleigh**
- **Iceland**
- **Hotpoint**
- **Your school or college**

While most businesses have one core activity, many also have other activities which may relate to other sectors. Marks and Spencer's core activity is selling clothes, food and other household goods. However, another area of activity for Marks and Spencer is financial services, where the company has activities in personal loans, chargecards, investments, life assurance and pensions.

Businesses often move into other areas of activity as a natural extension of their core activity. Many brewers, such as Courage, whose core activity is drink production, also own public houses, which are retail outlets. In this way, a business can expand into markets that complement and support its core activity. By owning public houses, Courage Breweries is able to ensure outlets – and customers – for its products.

Other businesses may move into activities that are unrelated to their core activity. For example, Unilever, which started out as Lever Brothers, makers of detergent and soap powders, now produces a wide variety of products including bleaches, deodorants and perfumes, cheese and dairy products and ice cream.

The process of moving into other areas of activity is called **diversification**. Diversification can be **lateral**, where the other activities are related to the core activity of the business, as with Courage Breweries, or **conglomerate**, where they are unrelated, as with Unilever.

Lateral diversification is usually undertaken to support and expand the core activity of the business. Conglomerate diversification may be undertaken to counter a possible decline in the core activity of a business. For example, British American Tobacco has diversified into alternative activities such as financial services, as there has been a considerable decline in demand for its tobacco products over the years. Conglomerate diversification may also be undertaken to allow businesses to move into areas of activity that are showing signs of growth or becoming more common. British Telecommunications, for example, has moved into new areas of activity such as internet access provision.

CASE STUDY

Esso UK plc

Esso UK is a major business operating in the oil and gas industries. It produces approximately one tenth of the total United Kingdom oil and gas output and one sixth of the output of petroleum products.

Esso UK plc is a public limited company. Its shares are owned by the Exxon Corporation, which therefore owns the company. There are two subsidiary operating companies: Esso Exploration and Production UK Ltd, and Esso Petroleum Company Limited. Both are private limited companies wholly owned by Esso UK plc. The activities of Esso Exploration and Production include exploration for and production of crude oil and natural gas. The activities of Esso Petroleum include research and the refining, distribution and marketing of petroleum products. Esso Exploration and Production operates in the primary industrial sector. Esso Petroleum operates in the secondary and tertiary sectors.

Esso has interests in oilfields in the North Sea and elsewhere on the United Kingdom continental shelf. The company largely operates these oilfields either with or on behalf of other oil companies, such as Shell. Esso is responsible for about 25 per cent of the activity in the North Sea oilfields. It expects to continue this level of investment and activity in the future. Esso is not involved in any onshore exploration in the United Kingdom.

Natural gas from fields in the northern North Sea is piped to St Fergus in north east Scotland. Here methane is separated and distributed to customers via the British Gas pipeline. The remaining mixture of ethane, propane, butane and heavier hydrocarbons is

piped to Mossmoran in Fife, where it is further separated into its individual components. Natural gas from fields in the southern North Sea are piped to a processing terminal at Bacton in Norfolk. Crude oil from the northern oil fields of the North Sea is transported by pipeline or tanker to the oil terminal at Sullom Voe, on Shetland.

Esso has an oil refinery at Fawley, near Southampton, which processes 300,000 barrels of crude oil a day. Processing is carefully controlled and monitored by computer. Most of the refined petrol, gas oil, jet fuel and diesel is transported to Esso distribution centres at west London, Heathrow Airport, Gatwick Airport, Purfleet, Avonmouth, Manchester, Nottingham and Birmingham. This is mainly by pipeline, although some refined products are transported by road, rail and sea.

The company's distribution system covers the entire United Kingdom. It also uses a few **branded distributors**, independent companies which supply Esso products to customers in defined areas. Esso sells directly to more than 1,500 industrial customers, and to a further 80,000 through its branded distributors.

Esso sells petrol and diesel through some 2,200 service stations. The company owns about 1,000 service stations, the remainder are franchise operations. Esso's own fleet of around 100 road tankers supplies the service stations. Retail fuel sales account for more than 40 per cent by volume of Esso's sales of petroleum products. Most of the service stations also have shops, which sell not only motor oils and car accessories, but tobacco and confectionery, snacks and drinks, household products and even fast food. Esso is one of the largest retail chains in the United Kingdom. Every hour of every day of the year, Esso service stations serve around 34,000 customers.

There is a standby response team, of more than 70 trained professionals, ready to deal with disasters such as oil spills. Esso is also active in the community and involved with education.

Esso UK plc

1 What is Esso's main activity?

2 What other activities does Esso carry out?

3 Does Esso provide goods or services?

4 Which industrial sector or sectors does Esso operate in?

Build your learning

Summary points

- Businesses carry out one or more activities.
- The main activity of a business is called its core activity.
- The core activity of a business may be producing goods or services.
- The activities of some businesses involve producing both goods and services.
- Some business activities are becoming more common, others less so.

Key words and phrases

You should know the meaning of the words and phrases listed below as they relate to business activity. Go back through the last four pages of the unit to check or refresh your understanding.

- **Branded distributors**
- **Core activity**
- **Conglomerate diversification**
- **Diversification**
- **Lateral diversification**
- **Main activity**

Student questions

1 What is meant by the core activity of a business?

2 Why might a business diversify into other activities?

3 COLLECT THE EVIDENCE

The work that you complete for this activity will form part of your assessment evidence for this unit. You should refer to the grid on page 171 to see what you need to do to achieve a pass, merit or distinction. Remember, if you carry out the following activities now, you will have completed part of the work needed for your end-of-unit assessment. You are advised to do this now, to avoid overload at the end of the unit.

What to do

1. **Describe the activities of the two businesses you are investigating for this unit. State which are their core activities, and whether they are dealing with products or services or both.**
2. **Find out about the broad trends for these activities: are they becoming more common or less common? How do these trends affect the businesses you are investigating?**

Influences on business

Businesses in the United Kingdom do not operate in isolation. They are part of the wider economic and social environment, both of this country and the European Union and the wider world.

Figure 2.12: External influences on business

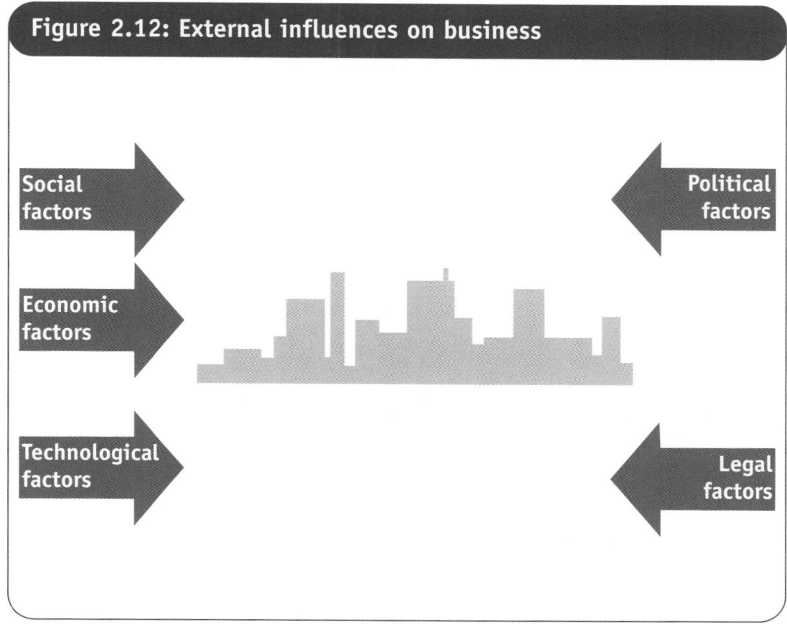

As Figure 2.12 shows, businesses are influenced by five principal factors. These are:

- **social factors**, such as the size and age distribution of the population, changes in lifestyles and socio-economic distinctions
- **legal factors**, such as health and safety and employment legislation
- **economic factors**, such as the free flow of goods and services within the European Union, increased competition within Europe and the world, levels of wages, inflation and unemployment
- **political factors**, such as government policy regarding issues such as privatisation, competition, taxation, and political trends and uncertainties
- **technological factors**, such as the development and introduction of computer technology, the adoption of new methods of marketing and selling such as e-commerce, and the impact technology has on production methods and employment levels.

In order to survive and grow, a business must recognise and respond appropriately to these influences. How it responds depends on the size and type of business, its activities and the sector it operates in, and its aims and objectives. Sometimes, the influences of specific factors mean that there has to be a trade-off between different objectives. For example, a business that seeks to maximise its profits through using the most up-to-date technology to increase productivity may find that it has to reduce its labour force, thus increasing unemployment. Increased unemployment reduces overall demand in the economy and may, therefore, have an impact on the profits of many businesses.

In the remainder of this unit, we consider two external influences on business in more detail. Each includes elements of all the five factors that we have identified as having an impact on businesses. We explore the effect of:

- location – how the position of a business affects its performance
- stakeholders – who the stakeholders are and how they influence the activities of businesses.

Location

The decision about where to locate a business is an important one, as the location of a business can influence its performance in many ways. Several factors must be taken into consideration, the importance of each varying according to the type, purpose and nature of the business. Factors that are important to retailers such as Marks and Spencer in looking for a site for a new store, are different to the factors that are important to a car manufacturer such as Vauxhall, considering where to build a new factory.

Business development plots marked on an aerial map of Telford

CASE STUDY

Marks and Spencer

Marks and Spencer's board approves plans to target the towns and regions considered suitable as locations for expansion throughout the UK. The job of actually finding viable sites falls to the company's estates division, which is based at head office in London.

The estates division's efforts are normally concentrated on either traditional town centre sites or more accessible edge-of-town locations. Acquisitions surveyors liaise with estate agents and property developers to identify a suitable site.

Although its edge-of-town stores – like the Metro Centre (Tyneside), Hedge End (Southampton) and Lisburn (Northern Ireland) – have proved highly successful, Marks and Spencer continues to seek sites in towns and the main thrust of its business remains in the high street.

Availability of space is one factor in deciding whether Marks and Spencer builds in the town centre or on the edge of the town. Other considerations are ease of access and car parking. Edge-of-town stores enable the company to provide on-site parking. They also provide it with the space in which to display its full range of merchandise.

When considering development opportunities, a detailed assessment of the area is drawn up by a special projects team, to make sure it is the right location in terms of potential profitability. To estimate the all-important turnover figure, the assessment includes researching the population and customer profile, the catchment area and the competition. Marks and Spencer also pays particular attention to local planning and environmental issues and meets local interest groups, incorporating their comments into the final proposal.

The majority of Marks and Spencer's properties are freehold or long leasehold, which protects it in part from the high increases in operating costs which face many retailers.

Alongside the work of building and fitting out the store, plans are also made to engage the people who will work in the store. The store manager, deputy manager, personnel manager and other senior management personnel will be men and women who are promoted and transferred from other Marks and Spencer stores. Other staff will be recruited locally.

Source: Adapted from *Bricks and Mortar (Building a Store)*, Marks and Spencer company information sheet.

Marks and Spencer

What factors do Marks and Spencer take into consideration when deciding where to locate a new store?

Any organisation that is considering starting a new business or expanding by moving to a new location must give careful consideration to a range of factors (see Figure 2.13).

Figure 2.13: Factors to be considered when choosing a business location

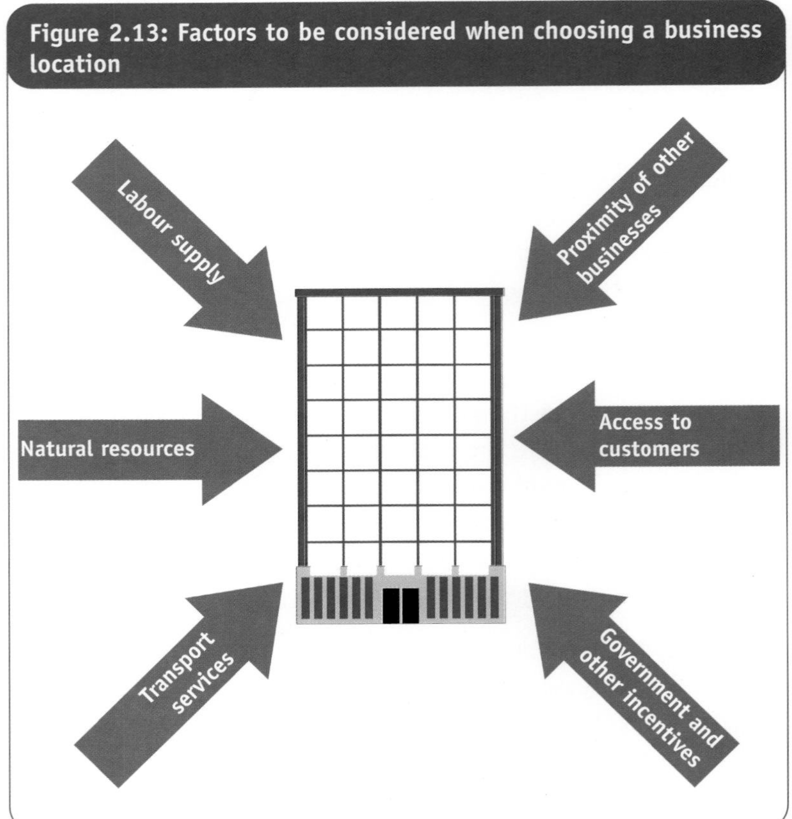

People and skills

All business and industrial organisations, apart from sole traders working on their own, need employees. When a business is considering a location – whether as a site to set up initially, to establish a new depot or factory, or to relocate (move) to – it must consider the availability of employees (the **labour supply**). It needs to consider:

- **numbers** – will the business be able to recruit enough employees for its needs?
- **skills** – do the employees who could be recruited locally have the right skills to do the work required?

People and skills

Visit your local jobcentre and look at the advertised job vacancies. Also check what types of jobs are advertised in local employment agencies and the employment section of your local newspaper. Make a list of the different types of job vacancy in your area and the skills employers are looking for. Is there a prevalence of one type of skill requirement?

What are the types of skills required for employment in the businesses you are investigating for this unit? Are they the types of skills needed for the jobs you have seen advertised? How common do you think those skills are in the area?

High unemployment in the late 1980s and early 1990s meant that there was a greater supply of labour available to businesses. However, unemployed people often lacked the skills that were needed by employers in their area. This was because, historically, certain types of industries had located in particular areas, leading to a concentration of particular skills. For example, textiles have traditionally been produced in Leicestershire, coal mined in certain areas of Nottinghamshire, Yorkshire and south Wales, and ships built in north east England, Scotland and Northern Ireland. As these traditional industries declined, there has not only been direct unemployment from factory closures, but the workers that have been made redundant have lacked the different skills needed for the jobs that were available. This has produced levels of unemployment above the national average.

In order to help this situation, local and national government have offered incentives to businesses to locate in areas of high unemployment (see below). On the face of it, this should make relocation to areas of high unemployment attractive to businesses. However, although a company would have access to a large supply of labour, the local people may not have the skills appropriate for that business. Businesses, therefore, tend to locate in areas where the available workforce has appropriate skills. This has a cumulative effect as can be seen in the growth of high-tech businesses along the M4 corridor in the Thames Valley.

Government and other incentives

While a prestigious modern office in the heart of the City of London may be highly desirable as a business location, the cost of the premises may well put them out of reach of the majority of companies in the United Kingdom. Increasingly, businesses of all kinds are moving away from the capital towards provincial centres. Cities such as Birmingham, Manchester and Nottingham are becoming centres of industry and commerce, a fact that is now having an impact on the price of commercial property in those areas.

On the other hand, the decline and closure of many manufacturing industries in some areas of the UK has led to an unequal distribution of unemployment between the regions. There is a similar unequal pattern across the rest of Europe. In order to rectify this situation, a variety of **incentives** have been developed by the European Union and by central and local government, which are designed to encourage new business into areas of high unemployment.

A regeneration scheme

The European Union provides aid through the European Regional Development Fund, which gives grants to projects concerned with developing areas of industrial decline, in some cases supporting businesses and improving transport links. The UK government has introduced financial incentives aimed at creating new jobs in areas of high unemployment. These incentives include free or subsidised rent on premises, subsidies per employee and grants for additional employees taken on. The overall level of aid to the regions has fallen in recent years, but many large businesses have located in depressed areas as a result of government action.

Financial incentives

Are there any incentives to businesses available in your local area, either from the government or the European Union? The planning department of your council or your local chamber of trade or commerce may be able to help you with this activity. You can find them listed in the Yellow Pages.

If there are incentives available, suggest reasons why they are being offered. If there are no incentives available in your area, where is the nearest area where incentives are available?

To qualify for regional aid from the government, a business must either locate in a designated development area, where a grant for the creation of new jobs is available, or in intermediate areas, where there may be financial aid.

The government has also provided some money for the regeneration of inner city areas. An example is London Docklands, where the decline of the docks had left a run down, almost derelict area. Government funding was used to reclaim the land and create the **infrastructure** (roads and communications) to make it an attractive area for commercial organisations. More examples of government-supported regeneration schemes may be found in many provincial cities.

On the waterfront: new residential development in the London Docklands

Local authorities have also sought to attract firms to their areas, particularly if there are high levels of unemployment. Measures taken include the easing of planning restrictions to allow new building development, the creation of business parks and retail parks to attract new businesses and large retail stores, respectively, normally with the incentive of a subsidised or rent-free period.

Financial help from local, national or European government is of particular interest to start-up manufacturing businesses, which often look for units on designated industrial parks. However, many national governments and local authorities compete keenly to attract investment from major foreign companies looking for new sites. For example, Toyota only decided to establish its new factory at Burnaston in Derby after considering the incentives available at a number of other locations in the UK and the rest of Europe.

Suppliers and raw materials

Many businesses, particularly those in the primary sector, are dependent on natural resources for their operation. An obvious example is mining. Coal mines must be located at the site of the coal reserves that are to be extracted.

In other industries, the availability of natural resources dictates the type of business activity. In agriculture, the type of farming – dairy, sheep, arable and so on – depends on factors such as the type of soil, its fertility and its suitability for different crops and grasses. Before the development of modern transport networks, manufacturing industries were generally located close to their sources of raw materials, while service industries needed to be close to their customers.

In general, all businesses must have good **access to suppliers and raw materials**. However, the development of fast rail links and motorway networks has tended to give businesses more freedom of choice over location. In practice, however, the availability of **transport links** influences the location of businesses in several ways.

- A manufacturing organisation which produces easily transportable goods from heavy or bulky raw materials is likely to locate itself close to its source of raw materials.
- A manufacturing organisation which produces heavy or bulky goods from easily transportable raw materials will locate itself close to its customers.
- A manufacturing organisation seeking to distribute its goods nationally or internationally will take the availability of transport facilities into account, perhaps locating close to a motorway junction or a port.
- A service industry which carries out its work on customer premises will consider the location of its customers, ease of access to them and the distance it is prepared to travel to provide its service.

The Japanese car giant Nissan chose to open a plant in north east England partly because of government incentives, but also because the site was close to motorway and rail links which could be used for distributing cars throughout the UK. The port facilities at Tyne and Wear were easily accessible for exporting to Europe.

The Nissan car plant, Sunderland

In south east England, manufacturing businesses are moving away from expensive town and industrial park locations to cheaper locations closer to motorway networks. The newly developed London Docklands only started to develop as a commercial centre once businesses were convinced that the transport network would properly serve the area. In the Midlands, new towns, such as Telford and Milton Keynes have also attracted businesses due to their easy access to the rest of the country via the motorway system.

Some businesses choose their locations in order to be easily accessible to their employees or customers. One of the reasons London developed as a major centre for business and commerce was the existence of a vast and complex commuter network which enables employees to work in the City or the centre of London while living in the suburbs. When the Disney Corporation decided to establish a theme park in Europe, it chose a location near Paris with easily accessible road, rail, air and ferry links with the rest of Europe.

Competition

No business organisation operates in isolation from other businesses, either as suppliers, competitors or customers. Historically, the location of other businesses has had a significant effect on the location of new businesses which are seeking to establish themselves.

Many areas have gained a reputation for a particular type of business. Examples include:

- Sheffield for producing stainless steel – a firm manufacturing stainless steel cutlery will benefit from being able to put 'made in Sheffield' on its product
- the City of London for banking and financial services – London has become the banking and financial capital of the world and a presence in the City is essential to the reputation of any major bank or financial institution
- the west Midlands for the car industry – the growth of car manufacturing in the west Midlands has led to the establishment of component and material suppliers in the area, such as Lucas Batteries and Dunlop Rubber.

In some cases, businesses can benefit from having a particular address. For example, in London, a private medical consultant who can afford a Harley Street address immediately gains prestige. Similarly, a firm of solicitors in Manchester will attract more clients if it has an office in Piccadilly rather than in Moss Side.

In the retail industry, large stores and supermarkets are often located in busy, out-of-town shopping centres and retail parks. With their ample car parking facilities, these locations suit the shopping habits of today's consumers, who tend to shop less frequently and need a car to carry their bulky shopping home. This has led to a decline in high street shopping, and many smaller cornershops are facing difficulties.

We have seen, then, that is often advantageous for a business to locate near other businesses, even when they are in competition, because of the reputation to be gained from locating in a particular area or because of the proximity of suppliers dedicated to a particular industry.

Customers

All businesses need **access to customers**. It is important, therefore, that a business gives consideration to where its customers are and how it will gain access to them. For some businesses, particularly in the retail sector, this means locating the business where the customers are, or where they expect to go for the type of goods and services the business provides.

The traditional high street: a focus for customers

Large stores and supermarkets are often found in busy out-of-town shopping centres and retail parks because that is where their customers want to go to shop. Smaller retail outlets, however, are also located near their customers. A small cornershop's customers are usually local residents, although it may attract passing trade if it is located on a busy road or near a bus stop. Similarly, businesses such as solicitors and local banks are located close to their customers or clients. They are often in prominent high street positions so that their location is well known and easily accessible to their customers.

Bluewater – one of a number of modern out-of-town retail complexes

As we have seen, some businesses choose a particular location because other businesses are already there. For other businesses, however, locating close to their customers is not so important. This may be the case with service industries where the service is carried out on the customers' premises, or with larger manufacturing companies whose customers are spread over a wide area, perhaps throughout the UK.

History and tradition

Sometimes a business's location is due to **history and tradition**. Some areas are historically associated with some types of industry. We have mentioned some examples already. Others include:

- Stoke on Trent, china
- Clydeside, shipbuilding
- Oxford Street, Regent Street and Bond Street in London, fashion
- Waterford in Ireland, crystal.

When an area becomes traditionally associated with a particular industry, having a location in that area may give businesses prestige and an impression of quality. Such an impression may, of course, be unwarranted – the fact that a stainless steel knife was produced in Sheffield does not mean that it is any better than a stainless steel knife produced in Manchester. Yet the expectation created in the customer by the knowledge that it was produced in Sheffield gives that knife a competitive edge.

Even when the original reasons for locating in a particular area are no longer valid, perhaps because new transport links have been constructed, or new sources of raw materials found, businesses may remain there due to inertia and the high cost of relocating.

Build your learning

Summary points

- Businesses choose location for several reasons.
- The location of a business can influence its success.
- Sometimes the factors influencing the location of a business may conflict.
- The importance of individual factors affecting the location of a business may change over time.

Key words and phrases

You should know the meaning of the words and phrases listed below as they relate to the location of businesses. Go back through the last 12 pages of the unit to check or refresh your understanding.

- **Access to customers**
- **Access to raw materials**
- **Access to suppliers**
- **History and tradition**
- **Incentives**
- **Infrastructure**
- **Labour supply**
- **Location**
- **Transport links**

Student questions

1 Explain in your own words how the location of a business can influence its success.

2 Why might one business want to locate close to its suppliers and raw materials, while another business might want to locate close to its customers?

3 How might the factors influencing the location of a business:

- conflict
- change over time?

4 COLLECT THE EVIDENCE

The work that you complete for this activity will form part of your assessment evidence for this unit. You should refer to the grid on page 171 to see what you need to do to achieve a pass, merit or distinction. Remember, if you carry out the following activities now, you will have completed part of the work needed for your end-of-unit assessment. You are advised to do this now, to avoid overload at the end of the unit.

What to do

1. **Identify the reasons that affect the location of the businesses you are investigating for this unit.**
2. **Why did each business choose its present location? Have any of these reasons changed? Are any reasons more or less significant now than they were originally? How do they affect the businesses now?**

Stakeholders

Stakeholders are individuals and organisations that have an **interest** in the running and activities of a business. The main types of stakeholders of a business are:

- customers
- employees (including managers)
- shareholders
- the local community
- the government.

Some stakeholders such as employees and managers are **internal**, that is inside the business, while others such as customers and shareholders are **external**, that is they are outside the business.

All stakeholders try to influence the activities of a business to get it to act in the way they want. While few stakeholders (except perhaps the government) have much individual power over the activities of a business, they often form alliances to increase the power they have. This is possible where the objectives of stakeholders are the same, or broadly similar.

CASE STUDY

Stakeholder influence

A textile company has a policy of disposing effluent waste into a local river. This pollutes the river and kills fish, but is an effective way of getting rid of the waste. It also contributes to the company's profits by keeping costs down.

This policy has concerned the local and wider community, which has objected to the damage to the environment and brought pressure to bear on the textile company. A pressure group has been set up to draw attention to the damaging activities of the textile company.

The final customers of the cloth produced by the textile company are members of the public. The company's own customers, such as clothing and fabric manufacturers, are concerned that their own businesses might suffer if they are seen to support activities which are damaging the environment. They are bringing pressure to bear on the textile company to prevent the pollution of rivers and threaten to take away their custom.

The textile company's shareholders, concerned that the activities of their company might lose it customers and profits, then join with the other groups in changing the company's policies on the disposal of waste.

At other times, the objectives of different groups of stakeholders conflict. For example, in recent years new technology has revolutionised the banking system. One of the major technological developments has been the introduction of automated cash dispensers, which are now seen not only outside bank premises, but also in supermarkets, airports and other places where customers might need cash quickly.

▶ Cash dispensers – good for customers, bad news for bank employees?

The availability of the cash dispensers, and their widespread acceptance and use, has led to a reduced need for bank staff to actually see customers in person. This in turn has led to a reduction in employment in banking, reduced personnel costs and increased profits for the banks.

While this is obviously in the interests of the banks' shareholders, who see their dividends increasing and therefore encourage further developments in technology, it conflicts with the interests of bank employees who may be made redundant. When the objectives of different groups of stakeholders conflict in this way, a compromise must be reached that will keep both sides happy. The interests of employees are usually represented by organisations such as trade unions, which negotiate with employers on behalf of their members (see page 43).

The main interests of the different groups of stakeholders, and the ways in which they can influence a business are shown in Figure 2.14.

Figure 2.14: The main interests of stakeholder groups and types of influence

Stakeholder	Areas of interest	Types of influence
Customers	Quality of product, value for money.	Customers can take their custom to competitors, thereby reducing the business's sales revenue.
Employees (including managers)	Good working conditions, including pay, job satisfaction, career and personal development.	Dissatisfied employees may not work efficiently – or not at all if they go on strike, or leave to work elsewhere.
Shareholders	High profits of the business in order to produce a high dividend; if the business is successful, its share price will be high, representing capital value to shareholders.	Shareholders vote on policy and the appointment – or removal – of directors at shareholders' meetings; if shareholders are dissatisfied with the performance of a business, or the way it is run, they may sell their shares, resulting in a drop in share price and increased danger of the business being taken over.
The local community	Environmental and nuisance matters, such as pollution, noise, vehicle damage to property, destruction of the environment and so on. The local community may also be interested in issues such as the effect on employment of business cutbacks or closures.	Pressure groups can be organised to lobby the business and other groups of stakeholders. Some pressure groups are set up for a particular purpose, such as to prevent the building of a bypass, while others, such as Friends of the Earth, are permanent organisations with specific objectives.
The government	The well-being of all sections of society, including employees and members of the public, and the environment.	The government can legislate on matters affecting people or the environment. Examples of legislation can be seen in employment and health and safety law, and consumer and environmental protection. Many items of legislation are now passed down from the EU.

Build your learning

Summary points

- All businesses have stakeholders.
- Some stakeholders of a business are internal and others are external.
- The stakeholders of a business try to influence its activities in accordance with their own interests.
- The interests and expectations of different groups of stakeholders may conflict.
- The interests of different stakeholders may change over time.

Key words and phrases

You should know the meaning of the words and phrases listed below as they relate to stakeholders and their influence on business. Go back through the last four pages of the unit to check or refresh your understanding.

- **Conflicting interests**
- **External stakeholders**
- **Internal stakeholders**
- **Stakeholders**
- **Stakeholders' interests**

Student questions

1 Identify the internal and external stakeholders of a business.

2 Describe how different groups of stakeholders can influence the activities of a business.

3 Explain, with examples, why the interests of one group of stakeholders might conflict with those of another.

4 How might the interests of stakeholders change over time?

5 COLLECT THE EVIDENCE

The work that you complete for this activity will form part of your assessment evidence for this unit. You should refer to the grid on page 171 to see what you need to do to achieve a pass, merit or distinction. Remember, if you carry out the following activities now, you will have completed part of the work needed for your end-of-unit assessment. You are advised to do this now, to avoid overload at the end of the unit.

What to do

1. **Identify the main groups of stakeholders in the two businesses you are investigating for this unit.**
2. **Describe the expectations and interests in the activities of the business of each stakeholder group and show any trends or changes in these.**
3. **Describe how each type of stakeholder influences each business and how the businesses are responding to their stakeholders. Explain any difference in the influence of stakeholders on one business.**
4. **Show how there might be conflicts of interest among different stakeholders in one of the businesses.**

Assessment check list

This unit is assessed on the basis of your portfolio. If you have completed the collect the evidence activities in this unit, you will have produced sufficient evidence to meet the requirements of assessment. You should present your evidence as a thorough and well organised case study of each of your selected businesses. Your case studies will include:

- a description of the types of ownership and the different liabilities of the owners of two businesses (page 129)
- a description of the industrial sectors in which your selected businesses operate, and current UK trends in their growth or decline (page 144)
- a description of the activities of your chosen businesses and current UK trends in their growth or decline (page 150)
- an analysis of the factors influencing the location of each business (page 164)
- a description of the different internal and external stakeholders in each business and how they influence the activities of the business (page 169).

You should use a range of information and present it suitably, using diagrams, tables and charts appropriately.

You should keep your completed case studies in your portfolio. When you are confident that you have finished everything to the best of your ability and to your satisfaction, you should write out a record of all the sources of information you have used, including books, notes from your tutor, information from your chosen business and so on. You should identify the information obtained and how you have used it.

The table opposite shows the assessment criteria, which set out what you need to do to achieve a Pass, Merit or Distinction for this unit.

Assessment grid

Section	To achieve a pass you must	To achieve a merit you must also	To achieve a distinction you must also
Ownership	Describe clearly the type of ownership of two contrasting businesses, the liabilities of their owners, and explain how the type of ownership suits the business activity.		
Industrial sectors	Describe briefly the industrial sectors that each of your chosen businesses is part of and identify the broad trends of growth or decline for that sector(s) in the UK.	Explain how trends in the growth or decline of a business sector in the UK are affecting one of the businesses you are investigating.	
Business activity	Describe fully the main activities of each of your chosen businesses, how they are carried out, and the trends of growth or decline for that type of activity in the UK.		
Influences on business	Explain why each business has chosen its location and which influences on location are most significant for the business now.	Explain why the influence of stakeholders on one business is different from their influence on the other.	Demonstrate a sound understanding of how and why external influences in the UK are affecting each business.
	Identify the stakeholders of each business and describe fully their main interests and any current changes to their interests and expectations, their influences on the business and how the business is responding to them.		Explain how there might be conflicts of interest among different stakeholders in any one business.

Cash
Date
Budget

Business finance 3

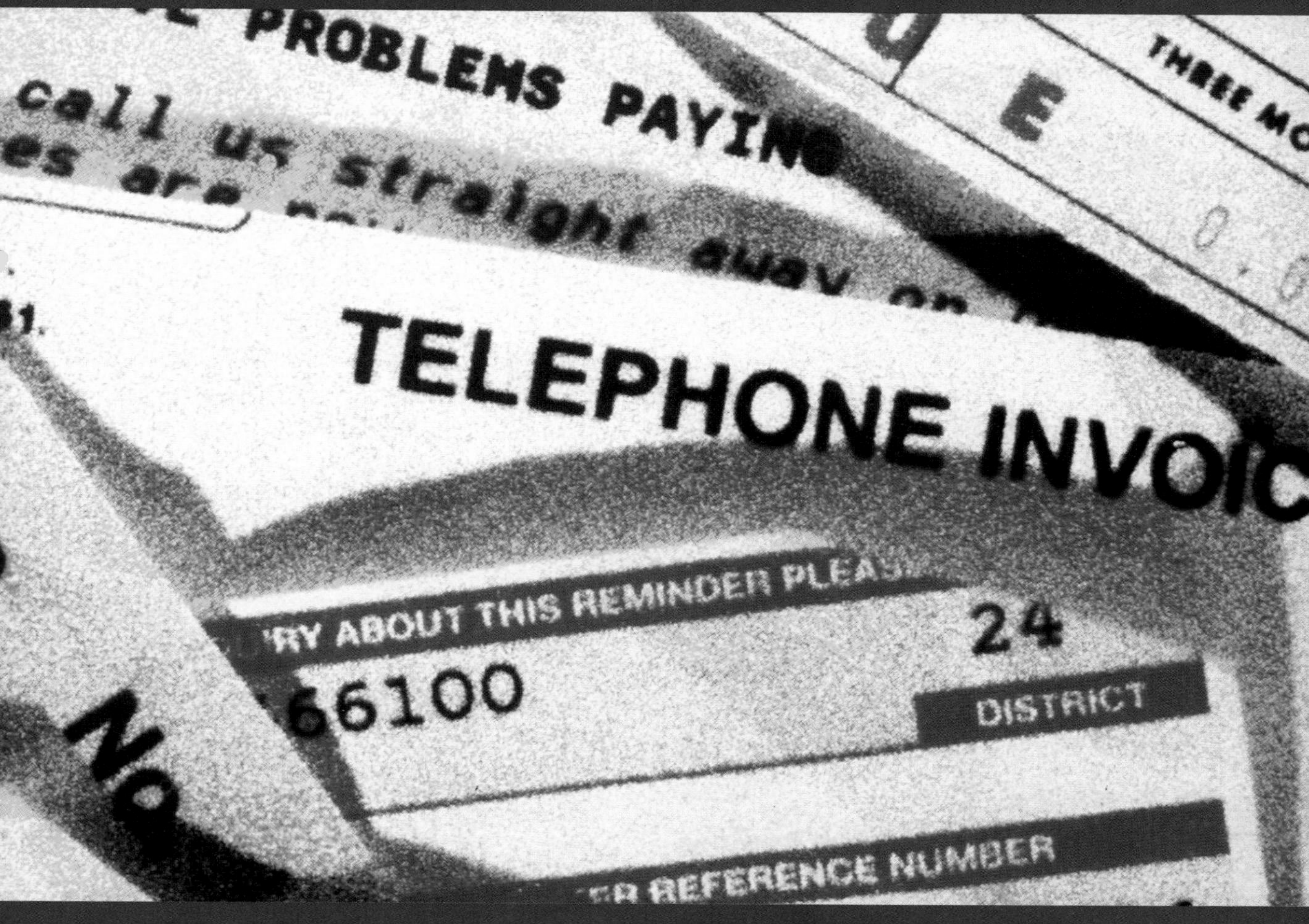

Producing goods and services costs money, which a business must recover from the revenue it receives from sales. In this unit, you investigate how businesses use cost and revenue figures to make decisions about producing new products. You will learn about the main types of cost and revenue for particular products and how to estimate cash flow and profit or loss. The breakeven point of a business is the level of sales required for the revenue received to exactly cover the costs incurred, and you will find out how this can be calculated. You will also learn about the documents that are involved in making a business purchase.

This unit is assessed by an external assessment. You will need to answer questions about:

- the costs and revenues of a business
- the use of cash flow forecasts
- measuring costs, revenue and profit using a breakeven calculation and a profit and loss statement
- financial documents used for buying and selling.

You will also need to be able to construct simple cash flow statements, calculate the breakeven point of a business, and calculate profit or loss using both breakeven and profit and loss statements.

Completing the collecting the evidence activities in this unit will help you prepare for the external assessment.

Covering the costs of a new product

One of the aims of businesses is to make a profit. However, all business activity costs money. Business **costs** include:

- raw materials and components out of which products are made
- the wages and salaries of the people who run the business and make the product
- electricity and power which is needed for heating and lighting as well as to run machinery
- factory and office costs, including rent and rates
- other costs such as market research, advertising, postage and telephone charges.

To cover these costs, the business sells the goods or services it produces. For example, British Energy plc is a large company that generates electricity. It sells the electricity it generates to the electricity companies that supply homeowners and businesses throughout the UK. In 1998, the cost of operating British Energy plc amounted to £1,377 million. The value of the electricity it sold was £2,067 million.

The money the business receives in return for the goods or services it sells is its income, or **revenue**. If the revenue of a business is more than its costs, it has made a profit. If the revenue of a business is less than its costs, it has made a loss. So you can see that British Energy made a very big profit in 1998.

The concept of profit and loss is shown in Figure 3.1. The revenues of companies A, B and C are shown by rectangles. Each company has the same total costs – this is illustrated by the horizontal total costs line. The revenue of company A (the red rectangle) is *less* than its costs – this company therefore made a loss. The revenue of company B (the blue rectangle) is *exactly equal* to its costs – this company has broken even. The revenue of company C (the blue and green rectangle) is *more* than its total costs – this company has therefore made a profit. Its profit is its total revenue minus its costs (represented by the green part of the revenue rectangle).

A business that makes a loss, and continues to do so over time, will have to close down – it will not have enough money coming in to pay its bills. Any business that is intending or planning to produce a new product, therefore, must find out if this is likely to make a profit. If the business is likely to make a profit with the new product, it will decide to go ahead. If the new product is unlikely to make a profit, the business will

Figure 3.1: Costs and profits

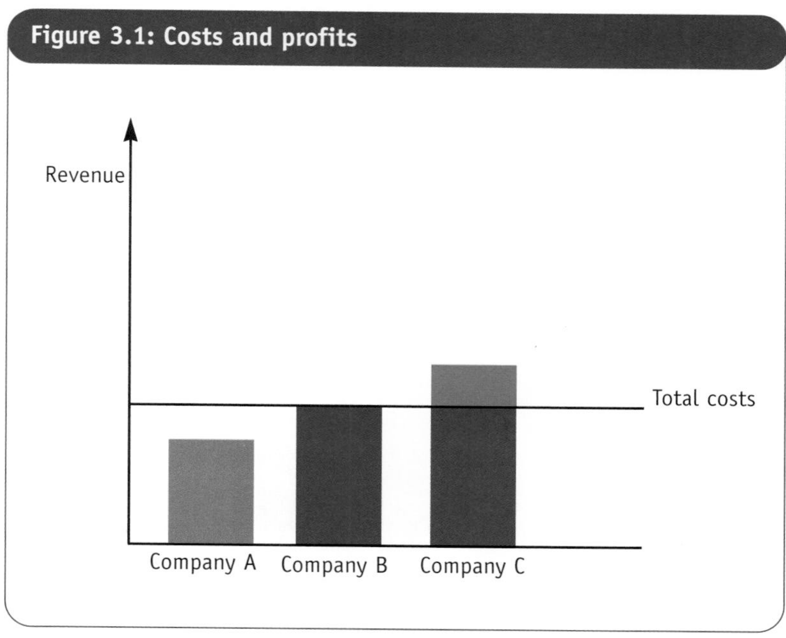

decide not proceed with it. The business may then try and develop a different new product that will produce a profit. All businesses – both new and established companies – must make these decisions about potential new products.

Sega, for example, spends a lot of money developing and producing new computer games. It needs to do this, as fashions in computer games change quickly. Its customers are always on the lookout for new games, wanting to stay ahead of the fashion. If Sega does not make a profit from new computer games, the company will soon find that it is in trouble as demand for its old games declines. Similarly, when Mary Tarsett decided to give up work and start her own teashop on the farm she was left by her uncle, she needed to know that the teashop was going to make a profit so that she could be sure that she had enough to live on.

To find out whether or not it is going to make a profit, a business needs to calculate the costs of producing the product and the revenue it will receive from selling the product.

First, let's consider the costs in more detail. The costs of a business fall into two areas:

- **start-up costs**, which are the costs that the business must meet before it starts producing and selling its products
- **running costs**, which are the costs that the business must meet in the course of the day-to-day process of producing and selling its products.

CASE STUDY

Tracy Fleming's new business

When Tracy Fleming was made redundant, she decided to try to set up her own business as a freelance computer programmer.

Tracy Fleming is a computer programmer who worked for Allman Computer Services, a computer consultancy serving businesses in the Midlands. After nine years in the job, during which Tracy had worked for a number of clients, the company decided to close its Midlands operation.

Several of her previous clients said they would use her services, so with her £10,000 redundancy payment Tracy thought she would have no difficulty in getting through the first year while she built up her circle of clients. When she went to her bank manager to tell her of her plan, however, Tracy got a bit of a surprise.

'I won't need a loan to start the business,' Tracy said confidently, 'but I realise that I shall have to have a business account.'

'What about start-up costs?' the bank manager, Laura Knights, asked. 'You will need to contact prospective clients by telephone or letter – so you will need to pay for telephone calls, stationery and postage even before you get any business. And what about advertising? The local paper could be useful, and it might be a good idea to have a brochure printed describing the services that you are offering and send it out to potential clients. That is a cost you will have to bear, too.'

'And how are you going to get to see clients? Your car and the petrol you use on business are a cost of your business now. So you see, there are many different start-up costs you will need to pay even before you start to do any work for clients – let alone begin to receive revenue from them.'

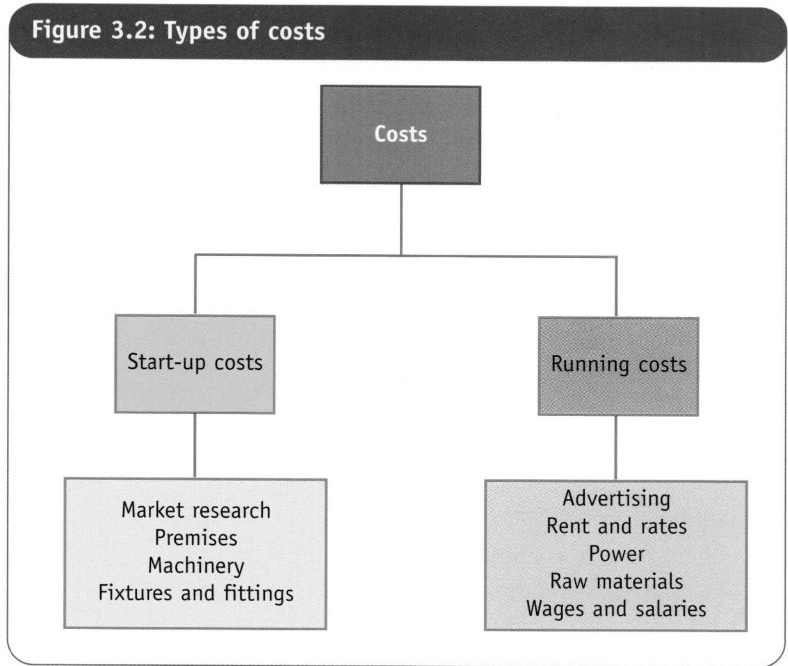

Start-up costs

The start-up costs are those costs that have to be met before a business can begin producing and selling its new product. Any business planning to produce a new product must identify the start-up costs. This is because these start-up costs will be incurred and must be paid before the business begins to receive any revenue from the product.

Typical start-up costs involved in planning a new product include:

- market research
- premises
- machinery
- fixtures and fittings.

Market research

One of the first things a business has to do when considering a new product is to carry out market research (see page 57). Market research enables a business to find out what type of product customers want, and whether the planned product fulfils this need. Market research may be carried out by the business itself, as part of the marketing function, or by an outside market research firm.

A business has to pay for the market research it undertakes. If it employs an outside market research firm, it will have to pay fees for its services. If the business carries out its own market research, it will have to pay for:

- salaries – to pay for the time of staff carrying out the market research (even if they are already employed by the business, the time spent on market research for the new product is a start-up cost of that new product)
- materials – all market research involves the use of some materials, such as paper for questionnaires or producing reports analysing the findings of the research
- other costs – including postage for sending out questionnaires, travel costs for visiting customers or interviewing people, telephone bills (which might be considerable if a telephone survey is carried out), and the cost of buying reports from organisations such as *The Economist*, Mintel and government departments.

Premises

When a business has carried out market research and established that its new product is what customers want, it must find premises where the new product can be produced. An existing business may be able to allocate a section of its current premises to the new product. For example, it may be possible to redesign the layout of the business's present factory to accommodate production of a new line. Where this is not possible, or where the business is itself new, it must buy or rent suitable premises.

A business that is starting up or expanding needs to find suitable premises

The premises needed depend on the type of product. A business that is planning to manufacture aircraft must have a huge hangar in which to work. A small business planning to assemble computers to customers' orders, on the other hand, may only require a small factory, possibly in shop premises. It will also need office space to carry out the administration of the business.

Not all new products require factories, of course. Somebody setting up in business as a mobile carpet cleaner only requires an office for administration – maybe even a room at home – since the carpet cleaning will be carried out at customers' premises.

Machinery

Producing goods and services requires machinery and equipment. Producing wooden furniture, for example, requires woodworking equipment such as lathes, vices, chisels and planes. A mobile hairdresser must have scissors, trimmers, hairdryers and styling brushes. He or she must also have a vehicle in which to carry the equipment and visit customers.

The type of machinery a business needs depends on the products it makes and the services it offers. Some businesses, such as light engineering companies, craft producers and design consultancies, only need a relatively small range of machinery and equipment. Other businesses, such as car manufacturers or oil refineries, must make a huge investment in sophisticated machinery before they can start production. This is beyond the scope of all but the largest firms.

Besides the machinery and equipment required to actually produce goods and services, most businesses also need other items of equipment such as computers, calculators and fax machines.

Fixtures and fittings

The premises also need various fixtures and fittings to enable business activity to be undertaken. Fixtures and fittings include:

- lighting, which must be adequate for the type of work – an architect working on detailed plans of a building will need brighter, more concentrated light than a machine operator
- electric sockets for machinery and equipment such as drills, computers and computer-controlled equipment
- gas points for heating, and any equipment that requires gas, such as gas-driven kilns
- telephones and telephone points
- office furniture such as desks and chairs.

CASE STUDY

Kellogg's new breakfast cereal: start-up costs

Like any business considering a new product, when Kellogg's is planning to produce a new breakfast cereal it first identifies the start-up costs.

The first start-up cost the company incurs is market research. Kellogg's must undertake in-depth market research to discover exactly what consumers would like in a new breakfast cereal. The research considers factors such as taste, fat and calorie content, and nutritional value, and the price customers are prepared to pay. Without this information, Kellogg's would not know if the new breakfast cereal is what consumers want or would buy.

Once the decision has been made to proceed, Kellogg's needs to find the premises, machinery and equipment required to produce the new breakfast cereal. Obviously, a large company like Kellogg's already has facilities and does not usually have to purchase new premises. However, the premises, machinery and other equipment are currently being used for other purposes and products, such as a different breakfast cereal.

Diverting the use of its facilities to the production of the new breakfast cereal means that they can no longer be used for their previous purpose. This involves a cost – a start-up cost of the new breakfast cereal. In financial terms, this cost is the revenue from sales of the product that was being made that will be lost when the premises, machinery and equipment are switched to production of the new breakfast cereal.

The new breakfast cereal may also require new machinery and equipment, particularly if the cereal has to go through a new process. (Producing Crunchy Nut Corn Flakes, for example, involves different processes than those used in producing Corn Flakes.)

The principal start-up costs, therefore, that Kellogg's must identify when planning a new breakfast cereal are:

- market research to find out what consumers want in a new breakfast cereal and the price that they are prepared to pay
- the cost of switching premises, machinery and equipment to production of the new cereal
- the cost of buying any new specialised machinery and equipment.

CASE STUDY

Tony's flower shop: start-up costs

When Tony Brundle was made redundant from his job as an electrician, his friend Stephen Irvine suggested Tony should open a flower shop.

Stephen has a restaurant in north London, and also does some catering at local offices. He constantly requires fresh flowers and arrangements and, knowing Tony's interest in flowers and gardening, thought this might be a good way to help them both. There was also a vacant shop not far from Stephen's restaurant that would be convenient.

Tony liked the idea of owning a flower shop. He could use his redundancy money to help finance the new venture, but had no other sources of capital. Living in a rented flat, he was unlikely to obtain much of a loan from his bank. With limited capital, Tony knew that identifying the start-up costs of the flower shop was critical, since he would have to pay these out of his own resources, before he even sold his first flower.

The first cost was market research. Tony wanted to know if there was a need for a flower shop and that the shop premises were in the right place to attract customers. Tony knew that Stephen would be a good customer, but he would need other customers if the shop was to be profitable. He hired a marketing consultancy to assess the likely custom and viability of the flower shop.

While the marketing consultancy was preparing its report, Tony identified the other start-up costs that he would incur. The main cost would be the shop premises. However, the shop was empty and it needed to be fitted out for use as a flower shop. This meant employing a shop fitter to construct racking and display stands and a large counter where flowers could be wrapped and payment taken from customers. Tony also wanted the room behind the shop, which had previously been used as a stock room and office, to be set out so that he could use it for making special flower arrangements for weddings and funerals. Tony also needed to buy an electronic till, a computer and telephone, as well as smaller items such as scissors, secateurs, a wrapping paper dispenser and waste bins.

The start-up costs of Tony's flower shop included:

- market research, to check the viability of the venture
- buying premises
- equipment, such as an electronic till, a computer and small items
- fixtures and fittings, such as display stands and counters.

Start-up costs

Knowing that you are studying business, some people have asked for your advice about start-up costs. In each case, make a list of the start-up costs involved in the venture that will be incurred before any revenue is received.

1 Your doctor's surgery is planning to open a small clinic in which it will offer a new range of services to expectant mothers and to people over fifty. The clinic will probably be in premises next door to the surgery. These premises are owned by the surgery but they are currently let to a hairdresser at a rent of £3,000 per year.

2 Michelle wants to buy her own small coffee shop in a nearby market town. She is intending to provide morning coffee, light lunches and afternoon teas for shoppers and people who work locally in shops or offices locally. Although Michelle is sure she can afford to undertake this project, her finances are limited, so she wants to know what her start-up costs are going to be.

3 Faizan is the works manager of a company that manufactures rattan furniture, which it sells through stores such as Homebase. He wants the company to diversify. He is putting a proposal to his board of directors suggesting that the company start producing pine furniture alongside the present rattan range.

Producing pine furniture requires different types of machinery to rattan. The company could commence production in its existing factory, although this would mean cutting down on existing production levels of rattan furniture, and Faizan favours renting a unit on a nearby industrial estate. He wants to know the start-up costs that would be involved:

- if the company switched to producing some pine furniture in its existing factory
- if it rented a unit on the industrial estate.

Running costs

Once the business has obtained the items it needs for start-up, it begins to incur **running costs**. Running costs are the costs that a business incurs in the course of the day-to-day process of producing and selling its products. Typical running costs include:

- advertising
- rent and rates
- power
- raw materials
- wages and salaries.

Advertising

Any new product or service must be advertised so that potential customers are aware of the product, and know where they can buy it. As with market research, advertising can be carried out either by the marketing function of the business itself, or by an outside agency. If advertising is carried out by an outside agency, the business must pay the agency's fees. If the advertising is undertaken by the business itself, however, it will have to pay for a number of things.

- **Time** – planning and carrying out an advertising campaign takes time and this is a cost in terms of the salaries or wages of those staff involved.
- **Materials and equipment** – advertising and promotion require appropriate materials and equipment. Designing a poster requires paper, pencils, paints, brushes and other artist's materials, or a computer with a graphics package. If photographs are to be used, a camera and film must be available. A computer with desktop publishing facilities may be needed to lay out an advertisement for a magazine or to design a brochure. If the advertisement is to be at a trade exhibition, items such as display boards and even drawing pins must not be forgotten. Television and radio advertisements require the hire of studios, video equipment and, maybe, actors and actresses.
- **Media** – in addition to the design and production costs, there is a cost involved in publishing advertisements. It can cost thousands of pounds to advertise in national daily and Sunday newspapers, and even more to run advertisements on television. Regional papers, television and radio are cheaper, but do not cover as wide an area. Trade and hobby magazines are also usually cheaper, but more specialised in their readership.

Rent and rates

Businesses that choose not to buy their own premises must rent somewhere. Renting can reduce start-up costs as it can be expensive to purchase business premises. However, businesses renting property will have to meet the running costs of paying the rent, usually on quarterly basis. There will probably also be a charge for the lease. (A lease is a contract granting the business the right to use the premises for a specified length of time.)

Regardless of whether premises are bought or rented, all businesses must pay rates to the local council. Business rates are designed to cover services such as maintaining roads and street lighting.

Power

Machinery and equipment need power to operate. Power is also needed to heat and light factories and offices. Types of power include gas (either natural or propane), electricity and coal.

Raw materials

Goods are produced from raw materials and components. These are items that are used up in the production process. For example, trainers are made from rubber, plastic and fibres; computers are made from metal, plastic, microchips and circuit boards; Big Macs are made from minced beef, bread, salad vegetables and dressings.

Figure 3.3: Cars are made from metals, plastics and other materials, components and paint

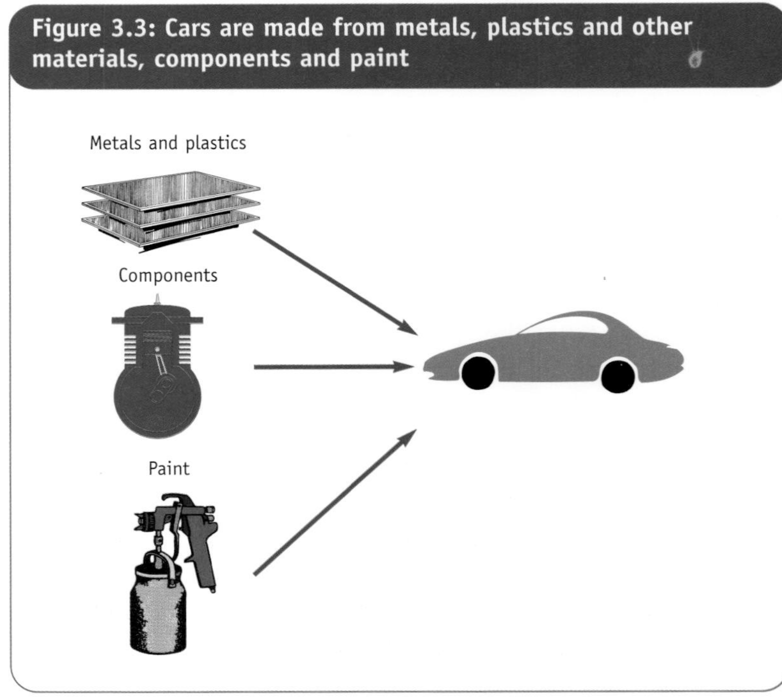

The more a business produces, the more raw materials and components it needs, and, consequently, the more it will spend on them. Even providing services can require essential materials. A hairdresser, for example, uses shampoo, conditioner, sprays and tints, while a haulier uses fuel and other vehicle oils.

Goods for resale

Retail businesses provide a service by selling goods that have been produced by other businesses. To do this, they must first purchase the goods from the producer. For example, a newsagent must buy magazines and newspapers from publishers. In the same way, in order to sell clothes, furnishings and foodstuffs to its customers, Marks and Spencer must buy these items from the manufacturers. (Although most items sold by Marks and Spencer are 'own label' – that is they carry the Marks and Spencer or St Michael label – they are made by other manufacturers.) In this way, shops and other retailers buy goods for resale. The cost of the goods forms a significant element in the running costs of retail businesses.

Wages and salaries

All businesses employ people. Employees are needed to plan production, purchase raw materials, buy goods for resale, operate machinery, deliver the goods or provide services, and carry out the administrative functions of the business. Employees of a business are paid wages or salaries in return for their work. The wages and salaries paid to its employees are part of the running costs of the business.

Other costs

Besides the costs we have already mentioned, businesses incur other running costs that must be met. These will vary according to the type of business. They include:

- insurance
- licences
- water
- telephone
- postage.

All businesses must have certain types of insurance, such as employee liability (if the business has employees) and property insurance. In addition, businesses that own cars or commercial vehicles must have vehicle insurance. They need to ensure that vehicles are licensed and must also have a special operator's licence if they own commercial vehicles over a certain size.

CASE STUDY

Kellogg's new breakfast cereal: running costs

As soon as Kellogg's begins production of the new breakfast cereal, it begins to incur running costs associated with the new product. As an established business, of course, Kellogg's is already incurring running costs in producing its existing products.

Kellogg's running costs are:

- raw materials – the maize, rice, sugar, honey, salt and other ingredients that go into its cereals
- wages and salaries – it must pay the operatives, supervisors and managers in the factory, the administrative staff, sales representatives and other marketing staff, advertising and financial staff
- rent and rates – on the factories and offices of the business
- power – to operate the machinery and food processing equipment such as ovens, as well as smaller office equipment such as computers
- advertising – Kellogg's advertising costs are enormous, covering advertisements on television, in magazines and newspapers
- other costs – such as packaging for the cereals, distribution to large shops and stores worldwide, and office costs such as telephone, stationery, postage and costs associated with company cars.

To make a profit, a business must receive sufficient revenue to cover its costs. It is important, therefore, for businesses to know what costs are associated with each product. This is part of the finance function.

As you can see, Kellogg's running costs are vast and complex. With so many products, the company wants to identify the proportion of each cost that can be attributed to specific products. In this way, Kellogg's can tell if it is still profitable to produce, for example, traditional Corn Flakes, or if it would be more profitable to switch production to another breakfast cereal.

CASE STUDY

Tony's flower shop: running costs

Having calculated the start-up costs of his flower shop, Tony Brundle decided to go ahead with the venture, although he chose to rent shop premises rather than to purchase them outright.

Tony decided to employ an assistant in the shop to help him at busy times (he hoped there would be lots of those), to cover for lunch breaks and to look after the shop when he was out buying flowers, doing arrangements for customers and doing the administration.

As soon as Tony's flower shop opened, it started to incur running costs. Identifying these costs are important for Tony. He must be able to check that they remain at a level that he can afford and that they do not suddenly start to rise. Obviously, Tony's flower shop is a far less complex business than Kellogg's, but when he sat down to identify the running costs he was surprised to find that there were almost as many separate areas of cost as in a large business.

The running costs Tony identified were:

- advertising – Tony decided to try to attract customers to the shop by advertising in the local paper
- rent and rates – Tony must pay a quarterly rent for shop premises (with the first quarter's rent paid in advance) and he also has to pay rates to the local council
- power – this is needed to light and heat the shop and to run equipment such as the electronic till
- stock for resale – Tony must buy flowers from local growers, from specialist suppliers, such as rose nurseries, and from other suppliers as far away as Jersey and Holland
- wages and salaries – Tony has employed an assistant and must pay her wages weekly
- transport – Tony has bought a small van for the business, so that he can make deliveries and collect items, and the insurance, fuel, servicing and other costs of running the van are part of the running costs of the business
- insurance – as an employer, Tony must take out employee liability insurance
- other items – other running costs include water, with flowers this is a very necessary commodity, and administrative costs such as telephone and postal charges, the cost of stationery (headed letter paper, printed invoices and so on) and bank charges.

Finally, Tony also wants to draw a regular amount for himself to live on. Although Tony is a sole trader (see page 104), and takes drawings out of the business rather than a set wage or salary, he must include his drawings as part of the running costs of the business.

Running costs

Look back at the activity on page 182. You were asked to identify the start-up costs for new products or services offered by three different businesses. Now identify and make lists of the types of running costs that will be incurred by each of these businesses.

Revenue from selling goods and services

Businesses only incur start-up and running costs if they expect to receive a revenue from selling their products. The **revenue** they receive is used to pay their costs but also needs to provide a profit for the business and must therefore be sufficient to cover these items.

Figure 3.4: Costs and revenue generated by three sports businesses

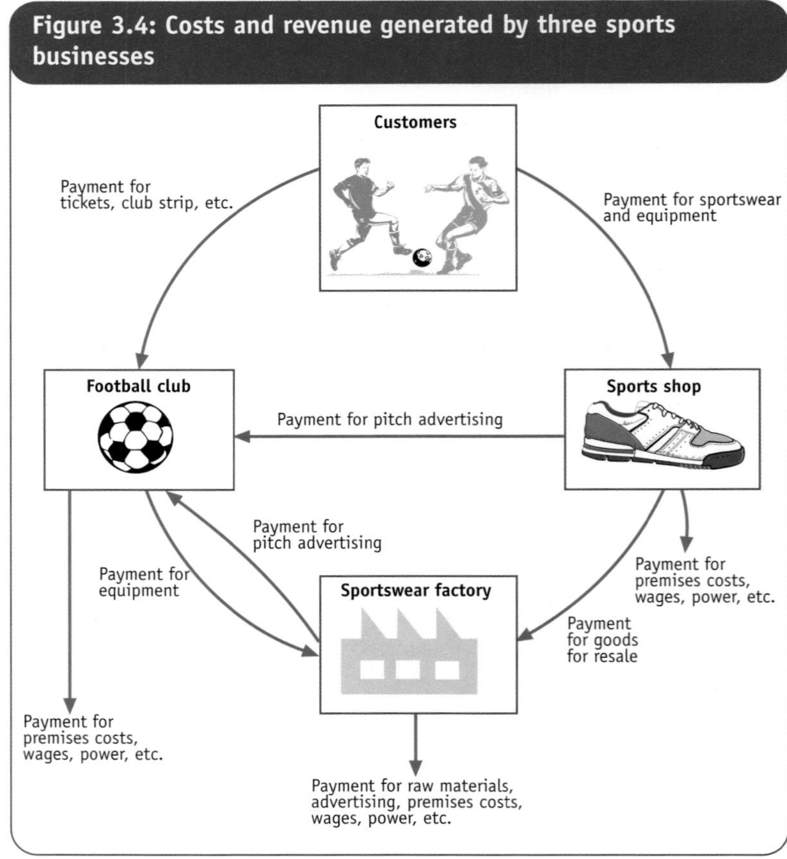

Let's consider an example. Figure 3.4 shows the costs incurred and revenue generated by three businesses involved in sports – a football club, a sports goods manufacturer and a sports shop.

A manufacturing company such as Nike receives revenue from selling trainers and sports equipment to retailers. It receives revenue from selling goods. From this revenue Nike must pay for:

- the raw materials and components from which its trainers are made
- advertising and promotion
- premises costs such as rates and rent
- power for lighting and heating its factories and offices and for running its machinery and equipment
- the wages and salaries of its employees.

A retail outlet, such as Sports Division, receives revenue from selling trainers produced by Nike, adidas, HiTec and other manufacturers. It receives revenue from selling its retail services. From this revenue, Sports Division must pay for:

- the trainers that it buys from the manufacturers for resale
- any advertising it undertakes, perhaps in the local paper
- premises costs such as rent and rates
- power for lighting and heating its shops and for running equipment such as electronic tills
- the wages and salaries of its employees.

A service industry, such as a football club like Manchester United, receives revenue from selling tickets to matches, sports clothing in the club strip, souvenir match programmes and advertising in the club ground. Since Manchester United does not actually produce any physical goods itself, it receives revenue from selling its services. Out of this revenue, the football club must pay for:

- the training equipment and other materials the club uses
- any advertising it undertakes, plus match programmes and souvenirs
- premises costs such as rent and rates on the club ground, offices and buildings
- power for lighting and heating its premises, including floodlighting the pitch, heating and lighting offices, club rooms and showers and for the tills at turnstiles and in the club shop
- the wages and salaries of its employees, including players, reserves, coaches, manager and administrative staff.

Some of the football club's revenue may be spent on Nike sports clothing and equipment, and the club may also receive revenue from Nike for advertising and promoting Nike products.

CASE STUDY

Kellogg's new breakfast cereal: revenue

Kellogg's will sell its new breakfast cereal to stores in the UK such as Tesco, Sainsbury's and smaller shops, many of them privately owned or perhaps franchises such as Spar shops and Today's stores. They will also sell the cereal to stores throughout the world.

Many Tesco customers like to eat Kellogg's cereals for breakfast. Some will want to try the new breakfast cereal. Tesco therefore needs supplies of the new breakfast cereal on its shelves for its customers to buy. Tesco in turn must buy the supplies of the new breakfast cereal from Kellogg's. The money Tesco pays for the cereal forms part of Kellogg's revenue.

Kellogg's can identify how much revenue it receives from sales of the new breakfast cereal in any given period – this is the total value of the new cereal sold in that period. It can also identify how much revenue it receives from sales of all the cereals it produces in any given period – this is its total revenue for that period. Since breakfast cereals are goods, Kellogg's receives revenue from selling goods.

Revenue from selling goods and services

In the previous activities in this section (see pages 182 and 188), you identified the start-up and running costs of three different business ventures. For each business venture:

- identify the source of its revenue
- state whether it receives revenue from selling goods or from selling services.

Note that the clinic (page 182) treats National Health Service patients, for whom it receives an annual payment from the government, and private patients, who pay individually for their own treatment.

Tony's flower shop: revenue

In his shop, Tony sells flowers that he has bought from growers and suppliers for resale.

He sells the flowers to individual customers, who know about his shop or just happen to be passing, who want a bouquet. He also sells to business customers like Stephen, who wants flowers for his restaurant.

The money Tony receives for the flowers he sells is his revenue. Although Tony sells flowers, and flowers are goods, he does not produce the flowers, but buys them for resale. Tony is therefore a retailer who, like all retailers, provides a service – that of selling the produce of others. Tony therefore receives revenue from selling a service.

Covering the costs of a business

If a business is to make a profit, its revenue must at least equal its running costs. The business must also cover its start-up costs. This is essential both for its survival and for the business to take advantage of any opportunities for growth that may occur.

There are three important aspects to be taken into consideration when calculating costs and revenue. These are:

- **cash flow** – the amount of actual cash coming into and going out of the business; a business must always ensure that it has sufficient cash to pay its bills as they become due
- **breakeven point** – the amount of a product the business must produce and sell in order to cover its costs
- **profit** – the amount of revenue the business has left after its costs have been deducted.

We examine each of these in turn in the next three sections.

Build your learning

Summary points

- Businesses that are planning to produce new products or provide new services must carefully work out the costs involved and the revenue they are likely to receive.
- Producing a new product or providing a new service will involve start-up costs and running costs.
- Start-up costs are those costs that must be met before the business can start producing and selling the new product or service.
- Running costs are those costs that are incurred through the day-to-day process of producing and selling a business's goods or services.
- Businesses receive revenue from selling goods and selling services.

Key words and phrases

You should know the meaning of the words and phrases listed below as they relate to the costs of businesses and new products. Go back through the last 18 pages of the unit to check or refresh your understanding.

- **Costs**
- **Revenue**
- **Running costs**
- **Start-up costs**

Student questions

1 Identify which of the following are start-up costs and which are running costs:

- **a** the metal used in the production of the first batch of a new car
- **b** the cost of setting up a new Marks and Spencer store
- **c** the fees of a market research agency hired to establish likely demand for a new product
- **d** the business telephone bill of a sole proprietor setting up in business as a mobile carpet cleaner
- **e** books bought by your local library
- **f** the wages and salaries of staff employed to open a new branch of Barclays Bank
- **g** the cost of adapting machinery designed to produce cases for desktop personal computers, so that it will produce cases for a new line of tower personal computers
- **h** the vehicle licence for the new van purchased by the mobile carpet cleaner for transporting equipment
- **i** a television advertisement telling people about a new car
- **j** electronic tills for Marks and Spencer's new store, to speed the service of customers and help in the day-to-day running of the store
- **k** the quarterly rent payment on an industrial unit taken by the mobile carpet cleaner for the day-to-day storage of his equipment and as an operating base of the business
- **l** electricity used for heating and lighting Marks and Spencer's new store.

2 Identify and make a list of the typical costs and revenues involved in the following business projects. You should state whether costs are start-up costs or running costs.

- A food company planning to produce a new range of fat reduced products.
- A woman planning to open a book shop in the high street.
- A supermarket planning to open a dry cleaners on its premises.

Student questions

3 Complete the table showing which businesses receive revenue from selling goods and which receive revenue from selling a service. The first line is completed for you.

Business	Purpose/type of business	Revenue received from selling goods or services
McDonald's	Fast food restaurants	Services
Rover Cars		
A rock band		
Esso		
Microsoft		
Lloyds TSB Bank		
British Airways		
Cadbury Schweppes		
Sainsbury's		
A leisure centre		

Using a cash flow forecast

A **cash flow forecast** is used to predict **cash flow**, the amount of money coming into and going out of a business over a period of time. Cash flow forecasts are normally calculated for a period of a year, subdivided into months.

- Money coming into the business is called **inflows**
- Money going out of the business is called **outflows**

Figure 3.5: Inflows and outflows

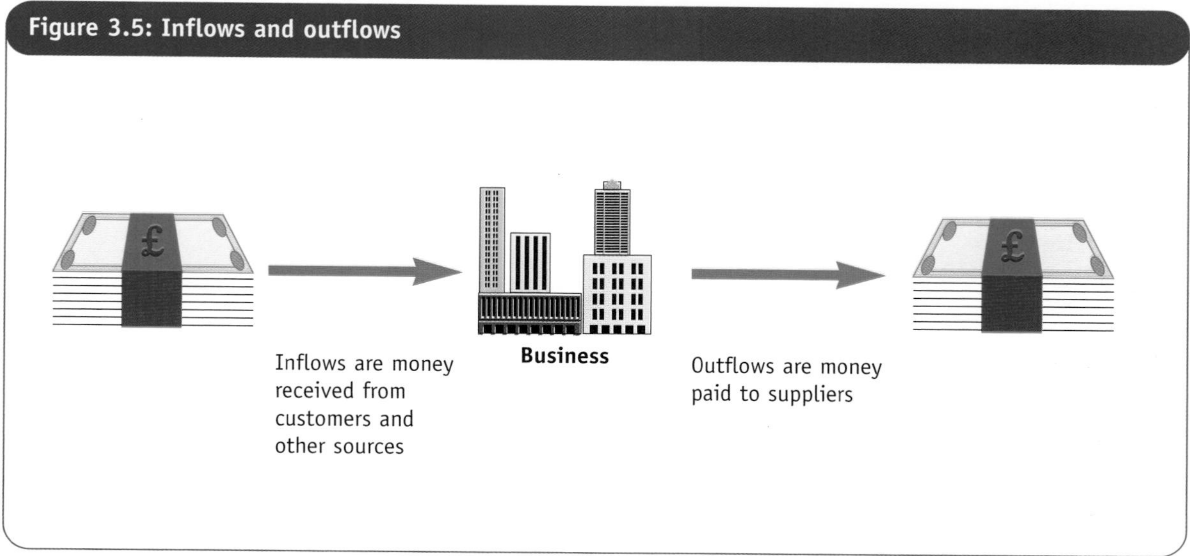

ACTIVITY

Your own cash flow forecast

An easy way to see how a cash flow forecast is calculated and to understand its importance is to construct your own forecast for the coming month.

Using the table on page 196, first list all the money you are going to receive (receipts) during the month from all sources, items such as wages from employment, allowances, loans and awards.

Next, list *everything* you expect to have to pay out (payments) in the month, items such as housekeeping or living expenses, fares, going out in the evenings, books and stationery, food, drinks, presents and so on.

Cash flow forecast

For period:

Receipts

Item	£
Total receipts	

Payments

Item	£
Total payments	
Receipts less payments	
Surplus/deficit:	

Is the money you have coming in more than the money you have to pay out in the month?

If it is, what do you think you might do with the surplus?

If it isn't, were you aware of this before you constructed the cash flow forecast, and how will you make up the shortfall?

How do you think a cash flow forecast might:

- help you save up for something you have always wanted?
- help you to be prepared for any unexpected items of expenditure?

For businesses, sources of inflows are:

- revenue from sales
- injections of capital, such as loans from banks and money put into the business by the owners
- grants from the government and other sources, such as business start-up grants, regional aid grants to encourage location in an area of economic decline and job creation grants.

Figure 3.6: Inflows

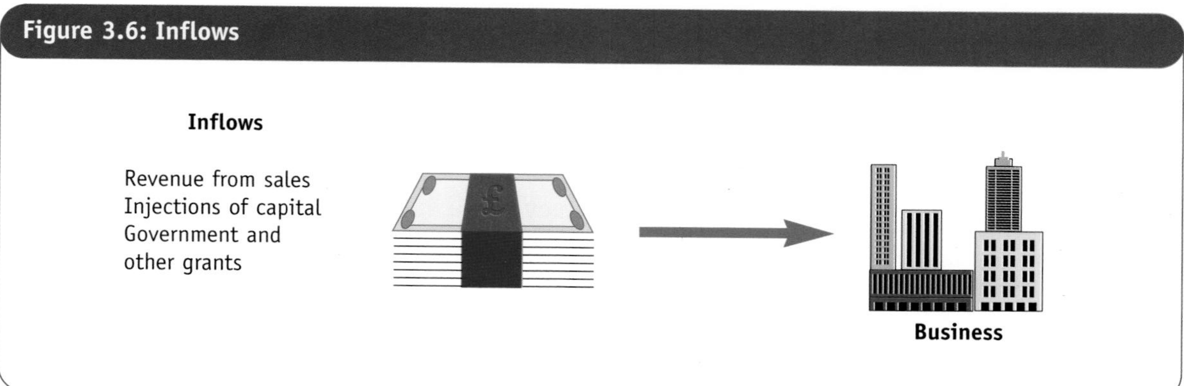

Outflows are payments the business makes for items of expenditure. These include:

- payments to suppliers of raw materials, new machinery and equipment
- rent and rates
- employees' wages
- payments to providers of services like telephone, gas and electricity
- advertising and promotion
- payments to the government for items such as taxes and national insurance contributions.

Figure 3.7: Outflows

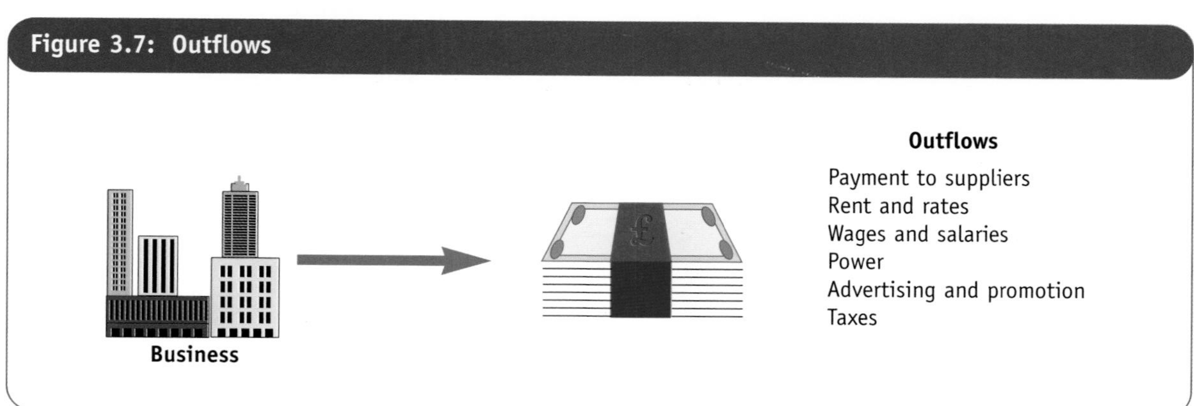

Having enough money coming in from all sources to cover payments as they become due is vital for any business. Constructing a cash flow forecast enables a business to see when money is expected to be received and paid out, so that if at any time insufficient money is coming in to cover payments due, appropriate arrangements for additional finance can be made. These arrangements might include arranging short-term loans or overdrafts with the business's bank.

For example, employees of a small manufacturer may be paid weekly. The employees expect to receive their wages at the end of each week. Their employer must therefore ensure that there is sufficient money available to pay the wages, since people are unlikely to continue working for a business if they do not get paid! Obviously, if the employees stop working, or leave the employer, production will cease, there will be no revenue from sales and the employer will soon go out of business.

Sometimes a business has to pay for raw materials before it has received the revenue for goods it has produced from those raw materials. A retailer may have to pay for goods it has purchased for resale before it has received revenue from selling them. If a business fails to pay a supplier because it does not

▼ Employees expect their employers to have enough cash to pay weekly wages

have enough money available to meet its bills, the supplier may sue to recover the money it is owed. Unless the business can pay, it may be declared bankrupt. This means that the business will be judged unable to meet its debts and it will be put into the hands of an administrator who may close the business down.

If, on the other hand, there are periods when there is more money coming in than is being paid out, the business can make use of this extra money, perhaps by investing it, or by buying new equipment or materials at advantageous prices.

It is important to remember that a cash flow forecast is quite different from a profit and loss forecast. A cash flow forecast is an estimate of the amount of money there is coming into and going out of a business, regardless of the actual levels of production or sales. A profit and loss forecast is an estimate of the excess of sales revenue over expenditure (or vice versa) during a period, regardless of whether any money has actually been received or paid out.

▲ Any extra money coming in to a business shouldn't be squandered

A cash flow forecast lists all anticipated inflows and outflows *in the month in which they are expected to be received or paid out*. In this way, businesses use cash flow forecasts to calculate the timing of inflows and outflows. You should note that besides running costs, a cash flow statement includes any payments for start-up costs and other capital items such as machinery and equipment.

A cash flow forecast takes account of the fact that although a business such as Sainsbury's receives payment for the goods it sells at the checkout at the time of sale, other businesses, such as Kellogg's – which supplies Sainsbury's with breakfast cereal for resale – may not receive payment for the goods it has supplied until a month or more after the date of sale.

In fact, most business purchases (that is purchases made by a business rather than a private customer) are made on the understanding that payment will not be made by the purchaser until some time after the goods have been received. This is called buying goods on credit. A standard practice is for payment to be due and made by the end of the month following the date the goods were received. Some businesses take even longer to pay for purchases they have made, in which case the payment becomes overdue. Obviously, all businesses try to keep overdue payments for goods they have supplied as low as possible.

Just as a business does not receive payment for all the goods or services it supplies at the time of sale, it does not pay for all the goods and services it purchases at the time of receipt.

- Some goods and services are purchased on the understanding that they will not be paid for until the end of the month after receipt.
- Some purchases, especially of major items such as machinery that must be specially made to order, require a deposit.
- Goods such as cars, as well as some small items such as stationery purchased from a small supplier, must be paid for at the time of purchase.
- Bills for items such as telephone, electricity and gas may be paid quarterly or monthly.
- Rent may be paid quarterly.
- Items such as insurance, vehicle licences and rates may be paid annually, or spread throughout the year.

You can see how difficult it can be to arrange for the timing of inflows and outflows to coincide. A cash flow statement is used to show any gaps, or shortfalls, between cash receipts and payments. If any temporary shortfalls are forecast, the business must arrange for an additional inflow of cash, perhaps in the form of a bank loan or an overdraft. If the shortfall is too great, or is likely to continue for too long, the business may decide not to produce a new product. Most growing businesses need additional funds at some time because of the difference in timing of cash inflows and outflows. If the timing of this need is predicted through the use of a cash flow forecast, the business finds the additional funds easier to arrange.

The beginning cash balance, or opening bank balance, for any period is the amount the business expects to have in the bank at the beginning of that period. The ending or closing cash balance, or closing bank balance, for a period, is the amount the business expects to be left in the bank after all inflows and outflows during the period have been taken into account. Cash flow forecasts are usually constructed to cover a full year. A year is a long time in business, however, and the forecasts are usually broken down into smaller periods, often of one month. By comparing the forecast cash flow with the actual cash flow for a period as soon as possible after the end of that period, appropriate action can be taken.

For example, a business which receives a lower revenue than forecast (perhaps a large customer has delayed payment for goods or services supplied on credit) but still has to pay the same items of expenditure (such as wages and salaries) may arrange for a temporary overdraft with its bank. Such arrangements alter the flow of cash into and out of the business, and mean that the cash flow for the following periods must be revised, as you will see from the case study.

CASE STUDY

Tony's cash flow forecasts

Tony Brundle is confident that he can make a success of the flower shop, but he realises that to begin with he will have a considerable amount to pay out with very little revenue coming in.

Tony therefore calculates a cash flow forecast for his first year of trading, estimating the amount of money he will receive and the amount he will have to pay out each month. He believes that this will enable him to identify any months in which he may not have enough cash to cover payments he has to make, so that he can make arrangements with his bank for additional finance to be available. Tony's cash flow forecast is shown in Figure 3.8.

For the purposes of the cash flow, Tony has assumed an increasing level of sales for the shop, with additional sales in April for Easter, and December for Christmas. The professional fees to be paid in January are for the market research Tony had commissioned, and the purchases figure of £20,000 also in January is for the shop fitting, payment for which is due in that month. Other items have been put in the months in which Tony expects to have to pay them.

Looking at the cash flow statement, Tony realises that although he is starting with a cash balance of £30,000, by the end of July he will be £9,100 overdrawn. This is a serious problem since, although he is expecting to be in credit again by the end of the year, he must make arrangements to cover payments that are due during the months when he does not have enough cash coming in. Tony therefore arranges with his bank for a loan of £10,000 in April, the first month he is likely to go overdrawn. Tony's bank is happy to make this loan because Tony has given them advance warning of his requirements.

The loan will give Tony the cash that he needs to cover all outgoing payments, but it will involve an additional outgoing payment of £509 per month in repayment of the loan plus interest. Tony must therefore recalculate his cash flow forecast as shown in Figure 3.9. This shows that he now has sufficient inflows of cash throughout the year to cover his outflows.

Figure 3.8: Tony's flower shop quarterly cash flow projection

	January	February	March	April	May	June	July	August	September	October	November	December
	£	£	£	£	£	£	£	£	£	£	£	£
Cash received												
Beginning cash balance	30,000	4,900	2,800	700	−4,300	−5,400	−6,000	−9,100	−7,200	−4,800	−4,900	−2,100
Cash sales	2,000	2,000	2,000	4,000	3,000	4,000	6,000	8,000	10,000	10,000	10,000	12,000
Loans												
Total cash available	**32,000**	**6,900**	**4,800**	**4,700**	**−1,300**	**−1,400**		**−1,100**	**2,800**	**5,200**	**5,100**	**9,900**
Cash disbursed												
Salaries and wages	750	750	750	750	750	750	750	750	750	750	750	750
Rent and rates	3,000			3,000			3,000			3,000		
Insurance	100	100	100	100	100	100	100	100	100	100	100	
Office supplies	50	50	50	50	50	50	50	50	50	50	50	50
Utilities												
Repairs and maintenance				500								
Goods for resale		2,000	2,000	3,000	2,000	2,000	4,000	4,000	5,000	5,000	5,000	6,000
Professional fees	2,000											
Travel	100	100	100	100	100	100	100	100	100	100	100	100
Purchases						500			500			500
Advertising	100	100	100	500	100	100	100	100	100	100	200	200
Other												
Total disbursements	**6,100**	**3,100**	**3,100**	**8,000**	**3,100**	**3,600**	**8,100**	**5,100**	**6,600**	**9,100**	**6,200**	**7,700**
Cash position												
Loan payment with interest												
Capital purchases	20,000											
Owner's withdrawal	1,000	1,000	1,000	1,000	1,000	1,000	1,000	1,000	1,000	1,000	1,000	1,000
Total cash paid out	**27,100**	**4,100**	**4,100**	**9,000**	**4,100**	**4,600**	**9,100**	**6,100**	**7,600**	**10,100**	**7,200**	**8,700**
End of month	4,900	2,800	700	−4,300	−5,400	−6,000	−9,100	−7,200	−4,800	−4,900	−2,100	1,200

Figure 3.9: Tony's flower shop recalculated cash flow projection

	January £	February £	March £	April £	May £	June £	July £	August £	September £	October £	November £	December £
Cash received												
Beginning cash balance	30,000	4,900	2,800	700	5,700	4,091	2,982	373	1,764	3,655	3,046	5,337
Cash sales	2,000	2,000	2,000	4,000	3,000	4,000	6,000	8,000	10,000	10,000	10,000	12,000
Loans				10,000								
Total cash available	**32,000**	**6,900**	**4,800**	**14,700**	**8,700**	**8,091**	**8,982**	**8,373**	**11,764**	**13,655**	**13,046**	**17,337**
Cash disbursed												
Salaries and wages	750	750	750	750	750	750	750	750	750	750	750	750
Rent and rates	3,000			3,000			3,000			3,000		
Insurance	100	100	100	100	100	100	100	100	100	100	100	100
Office supplies	50	50	50	50	50	50	50	50	50	50	50	50
Utilities												
Repairs and maintenance				500								
Goods for resale		2,000	2,000	3,000	2,000	2,000	3,000	4,000	5,000	5,000	5,000	6,000
Professional fees	2,000											
Travel	100	100	100	100	100	100	100	100	100	100	100	100
Purchases						500			500			500
Advertising	100	100	100	500	100	100	100	100	100	100	200	200
Other												
Total disbursements	**6,100**	**3,100**	**3,100**	**8,000**	**3,100**	**3,600**	**7,100**	**5,100**	**6,600**	**9,100**	**6,200**	**7,700**
Cash position												
Loan payment with interest					509	509	509	509	509	509	509	509
Capital purchases	20,000											
Owner's withdrawal	1,000	1,000	1,000	1,000	1,000	1,000	1,000	1,000	1,000	1,000	1,000	1,000
Total cash paid out	**27,100**	**4,100**	**4,100**	**9,000**	**4,609**	**5,109**	**8,609**	**6,609**	**8,109**	**10,609**	**7,709**	**9,209**
End of month	4,900	2,800	700	5,700	4,091	2,982	373	1,764	3,655	3,046	5,337	8,128

Build your learning

Summary points

- Businesses need to work out the money they have coming in and the money they have to pay out and when they will receive it and have to pay it out, so that they do not run out of money.
- If a business runs out of money it may not be able to continue producing its goods or providing its services.
- The money coming into a business – the inflows – may come from various sources including sales revenue, capital from the owners, loans from banks and government grants.
- The money going out of a business – the outflows – may go to pay for items such as raw materials, wages, rent, telephone, and new machinery.

Key words and phrases

You should know the meaning of the words and phrases listed below as they relate to the use of cash flow forecasts by businesses. Go back through the last nine pages of the unit to check or refresh your understanding.

- **Cash flow**
- **Cash flow forecast**
- **Inflows**
- **Outflows**

Student questions

1 Explain the importance to a business of using a cash flow forecast.

2 What are inflows and outflows?

3 How can preparing a cash flow forecast help a business decide whether to proceed with producing a new product?

4 Figure 3.10 shows the anticipated inflows and outflows of a business over the next year. Using the information in the table, construct a cash flow forecast for the business. If possible you should prepare your cash flow forecast using a computer spreadsheet package.

Figure 3.10: Anticipated inflows and outflows of Torrington and Hall Ltd

Opening cash balance	£45,000
Cash sales	£1,500 per month
Sales on one month's credit	£4,000 per month January – June, October and November, £6,000 July – September, £2,500 December (note these are the month in which the sales were made, not the month in which payment was received).
Salaries and wages	£1,250 per month
Rent and rates	£10,000 per year, paid in equal installments on 26 January, 26 April, 26 July, 26 October.
Insurance	£1,200 paid in July
Office supplies	£100 per month paid in cash
Utilities	£550 in June and September; £700 in December and March
Professional fees	£2,000 in February
Advertising	£100 per month, but £200 in June, July and August
Raw materials purchased on one month's credit	£2,000 per month January – June, October and November, £3,000 per month July – September, £1,500 December (note these are the months in which the goods were purchased, not the month in which payment was made).

Calculating the breakeven point

When a business is planning to produce a new product, it wants to know how many units of the new product it will have to produce and sell in a given period of time in order to cover the costs of producing them in that time. The **breakeven point** of a new product is the level of production and sales at which costs and revenues are exactly equal. It is the point at which revenue exactly covers costs and there is no profit or loss. If actual production or sales is at a level lower than the breakeven point, the product will make a loss. Conversely, if actual production and sales is at a level higher than breakeven, the product will make a profit.

For example, when Virgin planned to produce its new cola, calculating a breakeven point showed how many cans of the new cola it had to produce and sell in a given period of time in order for the costs of production to exactly equal sales revenue. If Virgin then produced and sold a higher number of cans of cola, it would make a profit.

Having calculated the breakeven point of a product, the business can decide whether it is able to produce and sell this number of units of the product in the time period. It needs to determine whether it has enough facilities, such as machinery and employees. If the business can produce and sell more than the breakeven level, then it will make a profit. This information helps the business decide whether or not to produce the product.

In the first section of this unit, we identified start-up costs and running costs. To calculate the breakeven point of a new product a business must identify costs as variable or fixed.

- **Variable costs** are those costs that are directly related to production, such as raw materials and the wages of the employees who are actually involved in producing the product. They are called variable costs because they vary directly with the level of production. The more units of a product, such as cans of cola, that are produced, the more raw materials, such as sugar and flavouring, are used and the higher their overall cost.
- **Fixed costs** are those costs, such as rent and rates, insurance, telephone charges, gas and electricity, and the wages and salaries of employees involved in the running of the business but not in the actual production of the product. Fixed costs are not related to and do not vary with the level of production. They are sometimes called overheads, and are costs that must be paid even if nothing is produced at all.

Figure 3.11: Variable and fixed costs

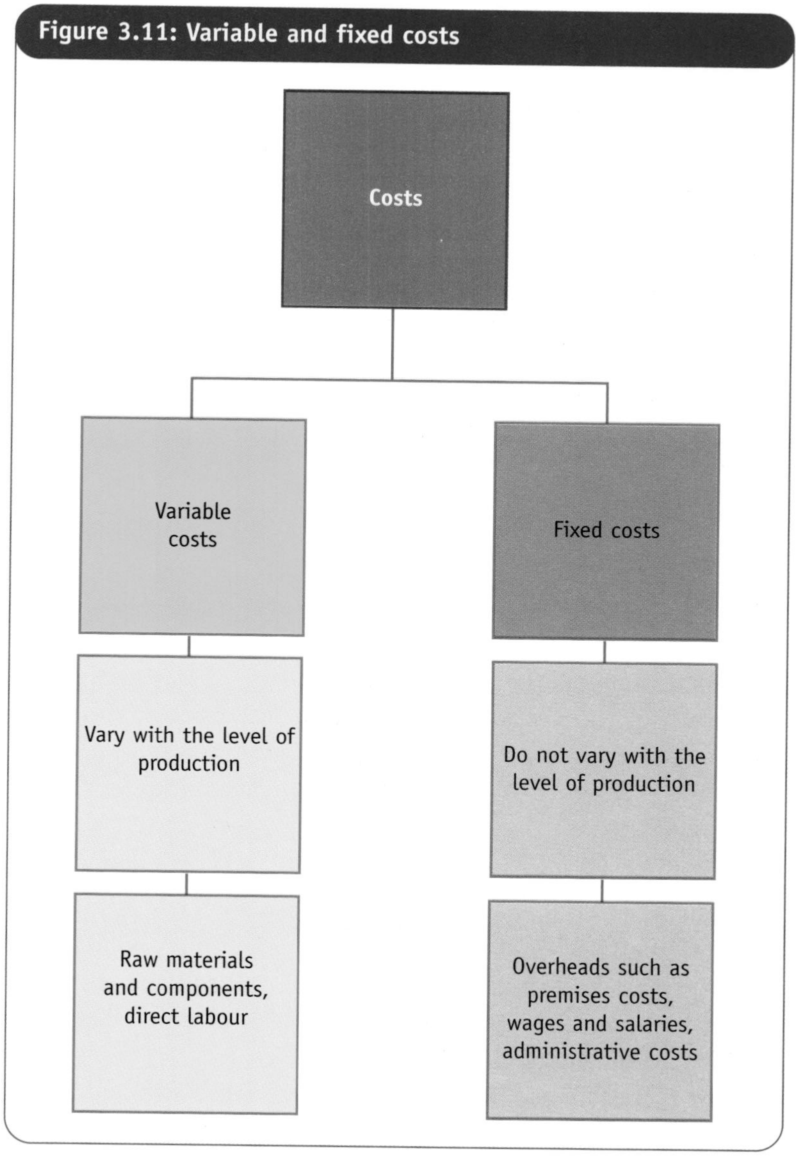

Care must be taken in allocating items such as fuel and licences for delivery vehicles. Although fuel costs increase with the number of deliveries made, and the cost of licences varies according to the number of vehicles owned by a business, they are not costs that are directly involved in the production of goods, and are therefore included with fixed costs. The same is the case with costs such as electricity and gas. Because these often contain a fixed element (the standing charge for connection) and a variable element (the cost of the actual electricity or gas supplied) they are sometimes referred to as semi-variable costs. However, for the purposes of a breakeven calculation, costs such as these are counted as overheads and treated as fixed costs.

Fixed and variable costs

Which of these costs are variable and which are fixed:

- the rent Tony pays for his shop premises
- the maize Kellogg's buys for its Corn Flakes
- staffing costs of Marks and Spencer's new store
- advertising a new car
- groceries bought by Tesco for resale
- telephone charges
- bank charges including interest on a loan that may increase if interest rates increase
- wages of Nike employees who operate the machinery that produces the soles of the business's trainers?

In addition to these costs, a business must calculate the **revenue** that will be generated from any given level of production and sales of the product. In order to do this, a business must know the price at which it will sell the product. This is then multiplied by any given number of units of the product. For example, if a business sells computer games at a price of £59 each, and wants to know how much revenue it will receive by selling 500 of these games, the calculation is

$$£59 \times 500 = £29{,}500$$

Calculating the breakeven point of a product is based on the idea that two elements are built into the price of the product. The first part of the price is to cover the variable costs of producing one unit of the product. The second part of the price is to go towards covering the fixed costs of the business.

The part of the price that goes towards covering the fixed costs of the business is called the **contribution**, as it contributes towards the fixed costs. Once enough units of the product have been sold to cover the fixed costs (the breakeven point) the contribution from each additional unit sold goes towards the profit of the business.

Figure 3.12: The elements of the price of a product

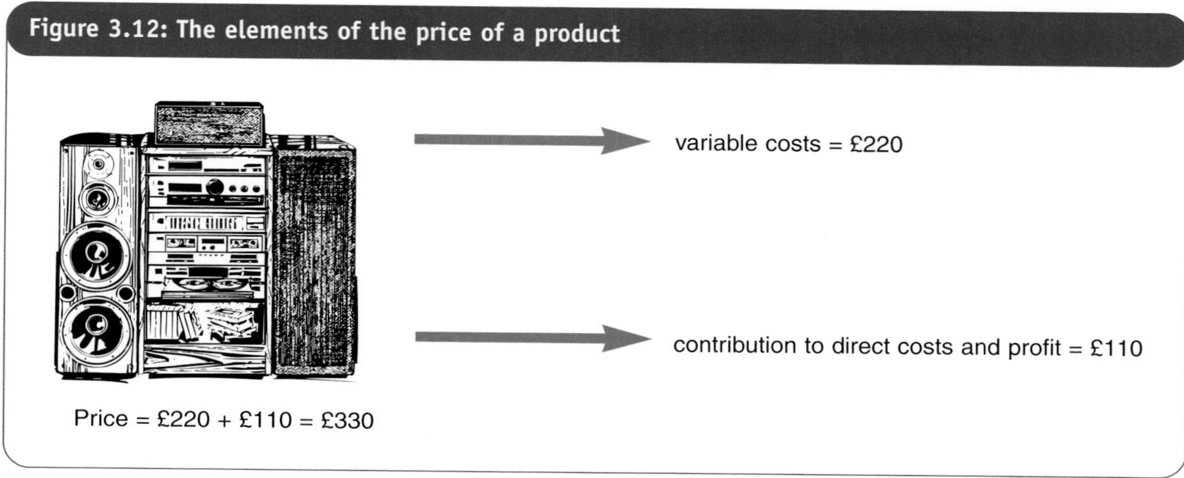

For example, Hopkirk and Sons of Edinburgh makes wooden filing cabinets, which it sells for £50 each. Hopkirk and Sons has calculated the variable costs of producing each cabinet at £7.50 for the wood and £12 for labour, £19.50 in all. Since the price of each cabinet, or unit of production, is £50, this leaves £30.50 to go towards paying the fixed costs of the business, and any profit.

There are two common ways that the breakeven point of a product can be calculated. It can be calculated using a breakeven chart or by using the **breakeven formula**:

$$\text{breakeven point} = \frac{\text{fixed costs}}{\text{selling price per unit} - \text{variable cost per unit}}$$

We shall consider each of these methods in turn.

Using the breakeven point formula

To calculate the breakeven point using the formula given above, you must know:

- the selling **price per unit**
- the variable costs per unit
- the total fixed costs.

Once these are known, the breakeven point is found by:

- subtracting the variable costs per unit from the selling price per unit to find the contribution
- dividing the total fixed costs by the contribution to find the breakeven point.

The breakeven point is thus the number of contributions (at one contribution per unit of production) required to cover the fixed costs of the business.

Hopkirk and Sons has calculated its fixed costs at £166,000 per year. Since it has already identified the contribution per unit as £30.50, its breakeven point is:

$$\text{breakeven point} = \frac{166{,}000}{£30.50} = 5{,}443 \text{ units}$$

Hopkirk and Sons therefore has to produce and sell 5,443 cabinets in order to break even.

There are two other important calculations that can be done using the contribution and fixed costs. To find out how much profit has been produced by a given level of production, this formula can be used:

$$\text{profit} = (\text{contribution} \times \text{units produced}) - \text{fixed costs}$$

In other words, multiply the contribution by the number of units produced and deduct the fixed costs to find the profit. Thus, if Hopkirk and Sons had actually produced and sold 6,000 cabinets its profit would be:

$$\begin{aligned}\text{profit} &= (6{,}000 \times £30.50) - £166{,}000 \\ &= £183{,}000 - £166{,}000 \\ &= £17{,}000\end{aligned}$$

To find out how many units must be produced to yield a **target profit**, this formula can be used:

$$\text{number of units} = \frac{\text{fixed costs} + \text{target profit}}{\text{contribution per unit}}$$

In other words, add the target profit to the fixed costs and divide the total by the contribution per unit.

If Hopkirk and Sons wanted to make a profit of £20,000, therefore, it would need to produce and sell:

$$\text{number of units} = \frac{£166{,}000 + £20{,}000}{£30.50} = 6{,}099 \text{ units}$$

Any change in the level of fixed costs, variable costs or selling price per unit will result in a new breakeven point and levels of profit or loss produced by given levels of production and sales. Such changes would require a recalculation of the figures.

Note that you will not be expected to remember these formulas in the assessment for this unit, but you must know how to use them. Any formula needed will be given to you during the assessment.

Using the formula

Breakeven calculations are useful in many situations to ensure that the costs of a project are covered and that some profit may be made.

Suppose that you are planning a disco to celebrate the end of term. It is obviously important that you cover the costs of the disco, but you would also like to be able to make a donation to student union funds.

◀ Planning the end-of-term disco

You have calculated the fixed costs of the disco (the cost of hiring the DJ and equipment, the cost of the hall, putting up posters around college and printing tickets) as £500. You are also going to have food costing £2.50 per head included in the ticket price. This is the variable cost of the disco. Asking around, you feel that tickets should be priced at £7.50.

Using the formula you calculate the break even point as:

$$\text{breakeven point} = \frac{£500}{£7.50 - £2.50} = \frac{£500}{£5.00} = 100 \text{ units}$$

This tells you that you must sell 100 tickets to break even. However, you would also like to make a donation of £100 to student union funds, and so this must be included in the breakeven calculation. The new calculation is:

$$\text{breakeven point} = \frac{£500 + £100}{£7.50 - £2.50} = \frac{£600}{£5.00} = 120 \text{ units}$$

This shows that you must sell 120 tickets in order to cover costs and have enough left to make the donation to student union funds.

You feel that this is no problem and proceed on this basis. Some time before the date of the disco, you are given some revised costs – the cost of the hall has gone up by £50, increasing your fixed costs, and the cost of the food has gone up to £3 per head. You do not feel that you can increase the price of the tickets, so you must calculate a new breakeven point. The new breakeven point is:

$$\text{breakeven point} = \frac{£600 + £50}{£7.50 - £3.00} = \frac{£650}{£4.50} = 144.44 \text{ units}$$

You now have to sell 145 tickets in order to cover your costs and make the contribution to student union funds.

You can now use this information to decide whether or not to proceed with the end-of-term disco. The question you must answer is – can you sell 145 tickets at £7.50 each? If the answer is yes, you can proceed in the knowledge that you will cover your costs and have enough left over for the donation. If, on the other hand, you do not think you can sell 145 tickets, you should decide not to go ahead unless you can either reduce some costs or increase the price of the tickets.

Using a breakeven chart

Once the fixed and variable costs of a product and the selling price per unit are known, the breakeven point can be plotted graphically on a **breakeven chart**. It is then an easy task to read off the profit or loss that will be produced by any given level of production and sales.

Figure 3.13 shows the breakeven chart for Hopkirk and Sons.

- Line DD represents the fixed costs: these remain constant for all units of output.
- Line CC represents the total costs (variable costs plus fixed costs): these rise as output rises. Note that the variable cost line starts at the level of fixed costs, since even when nothing is produced, the business still has to pay its fixed costs.
- Line AA represents revenue. This starts at 0, since there is no revenue when nothing is sold.
- Point B represents the breakeven point.
- The difference between the point on AA and the corresponding point on CC for a given level of production is the profit or loss produced by that level.

Figure 3.13: Breakeven chart for Hopkirk and Sons

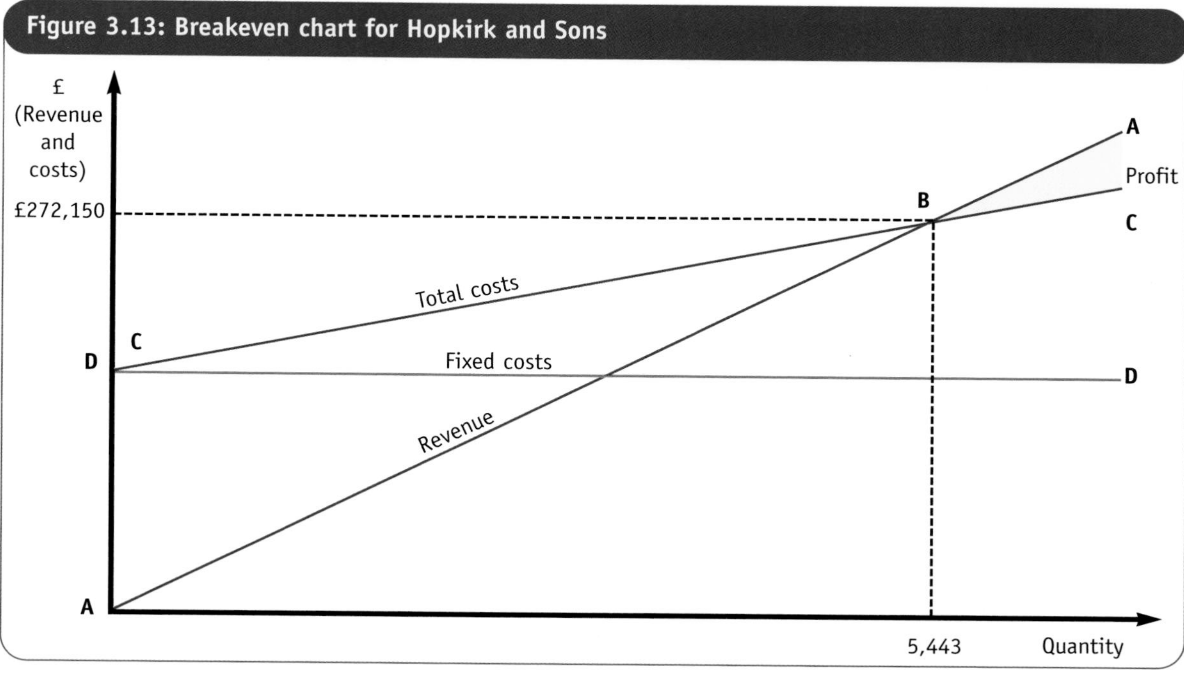

Any change in the level of fixed costs would result in a change in the position of DD (and therefore also of CC). Any change in the level of variable costs would result in a change in the slope of CC. Any change in selling price per unit would result in a change in the slope of AA. Such changes (as Figure 3.14 shows, see page 214) would alter the breakeven point and levels of profit or loss produced by given levels of production and sales. The new breakeven points in Figure 3.14 are indicated by the point B_1.

Using the breakeven chart

Construct three breakeven charts for the end-of-term disco we discussed on pages 211 and 212.

Your first chart should show the breakeven point excluding a donation to student union funds.

Your second chart should show the breakeven point including the donation to student union funds.

Your third chart should show the breakeven point at the new costs for the hall and food.

Check that your charts show breakeven points at the levels in the case study.

Figure 3.14: The effect of changes on breakeven point

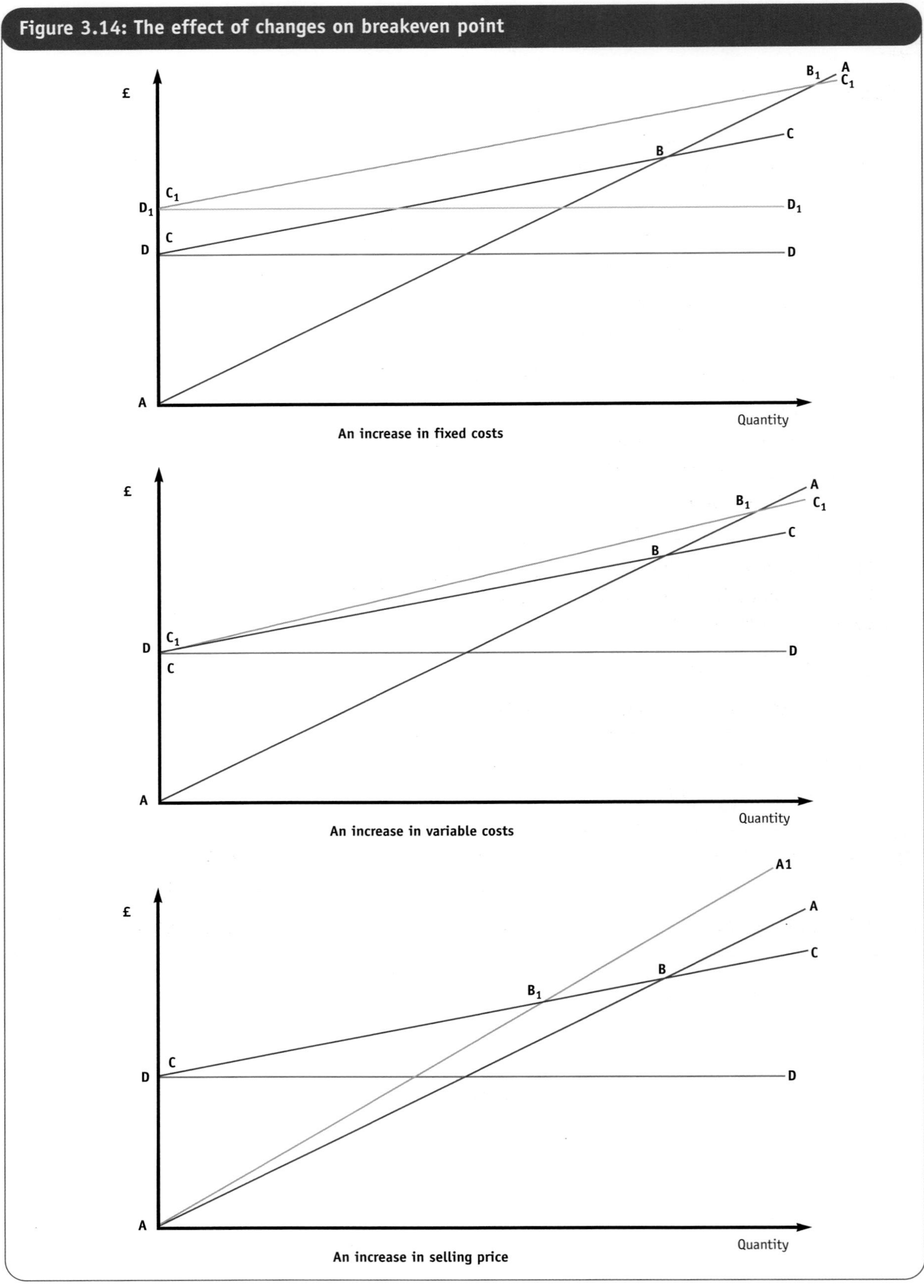

Build your learning

Summary points

- The breakeven point of a business or product is the point at which revenue from sales exactly covers the running costs of the business or product.
- Variable costs are directly related to production and vary as the level of production varies.
- Fixed costs are those costs that a business must pay regardless of how much is produced.
- A business may receive its revenue from selling goods or services.
- The total revenue of a business is calculated by multiplying the price per unit of production by the number of units produced.
- A breakeven calculation can be used to show the breakeven point, the level of profit produced by a given level of production, and the level of production required to yield a given profit.

Key words and phrases

You should know the meaning of the words and phrases listed below as they relate to breakeven calculations. Go back through the last nine pages of the unit to check or refresh your understanding.

- **Breakeven chart**
- **Breakeven formula**
- **Breakeven point**
- **Contribution**
- **Fixed costs**
- **Price per unit**
- **Revenue**
- **Target profit**
- **Variable costs**

Student questions

1 Explain why it is important for a business to calculate its breakeven point.

2 Explain the difference between fixed costs and variable costs. Give some typical examples of each.

3 Tony Brundle has identified the fixed costs of his flower shop at £46,000 for his first year of trading. He estimates that an average sale will be £20, £10 of which will go to cover variable costs.

a) Calculate the breakeven point of Tony's Flower Shop using the formula given on page 209.

b) Construct a breakeven chart for Tony's Flower Shop.

c) Calculate the effects on the breakeven point of:

- an increase of £5,000 in fixed costs
- an increase in average variable costs of £1 per sale
- an increase in the price of an average sale to £22.

d) Construct new breakeven charts to show these effects.

CASE STUDY

Ceri Thomas, costume jewellery maker

Ceri Thomas makes costume jewellery from a variety of materials in a small workshop. She estimates that the average cost of the materials she uses is £3 per item.

Ceri believes that she can sell all she makes at an average price of £15 per item. She wants to know how many she needs to make to cover her costs, including essential drawings of £10,000 for her day-to-day expenses, and to provide her with a profit for things like holidays and developing the business. Figure 3.15 shows her fixed costs.

Figure 3.15: Ceri Thomas' fixed business costs

Costs	£
Essential drawings	10,000
Stationery	100
Advertising	600
Rent and rates	4,000
Power	600
Telephone	430
Insurance	100
Capital equipment	250
Repayments of bank loan	200
Bank charges	100
Accountant's fees	400
Total fixed costs	**16,780**

Ceri has calculated her breakeven point to be:

$$\text{breakeven point} = \frac{£16{,}780}{(£15 - £3)} = \frac{£16{,}780}{£12}$$
$$= 1{,}399 \text{ units}$$

However, this calculation does not allow for any profit. Ceri feels she can comfortably produce 1,500 units of jewellery and wants to know how much profit this will produce. Since the first 1,399 units have covered all her fixed costs, the revenue from the additional 101 units that she can produce only has to cover the variable cost of producing them. Any additional revenue (the contribution, see page 208) is profit. Ceri has already calculated that the variable cost of producing one unit of jewellery is £3 and that the contribution is therefore £12. The profit Ceri will make by producing an additional 101 units of jewellery is therefore £1,212 (101 × £12).

Source: adapted from *Setting up and running your business*, Barclays Bank.

Estimating the profit or loss of a business

While it is possible to estimate the level of profit or loss of a business using a breakeven chart or calculation as Ceri Thomas did (page 217), it is often easier, clearer and more accurate to use a **profit and loss statement.** A simple profit and loss statement in standard format records:

- **sales revenue**– the money received from selling goods
- **cost of sales** – the variable costs of raw materials and the wages of those employees directly involved in production
- **gross profit** – sales revenue less the cost of sales, or profit before fixed costs are deducted
- **overheads and expenses** – these can be shown in as much detail as the business requires for its own planning and monitoring purposes
- **net profit** – that is the profit after variable costs and fixed costs have been deducted.

Figure 3.16 shows the profit and loss statement for Ceri Thomas. It is based on the production and sale of 1,500 items of jewellery. You should note that the profit given in the statement is slightly different from that given in the breakeven analysis, since the breakeven point for Ceri is not *exactly* 1,399 items.

Figure 3.16: Profit and loss statement – Ceri Thomas

Sales revenue	£22,500
Cost of sales	£4,500
Gross profit	£18,000
Overheads and expenses	£16,780
Net profit	£1,220

Unlike a breakeven calculation, a profit and loss statement does not use the concept of contribution, and it can be used accurately where there is more that one product and a range of contributions. Profit and loss statements are also useful in that they can be used to monitor the actual performance of a business against its planned performance. Any discrepancies are easy to identify and can therefore be investigated so that the appropriate action may be taken. Profit and loss statements are simple to produce using computer accounting and spreadsheet packages (see page 220).

Producing and monitoring a profit and loss statement

Hall and Jewell is a small computer consultancy, specialising in designing computer systems and selling them to small businesses. Sales revenue and expenses for last month were:

sales revenue	£24,613
rent and rates	£200
insurance	£100
direct wages	£2,546
other salaries	£2,900
maintenance	£653
heat, light and power	£101
cost of parts and materials, etc.	£15,829
postage, printing and stationery	£98
travelling	£149
telephone	£386
bank charges	£64
miscellaneous overheads	£487

Construct a simple profit and loss statement for Hall and Jewell and calculate its profit or loss for the month.

Even giant companies with complex business activities such as Marks and Spencer calculate their profit using a profit and loss statement. During the year ended 31 March 1997, Marks and Spencer calculated that:

- total sales revenue from stores, financial services and other sources were £7,841.9 million
- cost of sales totalled £5,103.8 million
- fixed costs and expenses were £1,037.9 million.

A simple profit and loss statement for Marks and Spencer is shown in Figure 3.17.

Figure 3.17: Marks and Spencer profit and loss statement 1997

	£ millions
Sales revenue	7,841.9
Cost of sales	5,103.8
Gross profit	2,738.1
Fixed costs and other expenses	1,700.2
Net profit	1,037.9

Using computers to produce financial information

Developments in computer technology and software mean that most businesses now produce financial documents and information using computers rather than manually in ledgers and account books. This is so even with quite small businesses, and many sole traders find it most convenient to keep all their financial records on a computer.

The use of computers in producing and calculating financial information depends on the software package used. Software applications range from spreadsheets which may be used to keep simple records of financial transactions, to complex integrated accounting software packages for recording and monitoring information. Sophisticated accounting software can be used to:

- make breakeven calculations and produce charts
- calculate and produce profit and loss statements
- monitor performance
- produce and record financial documents.

One simple application of information technology is using a spreadsheet to produce a profit and loss statement.

Figure 3.18: Computer spreadsheet

	A	B	C
1	A1		
2			
3			
4			
5			
6			
7			C7

A **spreadsheet** is like a sheet of paper. It is divided into boxes or cells into which information can be entered as it would be in a manual cash book (see Figure 3.18). Each cell has a reference number which is used to identify where information should be entered on the spreadsheet. For example, the cell with the reference number A1 is at the top left-hand corner of the spreadsheet; cell reference number C7 is the third cell from the left on the seventh row of the spreadsheet. Figure 3.19 shows a computer spreadsheet of the profit and loss account for Ceri Thomas (compare with Figure 3.16 on page 218).

Figure 3.19: Computer spreadsheet of the profit and loss account for Ceri Thomas

	A	B	C	D
1	Profit and loss statement			
2	Ceri Thomas			
3				
4				
5	Sales revenue			£22,500.00
6	Cost of sales			£4,500.00
7	Gross profit			£18,500.00
8	Overheads and expenses			£16,780.00
9	Net profit			£1,220.00

Once information has been entered onto a spreadsheet, the computer can do all the calculations for you. This is one of the benefits of using computers to record and monitor financial information. If you require a calculation to be made, the first step is to identify the cell in which you want the result of the calculation to appear. You then enter a special formula into this cell which tells the computer what calculation you require.

Different spreadsheet software packages require different formulae. It is important that you check the correct formulae with your tutor or the software information. However, to add the figures in a column, for example cells C7 to J7, and enter the total in cell K7, you will probably have to enter one of the following formulae in cell K7:

=SUM(C7:J7)
@SUM(C7:J7)

In many spreadsheet packages, it is possible to enter the appropriate formula by highlighting the relevant cells and clicking on an icon with the mouse.

Many computer software manufacturers produce spreadsheet software. Some of these packages are part of integrated applications suites. For example, Quattro is a spreadsheet package produced by Corel which forms part of the PerfectOffice suite. Excel, produced by Microsoft, is a spreadsheet package which forms part of the Microsoft Office Suite. Both these suites include word processing, presentation and other applications. Both spreadsheet packages are also available on their own.

▶ Many spreedsheet and accountancy software packages are available

As well as spreadsheet software, many **accounting software packages** are available, such as Sage, Quicken, and Quickbooks. Some of these are specifically designed for small businesses and are available from stores such as Dixons and PC World. Other, more sophisticated and specialised accounting and financial management software systems are available from businesses which specialise in computer systems for use by other businesses. Sometimes a large or complex business organisation employs a firm of computer consultants to develop and install computer systems, including accounting and other software, which meet the specific needs of the business.

There are several benefits of using computers to record and calculate profit and loss statements.

- Using a computer is quicker than producing financial information manually.
- Computers make calculations faster and more accurately.
- It is easier to make adjustments to information on a computer – and adjustments are usually recalculated automatically.
- Financial reports, such as profit and loss statements, can be produced quickly so that managers can respond quickly to problems and take appropriate action – such as to control costs that are higher than anticipated.

ACTIVITY

Using computers to produce financial information

Find out what computer spreadsheet or accounting package is available for you to use at your school or college.

Using the computer package, recalculate:

- the cash flow forecast of the business you constructed for question 4 on page 205
- the breakeven point for Tony's Flower Shop, and adjustments you made in the light of changes to costs and revenue for question 3 on page 216
- the profit and loss statement for Hall and Jewell that you constructed for the activity on page 219.

Find out about other accounting and spreadsheet software, such as Sage, Quicken, and Lotus. You can obtain information from stores such as Dixons and PC World, or you can contact the makers of the software themselves on the internet and find out about their products. The addresses are:

Lotus	**http://www.lotus.com**
Sage	**http://www.sage.com**
Quicken	**http://www.intuit.com**

Build your learning

Summary points

- The profit or loss of a business can be calculated using a breakeven chart or a profit and loss statement.
- A profit and loss statement shows sales revenue, cost of sales, gross profit, overheads and expenses and net profit.
- Most businesses use computers to record and calculate financial information such as cash flow forecasts, breakeven charts, and profit and loss statements.

Key words and phrases

You should know the meaning of the words and phrases listed below as they relate to calculating the profit or loss of a business. Go back through the last nine pages of the unit to check or refresh your understanding.

- **Accounting software package**
- **Cost of sales**
- **Gross profit**
- **Net profit**
- **Overheads and expenses**
- **Profit and loss statement**
- **Sales revenue**
- **Spreadsheet**

Student questions

1. Describe two ways of estimating or calculating the profit or loss of a business.
2. What is meant by cost of sales?
3. What is the net profit of a business?
4. What are the benefits to a business of using a computer to record and calculate financial information such as breakeven charts and profit and loss statements?
5. What types of computer software might a business use to calculate a profit and loss statement?

Investigating the flow of financial documents

The expenditure of a business is largely made up of purchases of goods, materials and services. A business must also pay wages and salaries to its employees for the work they do. In order that all purchases are carried out correctly and that accurate records of purchases can be kept for calculating profit and loss and other purposes, most business organisations have an established system of documents to be produced at various stages in the purchasing process. These help to ensure that the goods or services are purchased and delivered in the right quantity, and that the correct payment is made when it is due.

Most types of document are common to all organisations, although the format varies according to the requirements of specific organisations. The examples of documents in this section are from Trojan Horse Toys, a new business that has been set up to produce wooden toys that it will sell both directly to customers and through retail outlets. Similar documents are used by other business organisations.

The principal financial documents used to make a business purchase are:

- **purchase orders** – which request the goods from the supplier
- **delivery notes** – which are used by the supplier to confirm delivery of the goods
- **goods received notes** – which confirm receipt of the goods by the purchaser
- **invoices** – which are a request for payment for the goods issued by the supplier
- **credit notes** – which correct any errors on the invoice
- **statements of account** – which advise the purchaser of all invoices sent by the supplier
- **remittance advice slips** – which are used by the purchaser when paying invoices to detail which invoices are being paid
- **cheques** – which are used to arrange for payment to be transferred from the purchaser's bank account to the bank account of the supplier
- **receipts** – which are forms of confirmation that the supplier has received payment for the goods supplied.

Purchase orders

The first stage in the purchasing process, once the need for a particular product or service has been identified, is to place an order. For example, Trojan Horse Toys is running out of headed letter paper and must purchase some more. The paper is supplied by Eastfield Printers Limited. To purchase more headed letter paper, Trojan Horse Toys must order the paper from Eastfield Printers.

To do this, Trojan Horse Toys completes a **purchase order form** by entering details of the product it requires. The order form is then sent to Eastfield Printers by post or by fax. If necessary, Trojan Horse Toys can telephone Eastfield Printers to place the order, but in this case the order number (from the order form) and the date of the order should be quoted. This is so that when Trojan Horse Toys receives the goods, it can identify the order form that relates to the order. When an order is telephoned to a supplier for speed, the order form is sometimes sent to the supplier later as confirmation. The organisation that places the order keeps a copy for checking and accounting purposes. Figure 3.20 shows Trojan Horse Toys' order form for the headed letter paper.

Getting the bird

You work in the administration department of Lobley Stores, a small supermarket in Nottingham. Christmas is coming and the supermarket wants a supply of oven-ready turkeys for resale to its customers in the period leading up to Christmas.

Bradley's, a local farm, has offered the supermarket turkeys at 5p per pound, as long as Lobley Stores places the order now. You have been asked to place an order for 1,000 turkeys weighing 10 lbs and 1,000 turkeys weighing 15 lbs for delivery on 1 December. Complete an order form to send to Bradley's.

For this activity and the rest of the activities in this section you will need to design the appropriate forms. Do this on a computer if you can. Alternatively, your teacher may give you a copy of an order form to use.

Figure 3.20: Trojan Horse Toys' purchase order form

TROJAN HORSE TOYS LTD

PURCHASE ORDER

Order No
0001

Supplier	This order is CONFIRMATION of	Job No	Order Date
Eastfield Printers Ltd			8/9/2000

Delivery address if different from above	Any queries with this order contact	Delivery Date
	Ivan Helford	ASAP

Quantity	Description	Price
5 reams	Headed letter paper	£30 per ream

OUR ORDER NUMBER MUST BE QUOTED, OTHERWISE INVOICES WILL BE RETURNED UNPAID
Under COSHH Regulations Safety Literature covering all products on this order MUST be supplied

Signed for and on behalf of TROJAN HORSE TOYS LTD............I. Helford............ Date......8/9/2000......

NOTE: OTHER CONDITIONS OF PURCHASE SEE OVER

Delivery notes and goods received notes

Goods and services requested on an order form may either be delivered by the supplier or collected from the supplier by the customer. The headed letter paper ordered by Trojan Horse Toys is to be delivered by Eastfield Printers. When the paper is delivered, it is accompanied by a **delivery note** giving details of the items delivered. The person who receives the delivery on behalf of Trojan Horse Toys signs the delivery note. A copy of the delivery note, called a **goods received note**, is left with the delivery. Many businesses also produce their own goods received notes on which they enter details of the delivery. Trojan Horse Toys checks the details on the goods received note:

- against the goods actually delivered, to ensure that the details on the delivery note or goods received note are correct
- against the order form which refers to the goods delivered, to ensure that Eastfield Printers have delivered the right quantity of the correct goods.

Any discrepancies must be notified to the supplier at once by telephone, and confirmed in writing. The order number and the delivery note or goods received note number must be quoted when informing the supplier of any discrepancy. Figure 3.21 shows the delivery and goods received note for the headed letter paper.

Figure 3.21: Delivery and goods received note

No 123/

Eastfield Printers Ltd

DELIVERY AND GOODS RECEIVED NOTE

Supplier
Deliver to
Trojan Horse Toys

Description	Quantity	Order Number	Checked
Headed letter paper	5 reams	0001	

Received by (signature).. Date..

Getting the bird 2

The turkeys you ordered in the activity on page 226 have now been received by Lobley Stores. Complete a delivery and goods received note for them.

Invoices

Once the goods have been received and checked, they must be paid for. The supplier sends the purchaser a request for payment in the form of an **invoice**. The invoice gives full details of the goods or services for which payment is requested, including the order number and delivery note number. The invoice also shows the amount to be paid and how this has been calculated, including any VAT to be paid or discounts allowed, for example for prompt payment.

The invoice must be carefully checked:

- against the order form to ensure that it is for the correct goods and services and that the quantity, price and any discount shown on the order form are correct
- against the delivery note or goods received note to ensure that the goods and quantity on the invoice are those that were delivered.

The calculations on the invoice must be carefully checked to ensure that the invoice total is correct and that the purchaser is charged the correct amount.

A purchaser should notify the supplier of any discrepancies as soon as possible. The numbers of the appropriate invoice, delivery note, goods received note and order should be quoted. If the purchase invoice is correct and agrees with both the order form and the delivery or goods received note, it is authorised and passed as correct by a senior employee in the purchasing organisation who signs the document. The purchaser uses the checked purchase invoice:

- as authority to pay the supplier the amount shown on the invoice for the goods or services detailed on the invoice
- as a record of the outward financial transaction.

Figure 3.22 shows Eastfield Printers' invoice for the letter paper supplied to Trojan Horse Toys.

Figure 3.22: An invoice

Eastfield Printers Ltd

SALES INVOICE

Customer	Invoice No	File Ref.	Invoice Date	
Trojan Horse Toys Ltd	9756		12/9/2000	
Delivery address if different from above	**Customer Order No**	**Prod. Code**	**Despatch Date/s**	**Route**
	0001	XX	12/9/2000	VAN

Quantity	Description	Price	Per	Goods Value	VAT Rate
5 reams	HEADED LETTER PAPER	£30	REAM	£150.00	17.5%

Total Goods	£150.00
Total VAT	26.25
Invoice Total	176.25

TERMS STRICTLY NETT ONE MONTH

Getting the bird 3

Complete the invoice that Bradley's Farm sends to Lobley Stores for the turkeys it has supplied. There is no VAT on the cost of turkeys, but Bradley's farm has charged £50 plus VAT for delivery.

Credit notes

There are occasions when a purchase invoice is incorrect. For example:

- the goods or quantities on the invoice may not agree with those ordered or delivered
- the calculations on the invoice may be incorrect
- VAT may be charged incorrectly or at the wrong rate
- the amount of discount allowed may be incorrect.

If the purchaser notifies the supplier that an invoice is incorrect, the supplier sends either a **credit note**, which has the effect of reducing the amount due if the total on the invoice is too high, or an additional invoice if the total on the original invoice is too low. Some organisations prefer to cancel an incorrect invoice completely by issuing a credit note for the full amount of the invoice, and then to issue a new invoice for the correct amount. For example, one box of 250 sheets of headed letter paper supplied to Trojan Horse Toys by Eastfield Printers was damaged. Figure 3.23 shows the credit note sent by Eastfield Printers to Trojan.

Getting the bird 4

Ten of the 15 lb turkeys delivered to Lobley Stores are still alive and kicking and are being kept in a pen at the back of the stores awaiting collection by Bradley's Farm. Complete a credit note from Bradley's Farm to Lobley Stores for these turkeys.

Figure 3.23: A credit note

Eastfield Printers Ltd

CREDIT NOTE

Customer	Credit Note No	File Ref.	Credit Date	
Trojan Horse Toys Ltd	0001		14/9/2000	
Delivery address if different from above	**Customer Order No**	**Prod. Code**	**Despatch Date/s**	**Route**
	0001	XX	12/9/2000	VAN

Quantity	Description	Price	Per	Goods Value	VAT Rate
1 Box	HEADED	£30	ream	£15	17.5%

Total Goods	£15.00
Total VAT	£2.62
Invoice Total	£17.62

Statements of account

To help their customers check that all the invoices they have issued for goods or services supplied during a particular month have been received and are paid at the end of the month, most suppliers send a monthly **statement of account** to each customer. This lists all invoices and credit notes the supplier has issued to the customer during the month. The statement of account also shows any invoices issued during previous months which have not yet been paid by the customer and which are still outstanding on their account. The statement of account is not only a means of checking that all invoices have been received by a purchaser, but reminds the purchaser of what is owed to the supplier. Figure 3.24 shows the statement of account sent by Eastfield Printers to Trojan Horse Toys.

Getting the bird 5

Complete a statement of Lobley Stores' account with Bradley's Farm for the month in which the turkeys were supplied. The supply of turkeys is the only purchase Lobley Stores made from Bradley's Farm during the month and there are no invoices outstanding from previous months.

Remittance advice slips

A **remittance advice slip** is often attached to the statement of account. This contains details of the customer and lists the invoices shown on the statement. The customer indicates the invoices being paid and returns the remittance advice to the supplier, together with the payment. The supplier can therefore make sure that the payment is correctly allocated against the appropriate customer and invoices. Many customers operate computerised payment systems, and they prefer to produce their own remittance advice slips. These contain similar details and serve the same purpose. Figure 3.25 shows Trojan's remittance advice covering the delivery of headed letter paper.

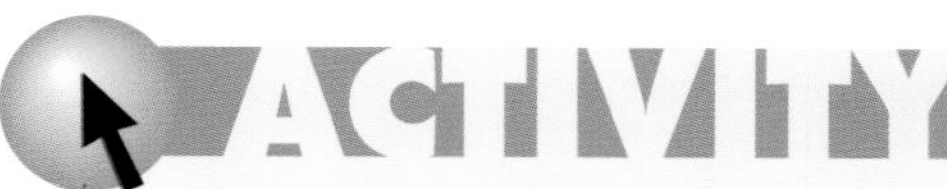

Getting the bird 6

Lobley Stores wants to pay Bradley's Farm for the turkeys. Complete a remittance advice showing what is being paid.

Figure 3.24: A statement of account

Eastfield Printers Ltd

STATEMENT OF ACCOUNT

TROJAN HORSE TOYS LTD	Any queries regarding items on this statement should be addressed to CREDIT CONTROL

Date	Item Reference	Debit	Credit	Balance	
12/9/2000	9756	£176.25			
14/9/2000	0001		£17.62	158.63	

Total Due £158.63

Please note that if no instalment dates are shown on invoices, payment is due within 30 days from invoice date.
If you have made any recent payment(s) which are not shown above, such payment(s) will be shown on your next statement.
All values shown are pounds sterling.

Figure 3.25: A remittance advice slip

Trojan Horse Toys **Remittance Advice**		
Pay To Eastfield Printers		
Date		*Value*
12/09/2000 14/09/2000	9756 0001	£176.25 –17.62
Total payment		£ 158.63 Paid by: Cheque

Cheques

Most businesses pay by cheque for the goods and services they purchase. Any individual or business with a current bank account can pay by cheque and many building society accounts also provide this facility.

A **cheque** is a form which is completed by the purchaser. The purchaser completes the cheque, signs it and gives or sends it to the supplier, together with the remittance advice if appropriate. The cheque instructs the purchaser's bank to transfer a stated amount of money from the purchaser's account into the account of the supplier, which may be at a different bank. In this way, a person or business has access to all the money in his or her bank account – and sometimes more, if he or she has arranged an overdraft facility with the bank.

The person or business who receives the cheque pays the cheque into his or her bank account using a paying-in slip. The transaction is then cleared through a central clearing house, and the money debited to (taken out of) the purchaser's bank account and credited to (put into) the supplier's bank account.

If there is not enough money in the account of the purchaser to cover the cheque, the cheque is returned unpaid to the supplier's bank and then to the supplier. In order to help prevent fraud, some retail businesses only accept cheques which are presented with a cheque guarantee card. This guarantees that the bank of a person or business who writes a cheque will honour the cheque and pay the amount shown into the account of the person or business receiving it, up to the limit of the card (normally £50 or £100).

The cheque drawn by Trojan Horse Toys in payment for the headed letter paper is shown in Figure 3.26.

Figure 3.26: A cheque

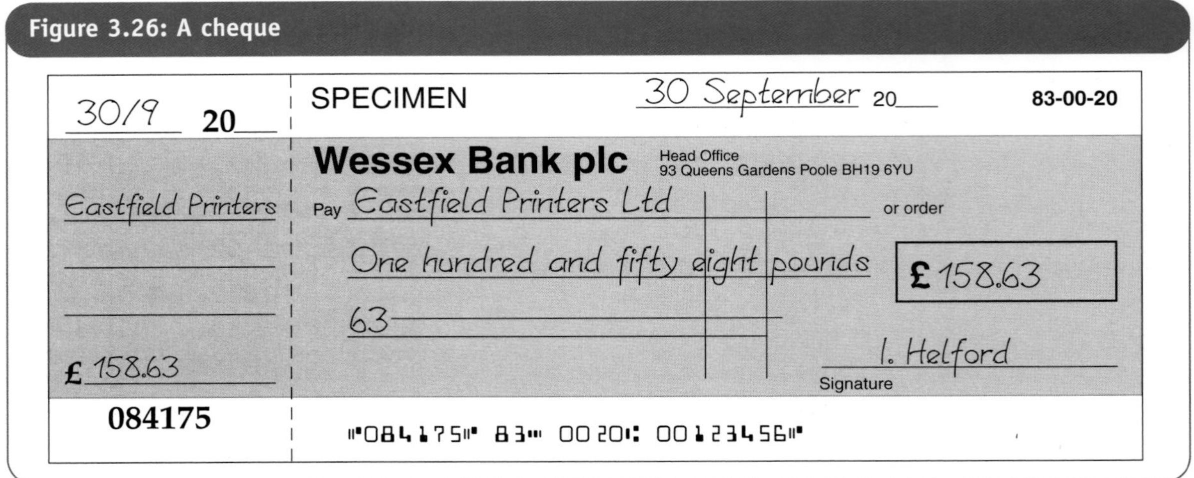
30/9 20__

Eastfield Printers

£ 158.63

084175

SPECIMEN 30 September 20__ 83-00-20

Wessex Bank plc Head Office 93 Queens Gardens Poole BH19 6YU

Pay Eastfield Printers Ltd or order

One hundred and fifty eight pounds 63

£ 158.63

I. Helford

Signature

⑈084175⑈ 83⑆ 0020⑆ 00123456⑈

Getting the bird 7

Complete a cheque for Lobley Stores paying Bradley's Farm for the turkeys. Note: the cheque should be made out for the amount shown on the remittance advice.

Receipts

A **receipt** is a written statement confirming that a payment has been made. It is important that some form of receipt is obtained so that it can be referred to later if there is any query about the payment or the goods purchased. Many types of document can serve as receipts. The following documents can all be used as receipts to show that a particular payment has been made.

- Receipts, such as till rolls and printed forms completed to confirm that a payment has been received. Printed receipt forms should be signed by the person who received the payment. When a customer pays an invoice, an acceptable receipt is given by the person writing 'received with thanks' or similar wording on the invoice and appending his or her signature and the date.
- Cheques do not need separate forms of receipt as a record of the date of the cheque, the amount and to whom it was made out is kept on the cheque counterfoil. Once the cheque is banked by the payee it goes through the banking system and a record of the payment appears on both the drawer's and the payee's bank accounts as proof of payment.
- Paying-in slips are used to pay money into a bank account. Some suppliers, such as British Telecommunications, British Gas and mail order catalogue companies, also issue their customers with paying-in slips to enable them to make payments directly into a bank or post office. Paying-in slips have counterfoils similar to those attached to cheques. This is stamped and initialled by the cashier at the bank or post office accepting the payment as a receipt for the payment.
- Bank statements also act as proof of payment, as cheques and cash paid into the bank account, and cheques drawn on the bank account are itemised.

Build your learning

Summary points

- When businesses buy goods or services, they use a number of financial documents.
- The financial documents used in making a business purchase are completed in sequence, and progress from the initial order to acknowledgement of payment.
- It is important that the financial documents are completed accurately and that all financial documents received by a business are checked for accuracy.
- Some businesses complete financial documents by hand, while others use computer programmes.

Key words and phrases

You should know the meaning of the words and phrases listed below as they relate to the financial documents used to make a business purchase. Go back through the last 13 pages of the unit to check or refresh your understanding.

- **Cheque**
- **Credit note**
- **Delivery note**
- **Goods received note**
- **Invoice**
- **Purchase order**
- **Receipt**
- **Remittance advice slip**
- **Statement of account**

Student questions

1 Describe the flow of financial documents used to make a business purchase, explaining the use of each document.

2 Why is accuracy important when completing financial documents?

3 Why should the business making the purchase check all financial documents sent by the supplier?

Assessment preparation

This unit is assessed by an external assessment. By completing all the activities and student questions in the unit you have covered everything you need for the assessment.

For the external assessment you will need to answer questions about:

- the costs and revenues of businesses (page 174)
- the construction and use of cash flow forecasts (page 195)
- measuring costs, revenue and profit, using a breakeven calculation and a profit and loss statement (page 206)
- the advantages to businesses of using computers to record and calculate financial information and to produce financial documents (page 220)
- the flow of financial documents used in making a business purchase (page 225).

You must also be able to:

- calculate and complete a cash flow forecast
- calculate the breakeven point of a business
- construct a breakeven chart
- complete a profit and loss statement
- complete financial documents used to make a business purchase.

Assessment grid

Section	To achieve a pass you must	To achieve a merit you must also	To achieve a distinction you must also
Covering the costs of a new product	Show you understand the difference between start-up costs and running costs, and between revenue from the sale of goods and the sale of services; identify typical items of cost and revenue.	Identify typical costs and revenues for specific types of business.	
Using a cash flow forecast	Identify which flows of money come into and out of a business; complete the main parts of a cash flow forecast.		Explain why it is important to prepare a cash flow forecast.
Calculating the breakeven point	Understand the difference between fixed and variable costs; create and interpret breakeven charts.	Calculate breakeven points from given data.	Show the effects of changes in fixed costs, variable costs and prices on the breakeven point and the level of profits; explain the reasons why costs and revenues might change.
Estimating the profit or loss of a business	Recognise the main elements of a profit and loss statement.	Calculate, from given data, total and average costs, revenues and profit or loss; complete a profit and loss statement accurately from given data.	
Investigating the flow of financial documents used to make a business purchase	Understand the use of financial documents, including who uses them, when and why; recognise financial documents, transfer given financial data to accurately complete these documents and check them for accuracy.	Understand the sequence in which financial documents are most commonly used; explain the advantages and disadvantages of using a computerised accounting system to generate financial documents.	
Other	Explain the advantages and disadvantages of using a computer spreadsheet for financial calculations.		Understand the significance of making errors in calculating financial data and in completing financial documents.

Index

Numbers in **blue** show the page on which the word is defined or used as a key word.